# NOTES for CATALOGERS

## A Sourcebook for Use with AACR 2

by
**Florence A. Salinger**
and
**Eileen Zagon**

**Knowledge Industry Publications, Inc.**
**White Plains, NY and London**

*Professional Librarian Series*

Notes for Catalogers: A Sourcebook for Use with AACR 2

**Library of Congress Cataloging in Publication Data**

Salinger, Florence A.
  Notes for catalogers.

  (Professional librarian series)
  Bibliography: p.
  Includes index.
  1.  Notes (Cataloging)-- Specimens.     2. Descriptive
cataloging--Rules.     3. Anglo-American cataloging rules.
I. Zagon, Eileen.     II. Title.     III. Series.
Z694.S244   1984          025.3'2          84-21770
ISBN 0-86729-099-4
ISBN 0-86729-098-6 (pbk.)

Printed in the United States of America

# Table of Contents

# ACKNOWLEDGMENTS

During the preparation of this work, a number of colleagues patiently answered our many questions, and grateful acknowledgment is made to all of them.

We owe a particular debt of gratitude to Charles T. Townley, our library director, mentor, and friend. His constant encouragement, support, and broad ranging knowledge were invaluable to us.

The following persons gave generously of their time and subject expertise: William J. Mahar, associate professor (Humanities & Music), John H. Joseph, associate provost and affiliate assistant professor (Education), Eton F. Churchill, assistant professor (Humanities & Multi-Media Journalism), Simon J. Bronner, assistant professor (American Studies & Folklore), and Michael J. Kalbaugh, instructional services officer, all of Pennsylvania State University Capitol Campus; Karl H. Proehl, head, Maps Section, University Libraries, Pennsylvania State University; Les Achey, head of cataloging, Mansfield University; and PALINET coordinators, Gale Eckerson, Anne Hudson, Anita Lingle, and Rian Miller-McIrvine. The resources of the libraries of Millersville University, Shippensburg University, and York College of Pennsylvania were made available to us, and for those we express our thanks.

Warm appreciation is extended to Vera Mae Fultz and Eileen E. Jackson for clerical assistance and to Susan A. Landucci for typing the manuscript. A special note of thanks is conveyed to Victoria A. Rogic for her assistance in the preparation of the index.

Research for this project was supported in part by a grant from The Pennsylvania State University, Capitol Campus Fund for Research.

Florence A. Salinger wishes to express appreciation to The Pennsylvania State University for awarding her sabbatical leave to research this work.

Florence A. Salinger
Eileen Zagon

Note notes, forsooth . . .
— *William Shakespeare*

# Preface

The present volume has evolved from *Monograph Cataloging Notes* (Florence Salinger and Eileen Zagon, White Plains, NY: Knowledge Industry Publications, Inc., 1981). Response to that endeavor encouraged us to write a second book with a broader scope, and to include notes illustrating all library materials covered by Chapters 1-12 of the *Anglo-American Cataloguing Rules,* second edition (*AACR 2*).

The purpose of this sourcebook is to aid the cataloger: (1) in making decisions concerning the appropriateness of particular notes, and (2) in acquiring suggestions for their phrasing and punctuation. It is designed to be used in conjunction with *AACR 2* and augments the examples presented there in the note areas in Part I. No effort has been made to give the rationale governing use and formulation of notes.

For the benefit of those libraries who look to the Library of Congress (LC) for leadership, LC cataloging practice is exemplified whenever it can be ascertained from cataloging records or from the continual interpretation of rules to be found in *CSB*.[1]

What might appear as inconsistency in the spelling of certain words is the result of either usage, tradition, or quotation—for example, "catalog" versus "catalogue." In general, LC prefers the American usage "catalog." When the spelling of "catalogue" is dictated by tradition, however—as it often is when relating to exhibitions—LC uses this form. When it is found in a quoted note, the word is spelled as it appears. There is also a diversity of style in phrasing and punctuation among chapters; style seems to be idiosyncratic, but it is consistently so from material to material.

---

1. *Cataloging Service Bulletin.* (Washington, DC: Library of Congress, Processing Services, 1978-   ).

The chapters and sections of this work correspond to those of *AACR 2*. Each example is identified by a number composed of the chapter number, a colon, and a consecutive number (e.g., 2:247). Each example number thus reflects a particular chapter.

While each material or type of publication covered by *AACR 2* is generally represented, early printed monographs were excluded because of their narrow scope and highly specialized nature. Readers may be surprised to find the inclusion of Chapter 1, "General," comprising 31 examples. These represent valid notes on materials for which there is no rule accommodation within their respective chapters in *AACR 2*. Chapter 1 also comprises a few kit examples—typical notes used when cataloging items made up of several types of material. We point out, however, that other examples or combinations of examples throughout this book are also suitable and may be used for kit notes.

Indeed, notes applicable to any one material may very well suit or suggest themselves for another material, and all should be examined carefully for that purpose. Similarly, we chose to omit sections from various chapters when they duplicated those shown in other chapters; for example, the sections on dissertations. Although dissertations may be issued in formats other than print, dissertation notes remain the same from format to format, and are shown for printed monographs only.

Chapter 4, "Manuscripts," stands out as the one major deviation from *AACR 2* in this sourcebook. The Library of Congress and others in the manuscripts and archives community also use another guide that both augments and departs from *AACR 2* for cataloging modern manuscript and archival material.[2] Because it is regarded as more adequately meeting manuscript cataloging needs, this guide is followed in the examples in Chapter 4.

Chapter 9, "Machine-Readable Data Files," is presented with a caveat. Guidelines issued by national cataloging leaders to accommodate microcomputer software were not available during the preparation of this work, and the authors were obliged to create the respective notation. To the best of our knowledge the examples for microcomputer software conform to the guidelines.[3]

Chapter 12, "Serials," provides a large number of notes which we hope will fulfill the need for models in this area, where complexity abounds and is compounded by frequent changes in title and history.

---

2. Steven L. Hensen. *Archives, Personal Papers, and Manuscripts: A Cataloging Manual for Archival Repositories, Historical Societies, and Manuscript Libraries.* (Washington, DC: Library of Congress, Manuscript Division, 1983).

3. American Library Association. Committee on Cataloging: Description and Access, *Guidelines for Using AACR2, Chapter 9 for Cataloging Microcomputer Software.* (Chicago: American Library Association, 1984).

A subject index is provided. Although detailed in index entries, it is selective: examples of a certain subject may recur throughout the chapters, but only a representative selection of examples is referenced in the index.

In conclusion, we ask our readers to use these notes solely as models, keeping in mind *AACR 2*'s counsel that examples used are illustrative and not prescriptive. These notes are intended as models for suitability, wording, and punctuation. We offer them in the hope that they can be used or adapted with ease, and that this volume will prove to be a valuable resource for catalogers.

*To Ian*
*—E.Z.*

*In memory of Nicholas J. (Mickey) Salinger*
*—F.A.S.*

# 1

# General

## NATURE, SCOPE, OR ARTISTIC FORM OF THE ITEM (1.7B1)

1:1        "First newspaper published and edited by women."
           (Serial)

1:2        "First daily in Philadelphia."
           (Serial)

1:3        Newsletter devoted to the art and artists of political
           cartooning.
           (Serial)

1:4        Magazine of television history.
           (Serial)

1:5        Each report summarizes the preceding year and presents a
           plan for the ensuing 5-year period.
           (Serial)

1:6        Each volume devoted to a particular subject.
           (Serial)

1:7        Review of the activity of the Patent Office.
           (Serial)

1:8        Index of articles about Hong Kong in selected Hong Kong periodicals.
           (Serial)

1:9        1968 used as base year.
           (Serial)

1:10       Data categorized by school district.
           (Serial)

## LANGUAGE OF THE ITEM AND/OR TRANSLATION OR ADAPTATION (1.7B2)

1:11       Directions given in French.
           (Three-dimensional artefact)

1:12       Instructions in Spanish and English.
           (Three-dimensional artefact)

1:13       Guide in English and French.
           (Three-dimensional artefact)

## STATEMENTS OF RESPONSIBILITY (1.7B6)

1:14       Transcribed by Algernon Charles Swinburne.
           (Manuscript)

## EDITION AND HISTORY (1.7B7)

1:15       Originally published in samizdat form in Moscow, 1978-
           (Serial)

1:16       Some numbers issued in rev. ed.
           (Serial)

1:17       Vols. for        lack ed. statement.
           (Serial)

1:18    Revised Jan. and July.
            (Serial)

1:19    A complete revision and a consolidation into 1 alphabet of
        biographical materials originally appearing in the quarterly
        Contemporary authors, v. 1-      published 1962-
            (Serial)

1:20    Expanded and edited papers selected from: Geochimica.
            (Serial)

## MATERIAL SPECIFIC DETAILS (1.7B8)

1:21    Monthly (tape subscription service).
            (Machine-readable data file)

## "WITH" NOTES (1.7B21)

1:22a   With: The Parthenon. Mounted together subsequent to
        publication.
            (Graphic material; title proper: Temple of Athena Nike;
            note on first item)
            *For LC's interpretation on the use of "With" notes see
            Cataloging Service Bulletin, no. 22, fall 1983, p. 20*

1:22b   With: Temple of Athena Nike. Mounted together sub-
        sequent to publication.
            (Note on second item)

1:23a   With: Bagels. ICBM. Polar. Polygraph. Radar. Slope.
        Snark.
            (Machine-readable data file; title proper: Algebra; note
            on first item. Examples 1:23a-b illustrate AACR 2 rule
            1.1G4)

1:23b   With: Algebra.
            (Note on second and subsequent items)

## MULTIMEDIA/KITS (1.10C3)

1:24        Title of filmstrip: What about unemployment?

1:25        Posters have descriptive notes in English, French, German, and Spanish.

1:26        Text available in Spanish and English; sound cassette primarily in Spanish; other material in English.

1:27        Summary: A collection of texts and flash cards originally published separately and distributed by Educators Publishing Service as a kit. For use in teaching language skills to adolescents with Specific Language Disability.

1:28        Includes wall chart, flag in folder, worry beads, stamps, coins, and book entitled: Getting to know Saudi Arabia / by Ted Phillips.

1:29        Contains: 1 teacher's book, 8 display photographs, 3 wall charts, 2 decision-making games, 2 work cards, 8 documents, 2 sets of role-play cards, anthology of prose and poetry.

1:30        Contents: What do you see? (1 videocassette (30 min.) : sd., col.) -- A hospital experience (74 slides : col.).

1:31        Contents: Phenakistiscope (visual wheel) / H. Frampton -- 100 year calendar (51 x 96 cm.) / On Kawara -- 6 prison poems (8 p. ; 18 cm.) + 1 sheet of paper with doodles on it (34 x 24 cm. folded to 24 x 17 cm.) / Rotella -- Asylum manuscripts (on brown paper towels ; 24 x 25 cm.) / Princess Winifred -- Excerpts from "Drift study" (1 sound tape reel (60 min.) : 7 1/2 ips, mono. ; 5 in.) / L. Young.

# 2

# Books, Pamphlets, and Printed Sheets

## NATURE, SCOPE, OR ARTISTIC FORM (2.7B1)

2:1      A novel.

2:2      Novel in Malay.

2:3      A play.

2:4      Poem.

2:5      Chiefly poems.

2:6      Short stories and essays.

2:7      Song texts.

2:8      Songs, without musical notation.

2:9      Cartoons originally published in the New Yorker.

2:10      Interviews and cartoons by S. Gross and others.

2:11      Art reproductions of chalk drawings of La Scala scenes.

2:12      Reproduction of the illuminations from the Rohan Book of Hours.

2:13    Folk tales told to Jean-Claude Dupont by Isaïe Jolin.

2:14    Recipes originally published in the Sandlapper magazine.

2:15    Vol. 2: tables.

2:16    Chiefly tables.

2:17    Vol. 2 chiefly tables.

2:18    English-Latin phrase book.

2:19    Sales catalog.

2:20    Student project of Groveton High School, Fairfax Co., Va.

2:21    Program souvenir of the conference.

2:22    "A transcript of proceedings, the ATLA mid-winter meeting, Monaco, February 8, 1978"--P. ii.

2:23    Transcript of the trial of Patricia Campbell Hearst, U.S. District Court, California.

2:24    Edited transcriptions of debates between the authors, in 1976 and 1977.

2:25    Prepared by the editor from tape transcriptions of a series of lectures given by Dr. Baade at Harvard Observatory in 1958.

2:26    Biography.

2:27    Biography of George Cram Cook, written by his wife.

2:28    Autobiographical.

2:29    Nineteen autobiographical stories about the author's childhood in Poland from 1908 to 1918.

2:30    A novel based on the life of Harry Rimmer.

2:31    Chapters 5-8 of Franklin's My dear girl, comprising his correspondence with Mary Stevenson Hewson.

2:32        Consists of pt. 2, Relations between the individual and his government, of Cases in constitutional law. 5th ed. 1979.

2:33        Consists of 2 essays: My style of drawing birds, published in Audubon and his journals / Maria R. Audubon. 1897; and, Method of drawing birds, published in the Edinburgh journal of science, v. 8, 1828.

2:34        Special number of: The Review of economic studies.

2:35        Special number of: Documentation législative africaine / issued by the Centre de recherches, d'études et de documentation sur les institutions et la législation africaines.

2:36        Contains only 6 stories.
(Title proper: 7 opowiadań)

2:37        Collection of the Flash Gordon comic strip covering the period of Apr. 12, 1936-Oct. 30, 1938.

2:38        "This collection of essays appears . . . as the September 1975 issue of Forum der letteren."

2:39        A compilation in original printings, of various memoranda, letters, speeches, documents, and publications by the author on improving certain public buildings.

2:40        A selection of colored illustrations from Prisse d'Avennes' L'art arabe d'après les monuments . . . (Paris, 1877) and from La décoration arabe (Paris, 1885); with a publisher's note and captions in English.

2:41        Selection of articles from Psychology today magazine.

2:42        Articles taken from Vital issues.

2:43        Selections from issues of El Reno American.

2:44        Selection of articles originally published in the New Yorker, 1927-1933.

2:45        Selections from the author's psychic readings, which originally appeared in the first 7 issues of the Journal of the Association for the Understanding of Man.

2:46        Selected from the author's Economics.

2:47    A selection from the Encyclopedia of library and information science, v. 21, p. 176-240.

2:48    Selections from John Grimestone's Commonplace book (ms. Advocates' Library 18.7.21., in the National Library of Scotland).

2:49    Selections from 1-2 Samuel and 1 Kings.

2:50    Chiefly selections from the New Testament.

2:51    Sculptors: David Annesley, Walter Darby Bannard, Willard Boepple, Anthony Caro, Brower Hatcher, Colin Kerrigan, Kenneth Noland, Jules Olitski, Nicholas Pearson, Larry Poons, David Smith, Margaret Swan, Roger Williams, Isaac Witkin, James Wolfe.

2:52    Essays written to accompany the exhibition at the National Portrait Gallery.

2:53    Exhibition catalogue with biographical notes.

2:54    Catalog of an exhibition held May 4-21, 1973.

2:55    Catalogue of an exhibition held at the University of Michigan Museum of Art, Dec. 5, 1971-Jan. 16, 1972; the 10th in a series organized by the Graduate Seminar in Museum Practice.

2:56    Catalog of the exhibition held Dec. 10, 1975-Feb. 15, 1976 at the Pierpont Morgan Library, New York; Mar. 16-May 2, 1976 at the Cleveland Museum of Art; May 28-July 5, 1976 at the Art Institute of Chicago; and Aug. 6-Sept. 17, 1976 at the National Gallery of Canada, Ottawa.

2:57    Catalogue, by L. Chalom, of an exhibition held Mar. 17-Apr. 10, 1968, Student Center Art Gallery, Seton Hall University, South Orange, N.J.

2:58    Issued in connection with the exhibition held May 14-Dec. 31, 1978 at the Danforth Museum, Framingham, Mass. in celebration of its 3rd anniversary.

2:59    "Published for the exhibition Graphicstudio U.S.F.: an experiment in art and education, the Brooklyn Museum, New York, May 13-July 16, 1978."

2:60    Exhibition held May 11-June 9, 1974 at the Santa Barbara Museum of Art.

2:61    An exhibition based on this book is scheduled to be held at the Whitney Museum of American Art, Oct. 14, 1976 to May 1, 1977, and at other museums at later dates.

2:62    Two presentations given at the annual meeting of the Commission, State College, Pa., Mar. 10-11, 1977.

2:63    Papers presented at a seminar in 1975, organized by the Democratic Socialist Club.

2:64    Papers presented at a meeting held in the Chemistry Dept., Sheffield University, April 17-19, 1972.

2:65    "The papers . . . were presented at a workshop given by the Council of Baccalaureate and Higher Degree Programs at Nashville, Tennessee on January 12-13, 1978, and repeated at Albuquerque, New Mexico, on February 27-28, 1978"--Introd.

2:66    Five of the 9 essays included were first presented at the Conference on Legal History held at Queens College on March 29-30, 1974, sponsored by the Historical Documents Collection of Queens College and the American Society for Legal History.

2:67    Chiefly papers presented at a symposium held in Oct. 1975 at the University of Cincinnati in cooperation with the University of Virginia.

2:68    Revised papers presented in their original form to the Conference on Social Change in Romania, held June 1977 at the University of California, Berkeley, sponsored by the Institute of International Studies.

2:69    Consists of edited papers from a conference held at the University of Oregon in Dec. 1968.

2:70    Outgrowth of a session of the Oct. 1977 meeting of the American Association for the Advancement of Slavic Studies.

2:71    "This book grew out of a conference on upland agriculture in northern Thailand, organized by the editors and held on the campus of Chiang Mai University in January 1970"--Pref.

2:72    Papers written chiefly in 1975 and early 1976 for a study conducted by the Office of Economic Affairs, Dept. of Housing and Urban Development.

2:73    Papers and documents filed before the U.S. Court of Claims and the U.S. Supreme Court.

2:74    Consists chiefly of Presidential decrees and documents issued by the Bureau of Internal Revenue.

2:75    "In memory of Arthur Sard"--P. [5].

2:76    Festschrift in honor of Zygmunt Gloger.

2:77    Written in honor of Frederick S. Tupper.

2:78    Contributions in honor and memory of Leopold G. Scheidl.

2:79    Volume of essays dedicated to Richard Hinton Thomas on his 65th birthday.

2:80    On cover: To Dr. Dayton C. Miller, in admiration and appreciation of his erudition and interest in the flute.

2:81    Presentation inscription to M. Hershel on cover.

2:82    Collection of articles presented to P.L. Anand, principal, Punjab University Evening College, on the occasion of his retirement from service.

2:83    Published on the occasion of the golden jubilee of the Landscape Institute.

2:84    Originally published in the May-June 1973 issue of the Mount Sinai journal of medicine as a commemorative issue in honor of Solomon A. Berson.

2:85    Memorial held at the Breitenbach residence in Chevy Chase, Md.

2:86    "This playlet was delivered as a lecture before the New York Theatre Guild, New York City, December 12th, 1928;

and before the League for Political Education, the Town Hall, New York City, December 17th, 1928"--Foreword.

2:87      Course held Dec. 1-3.

2:88      Hearings held Mar. 22-June 20, 1978.

2:89      Annotated.
          (Item is a bibliography)

2:90      Typescript (carbon copy).

2:91      Typescript (photocopy).


## LANGUAGE OF ITEM AND/OR TRANSLATION OR ADAPTATION (2.7B2)

2:92      Issued also in English.

2:93      Romanized record.

2:94      In various languages.

2:95      In English.
          (Title proper in Malay; parallel title in English)

2:96      In Kuki.

2:97      In Church Slavic.

2:98      In Slovenian.

2:99      In Konkani (Devanagari).

2:100     In Konkani (Kannada script).

2:101     In Serbo-Croatian (Roman) and Serbo-Croatian (Cyrillic).

2:102     Classical Greek and modern Greek.

2:103     In Japanese with some English, French, or Spanish.

2:104     In Chhattisgarhi; prefatory matter in Hindi.

2:105        In English; 2 essays in French.

2:106        In Tibetan; pref. in English.

2:107        In Polish, with summaries in English and Russian.

2:108        Czech or English; summaries in English, Russian, or
             Czech.

2:109        Basque or Spanish, with summaries in English.

2:110        German, Macedonian, or Serbo-Croatian, with summaries
             in English, French, German, Macedonian, or Russian.

2:111        English and/or Japanese texts.

2:112        Aramaic and English.

2:113        English and Hebrew. English translation by Lee and
             Murray Budney.

2:114        English and French, with occasional text in German,
             Italian, and Spanish.

2:115        Czech and Polish; prefatory matter, table of contents, and
             summaries in English and Russian.

2:116        Danish, English, and French.

2:117        Selections in Armenian.

2:118        Poems in the dialect of Minturno.

2:119        Examples and other citations in Arabic rendered in
             romanized form.

2:120        Introduction in English.

2:121        One contribution in French.

2:122        Partly also in Hebrew.

2:123        A few of the poems are in Swiss dialect.

2:124        Includes some papers in French.

2:125        Includes quotations in Sanskrit (Roman).

2:126    Includes poems in Italian with parallel English translations.

2:127    Includes papyri 626-658 in the original Greek, and English translations.

2:128    Includes 1 article in English and 7 in French.

2:129    Preface and table of contents also in English.

2:130    Descriptive text accompanying illustrations also in English.

2:131    Vol. 3 in French and German.

2:132    Appendix in Hindi and Sanskrit.

2:133    Summaries in Catalan and Spanish.

2:134    Some summaries in French and German.

2:135    Verse in Middle English; critical matter in English.

2:136    Poems in English and Spanish; plays in English.

2:137    Appendix, Survey questionnaires (leaves 33-50) in Arabic and English.

2:138    The poems are in Yiddish, Yiddish (romanized), and in English translation.

2:139    Preliminary and closing material in English and Spanish.

2:140    Legends in English, French, and German.

2:141    Text in German, Hungarian, Latin, and Slovak.

2:142    Text chiefly in Latin and Old High German.

2:143    Greek text with translation and commentary in Italian.

2:144    Text in Chinese; table of contents in Chinese and English; abstracts in English.

2:145    Text in Dutch and English, the former with summaries in English.

2:146    Text in English or German; summaries in both languages.

2:147    Text in English and French in parallel columns.

2:148    Parallel text in Czech, Latin, and Polish.

2:149    Latin, with interlinear English translation.

2:150    English and French, with French text on inverted pages.

2:151    English and Latin on facing pages.

2:152    English and French on opposite pages.

2:153    French originals and English rhymed versions on opposite pages.

2:154    English language translation of papers originally written in Russian.

2:155    Translation of: What is linguistics?

2:156    Translation of: Theorienstrukturen und Theoriendynamik. Originally published as: Probleme und Resultate der Wissenschaftstheorie und analytischen Philosophie, v. 2, pt. 2.

2:157    Translation with revisions of: Sprechen Sie lateinisch?

2:158    Translation of selections from: Psychiatrie.

2:159    "Translated . . . from . . . 'Kinder und Hausmärchen.' "

2:160    In large part a translation from: Le mythe de Sisyphe / Albert Camus.

2:161    Selected articles translated from the Persian.

2:162    Vocalized.
     (Vocalized is defined as: to furnish [as a consonantal Hebrew or Arabic text] with vowel or vowel points)

2:163    Text of the Ilyādhah vocalized.

2:164    Adaptation of: Anabasis / Xenophon.

2:165    "Adaptation of the 'Nun's priest's tale' from the Canterbury tales"--P. [3].

2:166    Adaptation of the traditional folk song.

2:167      Adapted from a folk verse.

2:168      "Adapted from Fairy tales from South Africa, by E.J. Bourhill"--Introd.

2:169      Prose version of: The Song of Roland.

2:170      A retelling of: The Lay of Havelok the Dane.

2:171      English versions of Pereira's poems by R. Lima.

2:172      Based on documentary film: Word is out.

2:173      Based on articles written for the New Yorker.

2:174      Based on papers presented at the Symposium on Acoustics and Spectroscopy held in Gdańsk in 1975.

2:175      Based on catalog of the same title published by British Council, London.

## SOURCE OF TITLE PROPER (2.7B3)

2:176      Cover title.

2:177      Spine title.

2:178      Caption title.

2:179      Colophon title.

2:180      Title from cover.

2:181      Title from label on cover.

2:182      Title from label mounted on cover.

2:183      Title from p. [1] of cover and spine, covered by labels, as above.

2:184      Title from verso of cover.

2:185      Title from spine.

2:186       Title from accompanying letter.

2:187       Title from portfolio.

2:188       Cataloged from portfolio.

2:189       Title supplied by cataloger.

2:190       Vol. 3 lacks collective title.

## VARIATIONS IN TITLE (2.7B4)

2:191       On cover: IEEE 1976 Power Engineering Society winter meeting.

2:192       On cover: New York World's Fair Armenian Folk Festival, May 31st, 1964.

2:193       Stamped on cover: Official audit report, Sept. 18, 1978.

2:194       On spine: WOL.

2:195       On spine: Datsun pick-ups, 1970-81.

2:196       On spine of binder: Law trial tactics.

2:197       Cover title: Lincolnshire structure plan.

2:198       Flyleaf title: Regional development guidelines for Muskingum County, Ohio.

2:199       Half title: Marc Chagall.

2:200       Spine title: Landlord-tenant law.

2:201       Title on spine: Religious thought and feeling in the Chansons de geste.

2:202       Title on verso of t.p.: In underground one can meet only rats.

2:203       Title on added t.p.: International trade and domestic employment.

2:204     Added t.p.: Genus Homo, its origin and subsequent evolution.
   (Title proper in Russian)

2:205     Title on p. [4] of cover: History of China.

2:206     Title on jacket: Edward the Third.

2:207     Title on accompanying memorandum: State payroll by election district, last half of 1978.

2:208     Caption title: Materials on landlord-tenant law for Detroit.

2:209     Running title: The Factories act, 1948.

2:210     Romanized title: Dar.

2:211     Original title: King Richard II.

2:212     Original title in Hebrew: Maḥberet.

2:213     Title also in Chinese.

2:214     Added t.p. in Korean.

2:215     Added Chinese t.p. in romanization: Chung yao ch'ien shuo.

2:216     Introductory volume, called v. 0, has also special title: The beginner's book.

2:217     Introductory volume issued without volume numbering has special title: Eröffnung des 5. Welt-Getreide- und Brotkongresses in der Deutschen Demokratischen Republik am 24. Mai 1970 im Kulturpalast Dresden.

2:218     Vol. 2 has also special title: Same real products.

2:219     Title on v. 2: The brain drain and taxation / edited by Jagdish N. Bhagwati.

2:220     Title on v. 2: Miso production. Lafayette, Calif. : New-age Foods Study Center.

2:221     Commonly known as: Alabama claims.

2:222    Also known as: Wallace.

2:223    Published also as: Les universités européennes 1975-1985.

2:224    American ed. published as: Different drummers.

2:225    British ed. published as: Denmark's day of doom.

2:226    Original ed. published as: Pelote, le petit mouton.

2:227    Original ed. published in English as: Sexual anomalies and perversions.

2:228    Previously published as: The book of American rankings.

2:229    Previously published as: Chief Joseph's own story. 1925.

2:230    Previously published as: Understanding Texas politics / Richard H. Kraemer, Ernest Crain, William Earl Maxwell. 1975.

2:231    Previously published as: A bibliography of the Chumash and their predecessors [with] The scientific expedition of Leon de Cessac to California, 1877-1879 / Henry Reichlen and Robert F. Heizer. 1964.

2:232    Previous eds. published as: Real estate : tax and financial aspects.

2:233    Published serially in Chicago tribune beginning Jan. 12, 1953 as: After the funeral.


## PARALLEL TITLES AND OTHER TITLE INFORMATION (2.7B5)

2:234    At head of title: Popular mechanics.

2:235    At head of title: Higher Education Act, Title II-C.

2:236    At head of title: Committee print.

2:237    Parallel title in Chinese characters.

2:238        Parallel title: Brijitto Rairī ten : 1959-nen kara 1978-nen made no sakuhin.

2:239        Title also in the association's other official languages.

2:240        Title also in English: Study on the behavior in the subject of traffic movements.

2:241        Titles on p. [3] in English, French, German, Russian, and Slovak; English title: . . . just stone and wood.

2:242        Added t.p.: The great English-Polish dictionary.

2:243        Added t.p. title: Yidishe literatur far onheybers.

2:244        Added t.p. title in Catalan: Pla comarcal de La Safor.

2:245        On verso of t.p.: Actual situation and needs of the scientific information in social sciences.
              (Title proper in Polish and Czech)

2:246        On verso of t.p.: Dizionaro poliglotto = Polyglot dictionary.

2:247        Subtitle: How I learned the secrets of mail-order marketing despite having made 25 horrendous mistakes.

2:248        Subtitle on cover: Projecte experimental de ciències socials de Catalunya.

2:249        Subtitle in colophon: [in nonroman script].
              (Use whenever possible according to AACR 2 rule 1.7A3)

2:250        Vol. 2 has subtitle: Sample population.

2:251        Edition of 1970 has subtitle: A plan for the garden.

2:252        Previous ed. has a slightly different subtitle.

2:253        "Preliminary findings"-- Cover.

2:254        "FY 1979"-- Spine.

2:255        "Presented in the Tuke Hall of Bedford College in London, 17th May 1976"-- T.p. verso.

2:256          Place and dates of exhibition from label on t.p.

2:257          The letter "u" in "uPIEEE-77" stands for the Greek
               letter "[mu]."


# STATEMENTS OF RESPONSIBILITY (2.7B6)

2:258          Author's name in Hebrew at head of title.

2:259          At head of title: Hungarian Office for Standardization.

2:260          Seal of the Pennsylvania State University at foot of title.

2:261          On t.p.: Centro Mexicano de Estudios en Far-
               macodependencia.

2:262          Statement of responsibility from label mounted above cap-
               tion title.

2:263          "Arthur D. Little, Inc."-- Cover.
               (Main entry; information does not appear in prominent
               source)

2:264          Author's name represented by rebus on title page.
               (Statement of responsibility reads: by [I.C. Stars])

2:265          "Written by Michael Watters and Barry Spinner"--Flyleaf.

2:266          "Prepared by Richard Sweet"-- Introd.

2:267          Produced by Ted Clark.
               (Information does not appear in prominent source)

2:268          Catalog by Dewey F. Mosby.
               (Information does not appear in prominent source)

2:269          By J.M. Franz, founder of the Kosmographische
               Gesellschaft? Cf. p. 23; also L. Euler. The Euler-Mayer cor-
               respondence, 1971.

2:270          Compiled by Thomas Tenison from the author's unpub-
               lished manuscripts.
               (Information does not appear in prominent source)

2:271      "Prepared by the Historical Services and Consultants Company, Houston, TX, under contract NASW-2590"--Foreword.

2:272      "Prepared for Agency for International Development, United States Department of State, and Ministry of Energy and Natural Resources, Government of Turkey, by United States Department of the Interior, Bureau of Reclamation"--Pref.

2:273      Translated by A. Chapman from a speech delivered in Washington in 1879.
          (Information does not appear in prominent source)

2:274      David C. Miller, principal author.
          (Information does not appear in prominent source)

2:275      Authors: A.J. Wolff and T.R. Grove.
          (Information does not appear in prominent source)

2:276      Authors: J.E. Lema and others.
          (Information does not appear in prominent source)

2:277      Contributions by various authors.

2:278      Statements of authorship vary.

2:279      Some of the studies prepared in cooperation with other authors.

2:280      "Dick Hobson, the author of this book . . . acknowledges the help of his collaborator, Mrs. Margaret Dodgson"--P. 5.

2:281      Prepared with the assistance of K. Barnhurst, D. Skellie, and J. Strauss.
          (Information does not appear in prominent source)

2:282      A report by an international group of energy experts.
          (Information does not appear in prominent source)

2:283      Authorship attributed to both Louisa Grace Ross and to Sir John Robinson.

2:284      Traditionally attributed to Robert Beverley. Cf. Virginia mag. of hist. and biog., v. 36, 1928, p. 344. Jefferson wrote "by Colō William Beverley" in his copy of the 2nd ed. Cf.

Library of Congress. Cat. of the library of Thomas Jefferson, 1952-1959, no. 1870.

2:285    "William Darton, in all probability, both wrote and illustrated the book"--Osborne catalog.

2:286    Authorship uncertain, has been attributed to Ramanujacharya.

2:287    Authorship much disputed, often ascribed to Cynewulf.

2:288    Work completed by R.A. Austen-Leigh.
    (Information does not appear in prominent source)

2:289    The blue pagoda was written by Hannes Bok to complete Merritt's The fox woman, which he left unfinished at his death.

2:290    Signed: A. Abeysinghe.

2:291    Signed at end: A Questionist.

2:292    Preface signed: Anth. Sparrow.

2:293    Text signed: Dorothy W. Sears.

2:294    The text is the Peter Alexander text.

2:295    Chairman: Earl of Snowdon.
    (Information does not appear in prominent source)

2:296    Translator statement stamped on t.p.
    (Translator's name appears in statement of responsibility)

2:297    "Illustrations . . . by Lucy Fitch Perkins"--Pref.

2:298    Includes additional material by Warren Blanding.
    (Information does not appear in prominent source)

2:299    The 1st pt. originally presented in 1959 by Robert Marshall as the Scott-Heron lecture; the 2nd pt. written and compiled by Kathleen N.M. Kelly.
    (Information does not appear in prominent source)

2:300    Vol. 1: Principal author of the articles, Alvaro Daza Roa.
    (Information does not appear in prominent source)

2:301      Vol. 2 by James B. Smith.

2:302      On cover of v. 2: By Adam Osborne.

2:303      Vols. 6-7 completed and edited by A. McCusker.

2:304      Stamped on t.p. of v. 2: By Laszlo Czirijak and George Pall. Edited by Thad P. Alton and Elizabeth Bass.

2:305      Vol. 1 translated by Charles Horowitz.
         (Information does not appear in prominent source)

2:306      Vol. 2 translated by A. White, with M. Higgins and C.M. Raphael.

2:307      First ed. by E.W. Johnson and C.B. Johnson. 1970.

2:308      First ed. edited by Melvin Mencher. 1973.

2:309      First-3rd eds. by G.H. Richert; 4th-5th eds. by G.H. Richert, Warren G. Meyer, and Peter Haines.

2:310      Previous ed. was written under the author's name as James Morris.
         (Author now known as Jan Morris after sex-change surgery)

2:311      Previous eds. prepared by U.S. Bureau of Naval Personnel.

2:312      Previous eds. of New trade names were by Ellen T. Crowley.

2:313      Authors' names in reverse order in previous eds.

2:314      Authors' names appear in the following order in the 1973 ed.: D.F. Bergwall, P.N. Reeves, N.B. Woodside.

2:315      Results of a project conducted by the Women's Action Alliance.
         (Information does not appear in prominent source)

2:316      Organized by the National Productivity Council (India) in collaboration with the Indian School of Mines, Dhanbad.
         (Information does not appear in prominent source)

2:317      "Project in collaboration with the IUCN Environmental Law Centre"--Pref.

2:318    "A report prepared in 1975 at the request of the Asian Centre for Development Administration, Kuala Lumpur"--P. 2.

2:319    Prepared under the auspices of the Public Works, Inc. under its earlier name: Boston Women's Collective.
        (Information does not appear in prominent source)

2:320    "Research project funded by the Committee for the Improvement of Instruction, the University of Nebraska at Omaha."

2:321    Sponsored by Chapter 3, District 10, of the Society of Logistics Engineers, and held Mar. 19, 1970.
        (Information does not appear in prominent source)

2:322    A research report prepared for the Massachusetts Dept. of Public Works in cooperation with the U.S. Bureau of Public Roads, agreement 1782.
        (Information does not appear in prominent source)

2:323    "Research project 3-5-71-155 conducted for the Texas Highway Department in cooperation with the U.S. Department of Transportation, Federal Highway Administration, by the Center for Highway Research, University of Texas at Austin."

2:324    "Sponsored by the Junior League of Memphis . . . and others"--Pref.

2:325    Sponsored by the Council of Thrombosis, American Heart Association and others.
        (Information does not appear in prominent source)

2:326    Workshop sponsored by the Law and Population Programme of the Fletcher School of Law and Diplomacy and by the Faculty of Law of the University of Nairobi.
        (Information does not appear in prominent source)

2:327    Organized under the joint sponsorship of the United Nations Economic Commission for Africa and others.
        (Information does not appear in prominent source)

2:328    Based in part on research by the Cambridge Group for the History of Population and Social Structure.

2:329     Based on: Bible. N.T. Mark V, 35-43.

2:330     Based on: El trovador / Antonio García Guitiérrez.

2:331     Based on: [Title / Statement of responsibility (in
nonroman script)].
    (Use whenever possible according to AACR 2 rule
    1.7A3)

2:332     Based on a manuscript by P. Collas.

2:333     Based on the letters and diaries of the author and his 3
brothers.

2:334     Based on a scenario by Auguste Mariette, which was
finished by Camille du Locle.

2:335     The libretto is based on the drama: Kabale une
Liebe / Schiller.

2:336     Libretto by F.M. Piave based on: Hernani / Victor Hugo.
Cf. Loewenberg. Annals of opera.

2:337     The biblical text is a revision of that prepared by the Ecole
biblique de Jérusalem.

2:338     Data for this study derived from the computerized
Association of American Medical Colleges Student Information System.


## EDITION AND HISTORY (2.7B7)

2:339     Edition statement from label on t.p.

2:340     Edition statement also appears as: Revised second edition.

2:341     Edition statement on cover corrected by mounted label:
Supplemental edition, 1975.

2:342     Includes other editions of some volumes.

2:343     Vol. 2: 3rd ed.; v. 3: 2nd ed.

2:344    Some volumes in revised editions.

2:345    Revision of: 3rd ed. 1975.

2:346    Revision of: 4th ed. Harrisburg, Pa. : Stackpole Books, 1967.

2:347    Rev. ed. of: Squash rackets for coaches and players. Sydney : Australia & New Zealand Book Co., 1977.

2:348    Rev. and enl. ed. of: A history of the Island of Jersey from cave men to the German occupation and after. 1950.

2:349    Revision and expansion of: A course in Moroccan Arabic. 1970.

2:350    Rev. and expanded version of the 1st pt. of the 1-vol. ed. of: Statistical theory in research / by R.L. Anderson and T.A. Bancroft. 1952.

2:351    Rev. and abridged version of: The joys of wine.

2:352    An abridgement of: I took a hammer in my hand. 1973.

2:353    Printed from the original ms. journal: The Town book.

2:354    First version published earlier in 1977 as: An opportunity for initiative.

2:355    Original ed. privately published in 1963.

2:356    First ed. published 1951.

2:357    First ed. published: Garden City, N.Y. : Doubleday (2 v.).

2:358    First ed. published earlier in 1977 as: The genealogies of two John Glenns.

2:359    Second ed. published as: Top pop records, 1955-1972. 1973.

2:360    Fourth ed. published in 1 v. as: Federal income, estate, and gift taxation. 1972; 5th ed. published in 2 separate volumes.

2:361    First-4th eds. published as: Obstetrical nursing / C.C. Van Blarcom.

2:362        First ed., issued anonymously. By Edmund Burke. Cf. New Cambridge bibl. of Eng. lit., v. 2, column 1184.

2:363        Previous ed.: Poona [India] : Arya Sanskriti Prakashan, 1969-1973 (4 v.).

2:364        German ed. published in 1970.

2:365        Previously published in: The Star.

2:366        Previously published in various periodicals.

2:367        Published in: Proceedings of a Symposium on Transient Ground Water Hydraulics, Fort Collins, Colo.

2:368        A combined ed. of 2 separately published works: Greenfield Village, and The Henry Ford Museum.

2:369        Illustrations originally published in: Paquebots / Michel Mohrt.

2:370        Detached from: The British journal of nursing, v. 78, no. 1944.

2:371        Part of the work was first published serially in the Maine bugle, July 1896-Oct. 1898.

2:372        "The first section of the history of Lyme's common was published in Patterns and pieces in 1976"--T.p. verso.

2:373        "Will be updated annually with a cumulative pocket supplement corresponding to the April 1 revision date of 21 CFR Chapter I"--P. iii.

2:374        "An updating of . . . [AIREA's] Case studies in apartment house valuation."

2:375        Updates: A selected bibliography of Alabama local planning and development documents, and A selected bibliography of Alabama county and regional planning and development documents; both issued by the office in 1974.

2:376        Updated ed. of: The James family of Wales and Bucks County, Pa., 1638-1974. 1st ed. 1974.

2:377        "An addendum to . . . Trilogy of murder."

2:378    Supplement to: The genealogy of John Marsh of Salem and his descendants, 1633-1888 / by Lucius B. Marsh.

2:379    Supplement to: The Boletín estadístico, no. 11-12, Nov.-Dec. 1974.

2:380    "A supplement to the Journal of monetary economics . . . containing papers presented at the April 1978 conference."

2:381    The first of 2 supplements to: Trade names dictionary / by Ellen T. Crowley. 2nd ed.

2:382    One of 27 papers which supplement: On further examination / by the Advisory Panel on the Scholastic Aptitude Test Score Decline of College Entrance Examination Board.

2:383    Continues: Fidelity & surety law bibliography, 1946-1971. 1972.

2:384    Continues the author's: Vintage films.

2:385    "Supersedes NBS special publication 386, 1973 edition [compiled by Jack M. Fath]."

2:386    Based on: Maryland, a guide to the Old Line State / compiled by the Writers' Program of the Work Projects Administration in the State of Maryland. 1940.

2:387    Based on: The Victorian solicitor / by Kenneth H. Gifford. 3rd ed. 1974.

2:388a    Sequel: Music and society since 1815.

2:388b    Sequel to: A social history of music, from the Middle Ages to Beethoven.

2:389a    Sequel: Northern Afghanistan, or, Letters from the Afghan Boundary Commission / C.E. Yate.

2:389b    Sequel to: England and Russia face to face in Asia / by A.C. Yate.

2:390    First volume of the author's trilogy, the subsequent volumes are: The Queen's sister; The Lady Cicely.

2:391    Final volume in a trilogy, the 1st of which is the author's The sunset warrior and the 2nd of which is his Shallows of night.

2:392  Third and final volume of autobiography, of which the 1st is Once is enough and the 2nd is More than enough.

2:393  Companion volume to: Who's who in consulting. 2nd ed.

2:394  Companion volume to the author's: Environmental law.

2:395  Companion work to: The law of contract / by G.C. Cheshire and C.H.S. Fifoot. 3rd Australian ed.

2:396  "Serves as a companion to Consultants and consulting organizations, 2nd edition"--Introd.

2:397  Prepared to accompany: Priests at prayer : a cassette tape program.

2:398  To be used in conjunction with: IATA regulations relating to the carriage of restricted articles by air / The International Air Transport Association.

2:399  May be used with the authors': All together now.

2:400  These papers are directly related to work reported in the editor's: Perception and measurement of scenic resources in the Southern Connecticut River Valley.

2:401  "This volume contains four appendices which present supporting material for the Secretary of Transportation's National highway safety needs report."

2:402  Facsimile of the 1870 manuscript in the Victoria and Albert Museum, London.

2:403  Facsimile, with letterpress transcription, of 6 paragraphs of aphorisms inscribed by the author in a copy of the 1st ed. of The crock of gold.

2:404  Reprint of an unspecified previous ed.

2:405  Reprint. Originally published: 1845.
    (Give only the date if original publisher is unknown)

2:406  Reprint. Originally published: New York : H. Holt, 1944.
    (Basic formal reprint note)

2:407  Reprint. Originally published: 2nd ed. London : Macmillan, 1935.

2:408        Reprint. Originally printed for: London : T.N. Longman, 1797.

2:409        Reprint. Originally published: Chapel Hill, N.C. : R. Adams, 1936.
                (Publisher is also author of item)

2:410        Reprint. Originally published: Bombay : Book Centre, [1965?].

2:411        Reprint. Originally published: London : London Print. and Pub. Co., 1958-1959.

2:412        Reprint. Originally published: Cambridge : Printed by J. Archdeacon for J. Deighton, 1785.

2:413        Reprint. Originally published: Brattleboro, Vt. : Stephen Daye Press, 1936. With corrections and additions.
                (Note expanded to show added information not included in body of entry)

2:414        Reprint. Originally published: Boston : Houghton Mifflin, 1928. With new introd. and new index.

2:415        Reprint. Originally published: Milwaukee : Bruce Pub. Co., 1954. With additional reading.

2:416        Reprint. Originally published: The secret of the universe. 10th ed. Grand Rapids : Eerdmans, 1955.
                (Note expanded to show title change and edition statement)

2:417        Reprint. Originally published: Counties of Howard and Tipton, Indiana (pts. 1-2). Chicago : F.A. Battey, 1883.
                (Note expanded to show specific part reprinted)

2:418        Reprint. Originally published: Mike, a public school story (pt. 2). London : A. and C. Black, 1909. Published separately as: Enter Psmith. 1935.

2:419        Reprint. Originally published: Quantum theory of molecules and solids, v. 2. New York : McGraw-Hill, 1965. With corrections and a new pref.

2:420          Reprint of pt. 2 of the ed. published in 1886 by Warner, Beers, Chicago; with complete index.
               (Original title shown as parallel title in body of entry; informal note used here to preserve clarity of meaning)

2:421          Reprint (pt. 1). Originally published: Books on persecution, terror and resistance in Nazi Germany. London : Wiener Library, 1949.
               (Note used when only part of the work in hand is a reprint)

2:422          Reprint (p. 1-112). Originally published: Journals kept in Hyderabad, Kashmir, Sikkim, and Nepal, v. 2, p. 151-262. London : W.H. Allen, 1887.

2:423a         Reprint (1st work). Originally published: Boston : T.O.H.P. Burnham, 1861.

2:423b         Reprint (2nd work). Originally published: Boston : Ticknor and Fields, 1860.
               (Notes used for reprint edition of two or three formerly independent works)

2:424a         Reprint (1st work). Originally published: London : Printed for F. and C. Rivington, 1794.

2:424b         Reprint (2nd work). Originally published: London : Printed for J. Johnson, 1803.

2:425a         Reprint (1st work). Originally published: London : Printed for the author and sold by E. Rich, [1787?].

2:425b         Reprint (2nd work). Originally published: London : Printed for the editor and sold by D. Brewman, [1791?].

2:426a         Reprint (1st work). Originally published with: The blue pagoda / H. Bok. New York : New Collectors' Group, 1946.

2:426b         Reprint (2nd work). Originally published with: The fox woman / A. Merritt. New York : New Collectors' Group, 1946.

2:426c         Reprint (3rd work). Originally published: New York : New Collectors' Group, 1947.
               (Title proper: The fox woman and The blue pagoda and The black wheel)

2:427a    Reprint (1st work). Originally published: The epistle exhortatorye of an Englyshe Christiane. Antwerp, 1544. (STC 1291).

2:427b    Reprint (2nd work). Originally published: A reply to Stephen Gosson's Schoole of abuse in defence of poetry, musick, and stage plays. 1579-1580. (STC 16663).

2:428a    Reprint (1st work). Originally published: Washington, D.C. : U.S. G.P.O., 1941.

4:428b    Reprint (2nd work). Originally published: Washington, D.C. : U.S. G.P.O., 1939.

2:428c    Reprint (3rd work). Originally published: Washington, D.C. : U.S. G.P.O., 1940.
          (Notes used when reprint edition has a collective title; individual titles should be included in contents note)

2:429    Reprint of works originally published 1920-1940.
          (Note used when reprint edition combines more than three formerly independent works)

2:430    Facsim. reprint. Originally published: London : Imprinted by Felix Kyngston for William Welby, 1612.

2:431    Originally published: In the fullness of time. Berne, Ind. : Berne Witness Co., 1948.
          (Omit the introductory word "Reprint" when in doubt as to whether new edition is a reprint)
          *For reprint notes expanded to include series statement see Series (2.7B12)*

2:432    Reprinted from: Munsey's magazine, Dec. 1900.

2:433    Reprinted from: Joachim Joesten's Truth letter, v. 3, no. 19, June 15, 1971.

2:434    Reprinted from: Prairie farmer's Reliable directory of farmers and breeders, Jackson and Williamson Counties, Illinois. 1920. With added index.

2:435    Pages 113-131 reprinted from: Proceedings of the Royal Geographical Society, no. 6, June 1881, p. 326-340.

2:436    Prepublication issue of chapters 1-3 of 1st American ed.

2:437          "Three hundred copies."

2:438          "250 exemplaires."

2:439          "Seventy-five copies have been printed."

2:440          "400 copies printed."

2:441          "Printed: 400."

2:442          "Limited to 110 copies."

2:443          Limited ed. of 20 numbered copies.

2:444          "420 copie numerate."

2:445          Edition of 100 copies, signed by the author.

2:446          "300 copies soft cover and 50 copies hard cover"--P. [2].

2:447          "175 copies printed for Abe Lerner by Ronald Gordon at the Oliphant Press in New York as a keepsake for presentation September 28, 1978, to members of the Double Crown Club in London"--P. [8].

2:448          "Issued in a first printing of 375 copies signed by the poet. Three hundred numbered copies are for distribution by the poet and publisher, of which numbers 1-62 are bound in vellum and include a poem in holograph. The remaining 75 copies will be issued later as part of boxed sets"--Colophon.

2:449          "Eleven sets of plates plus that required for copyright were produced."


## PUBLICATION, DISTRIBUTION, ETC. (2.7B9)

2:450          Imprint from t.p. of v. 2.

2:451          Imprint stamped on cover.

2:452          Imprint statement in Chinese characters.

2:453          Some imprint information from label mounted on p. [2] of cover.

2:454        Imprint under label reads: Oxford : Clarendon Press.

2:455        Vol. 2 has imprint: Boston : Boston Book Co., 1892.

2:456        Vol. 1 lacking imprint.

2:457        Publisher from label on t.p.; publication date and ISBN from label on verso t.p.

2:458        Publisher named on cover.

2:459        "Published by the Controller of Publications, Delhi"--Pref.

2:460        Photocopy imprint from label mounted on cover.

2:461        Photocopy. High Wycomb, England : Published on demand by University Microfilms, [197-]. 22 x 28 cm.
*For LC's interpretation on cataloging macro- and microreproductions see Cataloging Service Bulletin, no. 14, fall 1981, p. 56-58*

2:462        Photocopy. [S.1. : s.n., 1980?].
*See annotation for 2:461*

2:463        Vol. 2 published by: Washington, D.C. : American Chemical Society.

2:464        Vol. 2 published by the centre under its later form of name: Centre régional de documentation pédagogique de Marseille.

2:465        Published simultaneously in Australia.

2:466        Published in conjunction with the United Nations.
(Information does not appear in prominent source)

2:467        "Published in cooperation with the Asia Society, New York"-- Foreword.

2:468        "Published for The Trustees of the Sea Fishes of Southern Africa Book Fund."

2:469        "Privately printed."

2:470        "Privatdruck."

2:471      "Privately printed for A.J.A. Symons"--P. 13.

2:472      Distributor stamped on p. [4] of cover.

2:473      Distributor statement stamped on half t.p.

2:474      Distributor from label on flyleaf.

2:475      Distributed in the U.S. by: Atlantic Highlands, N.J. : Humanities Press.

2:476      Distributed in the U.K. by: Hemel Hempstead, England : Prentice-Hall International, International Book Distributors.

2:477      "Distributed by Serendipity Books, Berkeley"--Dust jacket.

2:478      "Sole distributors for the USA, Motorbooks International, Osceola, Wis."--Jacket.

2:479      Not available for distribution in Great Britain.

2:480      Label mounted on leaf following t.p.: Distributed in the U.S. by Charles River Reprints, Boston, Mass.

2:481      Label on p. iii: Transatlantic Arts, Levittown, N.Y., sole distributor for the U.S.A.

2:482      Label mounted on spine: Exclusive distributor, ISBS, Inc., Forest Grove, Or.

2:483      Vol. 3 distributed by: New York : Harper & Row.

2:484      Vol. 2: For sale by the Supt. of Docs., U.S. G.P.O.

2:485      Date from label on verso of t.p.

2:486      Publication date stamped on t.p.

2:487      Copyright statement changed in ms. on verso of t.p. of v. 1 to read c1978.

2:488      Deposited for copyright, July 5, 1886.

2:489      "August 1979."
           *For LC's interpretation on dates of release or transmittal see Cataloging Service Bulletin, no. 17, summer 1982, p. 14*

2:490        "Date issued, March 1977."
             *See annotation for 2:489*

2:491        Vol. 1 issued Dec. 1, 1979; v. 2: Apr. 1979.
             *See annotation for 2:489*

2:492        A projected 3rd volume was mentioned in pref. of v. 2,
             not yet published (Feb. 1912).

2:493        Part 1 not published.

2:494        No more published.

2:495        No more published?


## PHYSICAL DESCRIPTION (2.7B10)

2:496        "Published in large print."

2:497        Folding book; 31 x 127 cm. full size, folded to 31 cm.

2:498        Cyclostyled.

2:499        "Reproduced from a photographic copy of the pages of a
             hand made book of text and rubbings."

2:500        Thumb-indexed.

2:501        Loose-leaf for updating.

2:502        Consists of 4 separate pamphlets.

2:503        Sold as a set in 3-ring binder.

2:504        Each volume issued in a case.

2:505        Issued in portfolio; title from portfolio; text part in quires.

2:506        Maps in portfolio.

2:507        Issued in a split-page format.

2:508        Three columns to the page.

| | |
|---|---|
| 2:509 | Second work on inverted pages. |
| 2:510 | On double leaves, traditional oriental format. |
| 2:511 | Alternate leaves of braille and print. |
| 2:512 | Printed on 1 side of leaf only; the printed leaves, numbered in duplicate, facing each other. |
| 2:513 | Most right-hand pages bear the same numbers as the left-hand pages with the addition of the letter "a." |
| 2:514 | Paging irregular, following starred paging of original edition, inset in the margin of the text. |
| 2:515 | Page 190 incorrectly numbered 192. |
| 2:516 | Pages numbered in opposite directions. |
| 2:517 | Opposite pages (p. 2-147) numbered in duplicate. |
| 2:518 | Pages also numbered 223-256. |
| 2:519 | Pages also numbered 168-186 continuing the paging of the preceding number. |
| 2:520 | Continues the pagination of the author's: Nurses in nursing homes. |
| 2:521 | Alternate pages blank. |
| 2:522 | Pages 502-504 blank. |
| 2:523 | Verso of each page blank for notes. |
| 2:524 | Pages [98]-[100] blank for "Notizen." |
| 2:525 | Thirty-nine pages are blank for notes. |
| 2:526 | Page 656 reserved for future expansion. |
| 2:527 | Pages 371-433 deleted by censor. |
| 2:528 | Advertising matter included in paging. |
| 2:529 | Six tables on 3 folded leaves in pocket. |

2:530    One folded leaf of plates inserted.

2:531    Twelve leaves of plates inserted in envelope.

2:532    The illustrations are hand-colored.

2:533    Printed wrappers with 3 illustrations.

2:534    "The cover is an original lithograph by Claire Van Vliet."

2:535    Illustrations on lining papers.

2:536    The ill. is on p. [1]-[2], repeated on p. [17]-[18].

2:537    Map on lining paper.

2:538    Col. maps on lining papers.
         (Physical description area reads: maps (some col.))

2:539    Map inserted in v. 1.

2:540    Folded map inserted.

2:541    Part of illustrative matter (4 folded leaves) in pocket.

2:542    Graph on folded leaf in pocket.

2:543    Overlay inserted.

2:544    Spirit masters are bound with transparencies.

2:545    Text on p. [2-3] of cover.

2:546    Text on inside front cover.

2:547    Text on inside back and back cover.

2:548    Includes back cover with foldout playing field and leaf of
         punchouts.

2:549    Additions and corrections in ms.

## ACCOMPANYING MATERIAL (2.7B11)

2:550    Accompanied by loose-leaf index volume.

2:551    Accompanied by a topographic map of Snow Shoe, Pa.

2:552    Accompanied by signed photograph of Kreisler.

2:553    Accompanied by guide "Environmental specifications and standards" (25 p. : charts ; 28 cm.), previously published separately in 1979.

2:554    Magnifying glass in pocket.

2:555    One stereopticon in pocket.

2:556    Accompanied by a mylar insert showing the coffins, mask, and mummy of Tutankhamun.

2:557    With 625 slides (b&w) to accompany v. 1.

2:558    Vol. 3 contains map (col. ; 30 x 26 cm.).

2:559    Kept up-to-date by pocket parts.

2:560    Kept up-to-date by cumulative pocket parts and pamphlets and by replacement volumes.

2:561    Pocket contains a pamphlet, Far-out fun (24 p.) and a game, Pachisea (1 folded sheet and 1 sheet of transfers).

2:562    Twenty slides (col. ; 7 x 7 cm.) of Chagall's works in pockets inside front cover.

2:563    Selected works by H. Hazaz ([12] leaves) inserted in pocket in v. 2.

2:564    "Notes from the editors" (22 p.) inserted at end.

2:565    "Chilton's fuel economy & tune-up tips" ([8] p.) inserted between pages 140 and 141.

2:566    "The Illiad of Homer; notes from the editors" published as supplement (23 p.) and inserted.

2:567        Erratum slip inserted.

2:568        Errata slips ([2] leaves) inserted.

2:569        "Addendum" and "Errata": [2] p. inserted.

2:570        Colophon inserted.

2:571        "Supplement" (8 p.) laid in.

2:572        Kept up-to-date by monthly supplements.

2:573        "Additional information" slip mounted on blank leaf following text.

2:574        The facsimile of the original typewritten manuscript (12 p.) mounted at end of book.

2:575        Issued in a box (63 x 48 x 8 cm.) containing also 6 sound discs (33 1/3 rpm, mono. ; 12 in. in case), 4 dioramas (47 pieces : col.), 4 souvenir booklets (12 p. each : ill. ; 15 cm. in case), and 2 art reproductions (photogravure, col. ; 60 x 45 cm.).

2:576        Souvenir booklets give a brief synopsis of each opera.

2:577        Dioramas are of sets from the operas Aïda and Il barbiere di Siviglia.

2:578        Mode of use of accompanying disk: Apple II or Apple II plus; 48K RAM; DOS 3.2 or 3.3.


## SERIES (2.7B12)

2:579        Series statement from jacket.

2:580        Series statement in v. 2 only.

2:581        Vol. 1 lacks series statement.

2:582        Vol. 3 issued without series statement.

2:583        Vols. 1 and 2 in series: Bibliographies of famous authors. Vols. 3-7 in series: Bibliographies of modern authors. Vol. 8 in both series.

2:584        Issued as a Cambridge Christmas book. Cf. The Cambridge Christmas books / B. Crutchley. 1976. p. [5].

2:585        "A Ronald Press publication."

2:586        "A Knowledge Industry Publications, Inc. book."

2:587        "A Nature biography book"--Dust jacket.

2:588        "DMS market intelligence"--Verso of t.p.

2:589        Series statement also appears as: Nursing photobook.

2:590        Series title romanized: Ningen sensho.

2:591        Series 2 romanized: Ch'ing shao nien fu tao ts'ung shu.

2:592        "A special volume of the series: Studies in medieval
culture."

2:593        Originally issued as monographs in series: Kings of jazz.

2:594        Reprint. Originally published: Philadelphia : Jewish
Publication Society, 1925. (The Schiff library of Jewish
classics).
             (Reprint note expanded to show series statement)

2:595        Reprint. Originally published: London : Gresham Pub.
Co., [191-?] (Myth and legend in literature and art).

2:596        Reprint. Originally published: Philadelphia : G. Barrie,
1900. (The masterpieces of George Sand / George Sand ; v. 1).

2:597        Reprint. Originally published: State College, Pa. : Pennsylvania State College, 1940. (Pennsylvania State College
studies ; no. 7).

2:598        Reprint. Originally printed for the society by: Edinburgh :
W. Blackwood, 1889. (Scottish Text Society publications ;
no. 6-7, 17).

2:599        Reprint. Originally published for the Early English Text
Society by: London : H. Milford, Oxford University Press,
1927. (Original series / Early English Text Society ; no. 169).

2:600        Reprint. Originally published: Edinburgh : W. Blackwood,
1877. (Ancient classics for English readers. Supplementary
series ; v. 5).

2:601    Reprint. Originally published: Baltimore : Johns Hopkins Press, 1948. (Publications / Institute of the History of Medicine, Johns Hopkins University. Series 3, The Hideyo Noguchi lectures ; v. 6).

2:602    Reprint. Originally published: New York : Dell Pub. Co., 1966. (Laurel language library. Spanish series). With a new pref.

2:603    Facsim. reprint. Originally published: Modern chromatics, with applications to art and industry. New York : D. Appleton, 1879. (The International scientific series ; v. 26).
         *For reprint notes without series statement see Edition and History (2.7B7)*

# DISSERTATIONS (2.7B13)

2:604    Extra t.p. with thesis statement inserted.

2:605    Thesis statement from label mounted on cover.

2:606    Thesis (Ph. D.)--Dropsie College, 1917.

2:607    Thesis (doctoral)--Universität Stuttgart, 1980.

2:608    Thesis (M.S.)--Baylor University, 1972.

2:609    Thesis (M.A.)--University of Santo Tomas, Manila, 1980.

2:610    Thesis (licenciado en derecho)--Universidad de Chile, 1933.
         (Dissertation designated by the term used on the work)

2:611    Thesis (thèse complémentaire)--Bordeaux, 1967.

2:612    The authors' thesis (Ph. D.)--University of Denver, 1972.
         (Work of shared responsibility)

2:613    Ian S. Zagon's thesis (Ph. D.)--University of Colorado, 1972.
         (Text edited by the candidate)

2:614    Abstract of thesis (Ph. D.)--University of Illinois at Urbana-Champaign, 1977.

2:615     Summary of thesis--Royal Institute of Technology, Stockholm.

2:616     Condensed presentation of the author's thesis--University of California.

2:617     Revision of the author's thesis--Heidelberg, 1977.

2:618     Slight revision of the author's thesis (M.A.--University of Delhi, 1973) under the title: Market structure in Indian agriculture.

2:619     Revision of the 1st pt. of the author's thesis (University College of Swansea).

2:620     Translation and revision of the author's thesis (Freie Universität, Berlin, 1968) under the title: Normannen und Waliser bei Giraldus Cambrensis.

2:621     Issued also as Inaugural-Dissertation (Rostock).

2:622     Originally presented as the author's akademisk avhandling (Lund, 1962).

2:623     Originally presented as the author's thesis (Ph. D.--Catholic University of America, 1944).

2:624     Originally presented as the author's thesis (Ph. D.--University of Michigan) under the title: Anatomy of a city planner.

2:625     Submitted, together with papers previously published (listed on p. 7), as thesis (doctoral--Meerut University, 1980).

2:626     Some of the material presented as the author's thesis (M.A.--University of Keele).

2:627     Chapters 1-4 of the introd. originally presented as the editor's thesis (Bryn Mawr College, 1917).

2:628     Project initiated as editor's thesis (master's).

2:629     Outgrowth of the author's thesis (Ph. D.--University of Florida).

2:630     Data from author's thesis (Exeter).

2:631      Based on the author's thesis (M.A.).

2:632      Based on the author's thesis (Bombay University).

2:633      Spanish version of the author's thesis (Columbia University, 1975).

2:634      "A revised and updated version of a dissertation . . . presented in 1973 at Temple University, College of Education."

2:635      Thesis--Geneva (H.W. Ruelius, respondent).
             (Information does not appear in prominent source)

2:636      "Inaugural-Dissertation, Cologne"--Pref.

2:637      ". . . Habilitationsschrift, Marburg"--P. iv.

2:638      Revision of the author's Habilitationsschrift, Bonn, 1975.

2:639      "Rede, Salzburg: Festakt der Universität"--Foreword.

2:640      Accompanies "Programm" (Geburtstag des Königs)--Universität Bremen.

2:641      Separate from "program"--Lund.


# AUDIENCE (2.7B14)

2:642      Intended audience: Kindergarten children.

2:643      Intended audience: Biology, chemistry, and physics classes, grades 10-12.

2:644      Intended audience: Visually impaired.

2:645      Intended audience: Women returning to the work force.

2:646      For children aged 6-9.

2:647      For 10-12 year olds.

2:648      "A workbook for 6th form students"--Introd.

2:649    "Written specially for the foreigner . . . based on The new method English dictionary by Dr. West and J.G. Endicott."

2:650    A compilation to provide related background material for participants in the 3rd annual conference of the National Caucus on the Black Aged, held in Washington, D.C., Apr. 13-15, 1975.

2:651    "For presentation at a creative manufacturing engineering program."

2:652    For all interested in the use or manufacture of colors, and in calico printing, bleaching, etc.

2:653    "This extract from the forthcoming complete Orchestral music in print is devoted to works composed or arranged for students."

2:654    "Top secret."

2:655    Stamped on cover: Unclassified.

2:656    Open to researchers with permission of the Kennedy family.

2:657    May be duplicated, originals not to be detached from book.
             (Local note, for book of duplicating masters)

2:658    "Not issued for commercial purposes."


# SUMMARY (2.7B17)

2:659    Summary: Two children living on a sheep farm take care of their pet lambs, Penny and Pete.

2:660    Summary: Relates how Tiger came to lose his spots and how he eventually regained them--but with a difference.

2:661    Summary: Examines the different methods used by historians to gather facts and compile histories.

2:662    Summary: Explains how a ball-point pen works. Presents directions for constructing tools and devices with parts of pens and for using them in experiments and demonstrations.

2:663  Summary: Biographies of 10 professional quarterbacks: Fran Tarkenton, Roger Staubach, Bob Griese, Ken Stabler, Terry Bradshaw, Archie Manning, Ken Anderson, Bert Jones, Dan Fouts, and Jim Zorn.

## CONTENTS (2.7B18)

2:664  Bibliography: 8th prelim. page.

2:665  Bibliography: p. 72.

2:666  Bibliography: p. [3] of cover.

2:667  Bibliography: p. 24 (4th group).

2:668  Bibliography: p. ix-xxii.

2:669  Bibliography: p. [381]-382.

2:670  Bibliography: p. [46]-[47].

2:671  Bibliography: p. D1-D7.

2:672  Bibliography: p. [A]-B (2nd group).

2:673  Bibliography: leaf [57].

2:674  Bibliography: v. 1, leaves 114-115.

2:675  "Bibliographical notes": v. 1, p. 407-412; v. 2, p. 384-389.

2:676  "Bibliographical notes": v. 5, p. [593]-655.

2:677  Prefatory material includes bibliographical references.

2:678  Bibliographical references included in "Notes" (p. 292-309). Bibliography: p. 310-318.

2:679  Bibliography of the author's works: p. 228-229.

2:680  "A bibliography of Richard Wright's works": p. 191-205.

2:681    Bibliography of works by and about Dagny Juell: p. [3]-[5].

2:682    "The writings of Joachim Joesten about the assassination of President John F. Kennedy and related matters": leaf [18].

2:683    "A bibliography of Baroque literature studies, 1932-1976": p. [113]-137.

2:684    Discography: p. 26-28.

2:685    Filmography: p. A1-A4.

2:686    "List of sources used": p. xv-xvi.

2:687    "Mediography": p. 173-190.

2:688    Synopsis: p. vi-vii.

2:689    Synopses in German and English: p. vi-ix.

2:690    Engraved receipt form: p. [25].

2:691    "Alpha Omega hymn": p. 7 and p. 112.

2:692    "Music score": p. [59]-70.

2:693    Songs with piano acc.: p. 179-211.

2:694    "Descriptive catalogue of the etchings of John Taylor Arms": p. 55-76.

2:695    "Checklist of the exhibition": p. 313-334.

2:696    "Preachin' blues: a study of the life and music of Robert Johnson" / Bob Groom: p. 2-6.

2:697    "Directory of selected banks and financial institutions": [1-34] p. (last group).

2:698    Includes the original text and a modernized version.

2:699    Includes both the long and short texts.

2:700    Includes the text of "The rule of St. Augustine."

2:701    Includes selections from the Bhagavadgītā with English translations.

2:702    Includes all published as well as selected unpublished articles dealing with programmed instruction and computer-assisted instruction from 1954 through 1969.

2:703    Includes reproductions of the title pages of many of the articles.

2:704    Includes a diary written by F.N. Reckitt.

2:705    Includes quotations in Hindi and Sanskrit.

2:706    Includes lists of teas and other herbal preparations and Chinese herbs in romanized Chinese and Japanese and annotated Chinese characters.

2:707    Includes the California General corporation law.

2:708    Includes Tennessee property assessment newsletter, v. 1, no. 1: p. 1-9 (1st group).

2:709    Includes a bibliography.

2:710    Includes bibliographies.

2:711    Includes bibliographies and indexes.

2:712    Includes bibliographies, discographies, and index.

2:713    Includes bibliographical references.

2:714    Includes bibliographical references and indexes.

2:715    Includes index.

2:716    Includes tables.

2:717    "Appendix B: Printed writings by James Stephens": p. 420-458.

2:718    "Apéndices" (p. 347-[395]) consists of documents.

2:719    Appendices (p. 69-91): A. The German accounts -- B. The Portugese documents.

2:720        Appendix (p. [155]-180): The origin of geometry / by Edmund Husserl, originally published as: Die Frage nach dem Ursprung der Geometrie als intentional-historisches Problem. 1939.

2:721        Census tables cover periods between 1900-1970.

2:722        Vita.

2:723        Vita: p. [2] of cover.

2:724        Vita on label mounted on t.p. verso.

2:725        The 1st volume, unnumbered, consists of pref. and table of contents.

2:726        The main work, also issued separately, is followed by Teacher's guide and Reading guide / by Verna S. Fancett.

2:727        Contains an "Inventory of the library," chiefly in Latin; with prefatory matter, "Index of authors" with their works, and an "Index of incipits," / by K.W. Humphreys.

2:728        Contains Technical papers EM77-100--MM77-124.

2:729        Contains Technical papers AD78-741, etc. of the Society of Manufacturing Engineers.

2:730        Contains 3 parts; each part has also special t.p.: pts. 1-2. History of Sewickley Township (336 p.) -- pt. 3. History of Suterville (47 p.).

2:731        Consists of 2 titles: Killers attached to front cover, Lovers to back cover. Each part has special t.p.
             (Title proper: Lovers/killers)

2:732        Contents: Wordsworth -- Coleridge -- Hawthorne -- Longfellow.

2:733        Contents: Die Schlange aber -- Das Volleyballspiel -- Stilleben.

2:734        Contents: H.R. 6351 -- H.R. 7681 -- Comparison of H.R. 6351, H.R. 7681, and existing law.

2:735    Contents: Sioux history to 1890 / V. Douville -- History of St. Francis Indian Mission, 1885-1973 -- A listing by case and catalog numbers of select Sioux artifacts within this museum.

2:736    Partial contents: A toast / W.H. Auden -- The ambiguity of William Empson / M.C. Bradbrook -- Extracts from unpublished memoirs / K. Raine -- Mr. William Empson in Japan / R. Fukuhara -- An Empson bibliography / M. Megaw (p. [213]-244).

2:737    Partial contents: The European background / by Carl J. Friedrich -- The American scene / by Oscar Handlin -- Adjustment to the United States / by Hildegard Binder Johnson -- Bibliographical notes (p. [257]-268) -- Biographical dictionary of the Forty-eighters / by G.E. Zucker.

2:738    Contents: Oh America: Darkness. And Cherokee sundown. Note from Monticello. The big sellout! -- January 12th, 1967.
         (Includes section title)

2:739    Contents: Old Testament themes: The rescuing love of God / Q.R. Gordon. Aunt Hagar and her children / H.W. Creecy, Sr. Why do the righteous suffer? / C.W. Cone -- New Testament themes: The suffering God / E.P. Wimberly. What can Christianity do for me? / T. Hoyt, Jr.
         (Includes section title)

2:740    Contents: v. 1. 1604-1705 -- v. 2-4. 1705-1837.

2:741    Contents: v. 1. Humanities -- v. 2. Language and literature -- v. 3. History -- v. 4. Index.

2:742    Contents: [1] Alphabetical ownership volume, geographical cross index -- [2] Map volume -- [3] Aerial/Map volume.

2:743    Contents: [1] Arrest. Preliminary examination. Bail. Grand jury. Indictment and information -- [2] Process upon indictment and information. Arraignment. Waiver of jury trial. Trial jury.

2:744    Contents: v. 1. Descriptive survey -- v. 2. [without special title] -- v. 3. Township maps.
         (LC practice designating untitled volume)

2:745     Partial contents: pt. 1. Baptisms, 1563-1620. Marriages
          and burials, 1600-1620 -- pt. 2. 1621-1660 / J.R. Bulmer,
          editor and indexer.

2:746     Contents: t. 1. Textes -- t. 2. Commentaire / M.E.
          Boismard, A. Lamouille, et P. Sandevoir.

2:747     Contents: v. 1. Wildlife / E.G. Klinkhart and W.B.
          Driskell -- v. 2. Fisheries / R.F. McLean, K.J. Delaney, and
          B.A. Cross.

2:748     Contents: v. 1. Assessment and application / S.J. Rogers
          and D.B. D'Eugenio -- v. 2. Early intervention developmen-
          tal profile / S.J. Rogers . . . [et al.] -- v. 3. Stimulation ac-
          tivities / S.L. Brown and C.M. Donovan.

2:749     Contents: [Bd. 1] Der Findling -- Bd. 2. Der Zögling --
          Bd. 3. Der Vagabund -- Bd. 4. Der Glücksucher.

2:750     Contents: t. 1. Catalogue statistique = Statistical catalog
          -- t. 2. Catalogue démographique = Demographic catalog.

2:751     Partial contents: v. F2. Feature films, 1921-1930. Feature
          films, 1921-1930, credit & subject indexes (2 v.) -- v. F6.
          Feature films, 1961-1970. Feature films, 1961-1970, indexes
          (2 v.).
                    (Physical description area reads: 2 v. in 4)

2:752     Partial contents: v. 8. The structure and dynamics of
          psyche (2nd ed. 1969) -- v. 9. pt. 1. The archetypes and the
          collective unconscious (2nd ed. 1968) -- v. 9. pt. 2. Aion :
          researches into the phenomenology of the self (2nd ed.
          1968).

## NUMBERS BORNE BY THE ITEM (2.7B19)

2:753     Australasia supplement (2 v.) and British Isles supplement
          (2 v.) are each numbered as v. 23-24.

2:754     "Pub. no. 15-1738."

2:755     "Catalog 161."

2:756    "IEEE Computer Society, IEEE catalog no. 77 CH1265-8 C (vol. 2)."

2:757    "3411."

2:758    "TFT 78."

2:759    "COM.70/IV.17b/A."

2:760    Supt. of Docs. no.: Y 4.P 96/10:96-H 49.

2:761    "S.T.C. no. 14700"--Label mounted on cover.

2:762    "AWS A2.4-79, superseding A2.4-76, A2.2-69, and A2.0-68."

2:763    On spine: 3.

2:764    On cover: Preliminary report no. 5.

2:765    On label on t.p.: 79 TH0056-2-PWR.

2:766    "Contract #C35002 (79)."

2:767    "Contract SAE-8989 with the United States Office of Education, Department of Health, Education, and Welfare."

2:768    "Prepared for IDA in support of a study to be submitted to the Department of Defense under contract no. SD-50, task order T-23."

2:769    "Supported in part by a contract (no. N00014-67-C-0379) from the Office of Naval Research, U.S. Navy."

2:770    "IITRI project no. H-6031 in fulfillment of Illinois Law Enforcement Commission action grant A-70-96."

2:771    United Nations sales publication no.: E.67.I.2.

## COPY BEING DESCRIBED AND LIBRARY'S HOLDINGS (2.7B20)

2:772    Library's copy imperfect: Cover wanting.

2:773    Library's copy imperfect: All after p. 362 wanting.

2:774    Library's copy imperfect: P. 101-102 and p. [11-16] (2nd group) wanting; t.p. and p. 75-76 damaged.

2:775    Library's copy imperfect: T.p. mutilated, with part of the imprint missing; p. 7-8 (4th group) wanting.

2:776    Library's copy imperfect: Vol. 1, p. 486-511 missing.

2:777    Library's copy imperfect: P. 94 and 127 blank.

2:778    Two of the 24 art prints in library's copy are identical (Scholar evading women).

2:779    Library has v. 1-5, 8-10.

2:780    Library has no. 15.

2:781    Library set incomplete: Vols. 22, 25 wanting.

2:782    Library lacks no. 394.

2:783    Library's copy unnumbered.

2:784    "Copy number 7 of 33."

2:785    "Fifty copies have been printed . . . This is No. [35]"

2:786    Library has copy no. 19.

2:787    Library has copy no. 162, signed by author.

2:788    "No. 5 [signed] Jenny Joseph."

2:789    Library's copy has author's autograph on p. 1.

2:790    Library's copy has author's autograph and corrections of 4 misprints in his hand.

2:791    Library's copy signed and with notes by the author on endpapers.

2:792    Library's copy of v. 1 autographed by author.

2:793    Library's copy has author's typescript note to and portrait of Haute Tarkington Jameson inserted.

2:794    Library's copy annotated in margins by previous owner.

2:795        Library's copy has Guiteau's printed circular letter, offer-
             ing his services as lecturer, dated from Milwaukee in Sept.
             1878, ([1] leaf) laid in.

2:796        Library's copy is 1 of 50 bound in leather.

2:797        Gift of Mrs. Leonora McKim, Dec. 17, 1940.


## "WITH" NOTES (2.7B21)

2:798a       With: An assessment of solar energy / Paul Donovan.
             Washington, D.C. : U.S. G.P.O., 1972. Bound together
             subsequent to publication.
                 (Title proper: Passive solar buildings; note on first item)
                 *For LC's interpretation on the use of "With" notes see*
                 *Cataloging Service Bulletin, no. 22, fall 1983, p. 20*

2:798b       With: Passive solar buildings / R.P. Stromberg and S.O.
             Woodall. Albuquerque, N.M. : Sandia Laboratories, 1978.
             Bound together subsequent to publication.
                 (Note on second item)

2:799a       With: Excellent women / Barbara Pym. New York : Dut-
             ton, 1978 -- Sweet William / Beryl Bainbridge. New York :
             G. Braziller, 1975. Bound together subsequent to publica-
             tion.
                 (Note on first item; title proper: Quartet in autumn)
                 *For LC's interpretation on the use of "With" notes see*
                 *Cataloging Service Bulletin, no. 22, fall 1983, p. 20*

2:799b       With: Quartet in autumn / Barbara Pym. New York :
             Harper & Row, 1980. Bound together subsequent to publica-
             tion.
                 (Title proper: Quartet in autumn; note on first item)
                 *See annotation for 2:798a*

2:800a       With: Articles agreed upon by the arch-bishops and
             bishops . . . in the convocation holden at London in the year
             1562 / Church of England. London : Printed by J. Bill and
             C. Barker, 1662 -- Constitutions and canons ecclesiastical,
             treated upon by the Bishop of London . . . 1603 / Church
             of England. London : Printed by A. Warren for J. Kirton,
             1662 -- Constitutions and canons ecclesiasticall treated upon

by the Archbishops of Canterbury and York / Church of
England. London : Printed by R. Barker, 1640. Bound
together subsequent to publication.

(Title proper: A collection of articles, injunctions,
canons . . . ; note on first item)
*For LC's interpretation on the use of "With" notes see
Cataloging Service Bulletin, no. 22, fall 1983, p. 20*

2:800b    With: A collection of articles, injunctions, canons . . .
with other publick records . . . / Church of England. London : Printed by R. Norton for T. Garthwait, 1661. Bound
together subsequent to publication.

(Note on second and subsequent items)

2:801a    In an envelope with: An introduction to the performing
arts collections of the Library of Congress . . . an exhibition
at the Performing Arts Library / Library of Congress.
[Washington, D.C. : Performing Arts Library, 1979] -- The
Performing Arts Library of the Library of Congress and the
Kennedy Center / Performing Arts Library. [Washington,
D.C. : The Library, 1979]. Bound together subsequent to
publication.

(Title proper: The Performing Arts Library; note on
first item)
*See annotation for 2:798a*

2:801b    In an envelope with: The Performing Arts Library : open-
ing program . . . / Performing Arts Library. [Washington,
D.C. : The Library, 1979]. Bound together subsequent to
publication.

(Note on second and subsequent items)

2:802    Issued in case, with: The immense journey / by Loren
Eiseley.

2:803    No. 9 in a volume with binder's title: Middletown
memoirs.

2:804    Vol. 32, no. 4 of a collection with binder's title: Heindel
papers.

# 3

# Cartographic Materials

## NATURE AND SCOPE OF THE ITEM (3.7B1)

3:1        Cadastral map.

3:2        Partial cadastral map.

3:3        Smithfield map is a cadastral map. County maps are road maps.

3:4        Diagrammatic map.

3:5        LANDSAT satellite photomap.

3:6        "Map/brochure."

3:7        Perspective map.

3:8        Photomap.

3:9        Photomaps.

3:10       Pictorial map.

3:11       Bird's-eye view.

3:12       Worm's-eye views.

3:13      Panorama.

3:14      An atlas factice which forms part of the Gifford Pinchot Papers in the Manuscript Division.

3:15      "Provisional, not to be used for navigation purposes."

3:16      "These maps were prepared as an aid to fishing. They are not intended for navigational purposes."

3:17      "Situation shortly before the coronation of Leopold II"--P. 3.

3:18      "Aerial photography flown on 19.3.76 by J.A. Story and Partners Ltd."

3:19      Survey made 1775.

3:20      "Surveyed in 1886-87 and published . . . 1895. Revised in 1903 and published . . . 1905."

3:21      "About Australia's major urban areas . . . from the Census of Population and Housing of 30 June 1976"--V. 1, p. [1].

3:22      Maps cover the period 1960-1976.

3:23      Covers Little Whitestick Creek in Beckley (W. Va.).

3:24      Covers Philadelphia region.

3:25      Covers western half of Turkey.

3:26      Does not cover the Rutherford campus.
              (Title proper: Fairleigh Dickinson University)

3:27      Does not cover western Maryland.

3:28      Shows amateur radio station call-letter prefixes.

3:29      Shows highways, military, scheduled, and municipal airports.

3:30      Shows house numbering system.

3:31      Shows Japanese and Chinese settlements.

3:32     Shows oil and natural gas fields, pipelines, and lease
areas.

3:33     Shows oil wells and petroleum geology.

3:34     Shows radial distances.

3:35     Shows radial distances from Philadelphia.

3:36     Shows region near Hohwachter Bay in Ostholstein.

3:37     Shows television stations and service regions.

3:38     Shows transfer stations, landfills, dumps, salt storage facilities, and flammable liquid underground storage facilities.

3:39     Shows unidentified numbered rectangles.

3:40     Shows vegetation types.

3:41     Also shows existing land use and open spaces.

3:42     Also shows mineral deposits.

3:43     Also shows minor civil divisions.

3:44     Also shows natural zones.

3:45     Also shows Newcastle, Penryn, and Rocklin.

3:46     Also shows soil classes.

3:47     Selected buildings shown pictorially.

3:48     Selected points of interest shown pictorially.

3:49     Plate 8 has 3 labels mounted to show Gatun Locks, Pedro
Miguel Lock, and Miraflores Locks.

3:50     Does not show land capability.
         (Title proper: Chittenden County, Vermont, land
         capability plan)

3:51     Picnic spots not shown.
         (Title proper: Road map of picnic spots, environs of
         Madras)

3:52     Raised relief globe. Relief also shown by shading and spot heights. Depths shown by shading and soundings.

3:53     Relief model. Relief also shown by gradient tints and spot heights.

3:54     Relief shown by contours.

3:55     Relief shown by contours, shading, and spot heights.

3:56     Relief shown by formlines.

3:57     Relief shown by gradient tints, contours, and spot heights.

3:58     Relief shown by hachures and land form drawings.

3:59     Relief shown by shading and spot heights.

3:60     Relief shown by shading, hachures, and spot heights on some sheets.

3:61     Relief shown on some sheets by contours.

3:62     Relief shown pictorially.

3:63     Relief shown pictorially and by spot heights.

3:64     Relief shown by contours and spot heights. Depths shown by contours on some sheets.

3:65     Relief shown by contours and spot heights on some sheets. Depths shown by contours and soundings. Depths shown by gradient tints on some sheets.

3:66     Relief shown by hypsometric tints and spot heights. Depths shown by bathymetric tints and soundings.

3:67     Relief shown by shading and spot heights. Depths shown by contours, bathymetric tints, and soundings.

3:68     Relief shown by shading, gradient tints, and spot heights. Depths shown by gradient tints and soundings.

3:69     Relief shown by spot heights. Depths shown by contours.

3:70     Relief shown pictorially. Depths shown by soundings.

3:71        Depths shown by contours.

3:72        Depths shown by gradient tints.

3:73        Depths shown by soundings.


# LANGUAGE (3.7B2)

3:74        English and Arabic versions of the same maps, printed back to back on 1 sheet.

3:75        Consists of 2 maps, 1 in English and 1 in Arabic.

3:76        Cover title and title of accompanying text in Italian, English, German, French, and Spanish.

3:77        Legend in 6 languages.

3:78        Legend and scale statement in French.

3:79        Legend and authorship statement in French and romanized Chinese (Pinyin).

3:80        Names in Latin or English.

3:81        Place names in Korean and English.

3:82        Publication statement in English and Welsh.

3:83        Some notes in Swedish and English.

3:84        Some sheets in Finnish only.

3:85        Title in 6 languages. Legend in Spanish and English.

3:86        Title in German, English, and French. Legend in 12 languages.

3:87        Title in Romanian, romanized Bulgarian, English, and French. Legend in German, English, French, Romanian, and Bulgarian.

3:88        Romanized record.

3:89        Titles in English and Urdu.

3:90        Titles and legend in German, English, French, and Croatian.

## SOURCE OF TITLE PROPER (3.7B3)

3:91        Envelope title.

3:92        Panel title.

3:93        Title adapted from publisher's catalog.

3:94        Title derived from earlier edition.

3:95        Title derived from publisher's catalog.

3:96        Title from accompanying text.

3:97        Title from cover of 1979 ed.

3:98        Title from earlier ed.

3:99        Title from index cover.

3:100       Title from index map.

3:101       Title from label on case.

3:102       Title from leaf 1.

3:103       Title from p. 7.

3:104       Title from portfolio.

3:105       Title from publisher's catalog.

3:106       Title from slip case.

3:107       Title from verso.

3:108       Title slip affixed to verso.

3:109       Map title, date, and author from label.

3:110      Title does not appear on some sheets.

3:111      Lacks title and legend.


## VARIATIONS IN TITLE (3.7B4)

3:112      Alternate panel title: Loomis basin, Placer County's nicest place to live.

3:113      Alternate title: Verkehrswege in der Bundesrepublik Deutschland 1980.

3:114      Alternate title: South Africa = Suid-Afrika.

3:115      Base map title and authorship statement: Geologic map of region J, North Carolina / by William F. Wilson, P. Albert Carpenter III, and John M. Parker III.

3:116      Collective title of village maps: A guide to the villages of Wayne County.

3:117      Colophon title: Avtokarta Slovenije 1:350 000--1981.

3:118      Cover title: Buena Vista County, Iowa.

3:119      Cover title: Karta Stockholm = Map of Stockholm.

3:120      Cover title: Pianta-souvenir, Napoli, Pompei-Capri-Ischia : informazioni utili per il turista = Map : useful information for tourist.

3:121      Envelope title: Büro- und Verwaltungskarte Deutschland mit 96 Seiten Register.

3:122      Filing title in right lower margin: Chesterfield County.

3:123      Half title: Atlas géographique et physique.

3:124      In English, mounted on label: Map of proposed sea level canal at Panama, scale 1:50000, 1879 to 1885. . . . The map was made by M. Brochard's secretary, Monsieur F. Arme.

3:125      In upper margin: Old roads from Griffith's map 1794.

3:126      Legend title: How to read your map of Pennsylvania.

3:127      Panel title: Welcome to Pampa : hang your hat on the top o' Texas.

3:128      Panel title: Riyadh = [Madīnat al-Riyāḍ].

3:129      Panel title: Pianta guida di Venezia : nuova guida illustrata = Nouveau guide illustré = New illustrated guide = Der neueste illustrierte Führer.

3:130      Sections of map separately titled: Street map of San Diego -- Street map of eastern San Diego, El Cajon & La Mesa.

3:131      Sound cassette title: Instructions, OSU main campus tactual maps.

3:132      Text title: Greater Gouverneur, St. Lawrence County, New York State.

3:133      Title at head of legend: Scotland : scale: approx. 8 miles to 1 inch, 5 kms. to 1 cm., 1:500,000.

3:134      Title at lower margin: Atlantic City.

3:135      Title at upper edge: Prince Gallitzin State Park.

3:136      Title at upper neatlines: Nash and Edgecombe Counties.

3:137      Title in center of map: Raleigh.

3:138      Title in legend: Okpaku-third press map of Nigeria, political.

3:139      Title in preface: Scott Foresman world atlas.

3:140      Title in right lower margin: King George Co., Va. : November 1981.

3:141      Title in right upper margin: Conservation planning and application.

3:142      Title in upper margin: Welcome to St. Albans.

3:143      Title in upper margin: Jugoslawien = Yugoslavia = Yougoslavie = Jugoslavija.

3:144      Title in upper margin: [Title (in nonroman script)].
           (Use whenever possible according to AACR 2 rule 1.7A3)

3:145      Title in upper right corner: Gdańsk.

3:146      Title in upper left corner: West Seneca - Lackawanna.

3:147      Title on flap: Atlas régional Nord-Pas de Calais.

3:148      Title on map: Western Australia.

3:149      Title on plastic hanging rod: Palestine, natural.

3:150      Title on title sheet: Meadow Creek watershed, plan profile.

3:151      Title on verso t.p. and side flap: Atlas régional du Nord-Pas de Calais.

3:152      Title within neatline: Bluefield, W. Va., nature's air conditioned city, Bluefield, Va. / map prepared & sponsored as a public service by Greater Bluefield Chamber of Commerce.

3:153      Variant title: Welcome to historic and scenic Nebraska City.

3:154      Wrapper band title: Potential cycleroutes and disused railways in England and Wales.

## PARALLEL TITLES AND OTHER TITLE INFORMATION (3.7B5)

3:155      Title on case in Italian.

3:156      Title in upper margin in Greek letters.

3:157      Subtitle on tube: With street map and useful information.

3:158      Each sheet individually titled.

3:159      Stamped on title page sheet: Draft.

3:160      Dedicated: To his Grace John Duke of Argyll, Commander in Chief of his Majestys forces in North Britain, &c. &c. &c. This work is most humbly inscribed by his grace's most obliged & very humble servants, George Taylor, Andren Skinner.

## STATEMENTS OF RESPONSIBILITY (3.7B6)

3:161        At foot of title panel: Government of the District of Columbia, Marion Barry Jr., mayor, July 1982.

3:162        Adhesive label affixed to title panel: North Hills Area Chamber of Commerce . . .

3:163        "Gifford Pinchot"--Cover.

3:164        In compass rose: R & R maps.

3:165        In lower left corner: H.C.H. Himaanga.

3:166        In lower right corner: E.M.

3:167        On some sheets: G.M. Hoffman, asst. div. eng'r.

3:168        Stamped in left margin: Borough of Coopersburg, Office of the Secretary . . .

3:169        Stamped on title panel: Darlington Chamber of Commerce, Inc. . . .

3:170        Stamped on verso: OBCC, Ormond Beach Chamber of Commerce . . .

3:171        In lower margin: Annotations by Henry Brooks Price, 1932.

3:172        Annotated by H. Brooks Price as a working draft for his 1933 manuscript map of Maryland.

3:173        "Base by Slim Meyer, M.G. Cox Abstract Co., Pauls Valley, Oklahoma."

3:174        "Base compiled from latest USGS quad sheets."

3:175        "Base compiled from U.S.G.S. quadrangle sheets and Florida county general highway map, polyconic projection."

3:176        "Base modified from U.S. Geological Survey, 1980."

3:177        "Base information from USGS 7 1/2' quads."

3:178        Base map: Botswana 1:2,000,000 / prepared by the Department of Surveys and Lands, 1976.

3:179  Base map by: Commonwealth of Pennsylvania, Department of Highways, Harrisburg.

3:180  "Base map prepared by the Geological Survey in cooperation with the Soil Conservation Service."

3:181  "Base source: USGS topo quads 1:250 000 and General Highway Maps, West Virginia Department of Highways, 1978."

3:182  "Base Source: USGS-1:24 000 topographic quads dated 1965."

3:183  "Source: USGS 1:100 000 Norfolk and Plymouth Cos., Mass., base maps, dated 1976."

3:184  Cartographic assistance for Woodburn city map from Jeanne Newton, city of Woodburn.

3:185  Copyright: LMAG ZH.

3:186  "Copyright Fred F. Johnson."

3:187  Copyright "MCMXXCI Hearne Brothers."

3:188  "C[opyright] MCMXXCI Hearne Brothers."

3:189  "Copyright 1979 Susan Von Gruenigen"--Verso t.p.

3:190  "Copyright 1981, Girard Publishers, Inc. . . . Ventnor, NJ . . ."

3:191  Entire contents copyright by Hammond Incorporated.

3:192  On all maps: Copyright Collins-Longman Atlases.

3:193  On most maps: Copyright Rand McNally.

3:194  "Information furnished courtesy of Mr. Mel Bauer, city engineer."

3:195  Maps prepared by: Cartographia, Budapest; Esselte Map Service A.B., Stockholm; George Philip & Son, Ltd., London; Rand McNally, Rand McNally GmbH, Stuttgart; Teikoku-Shoin Co., Ltd., Tokyo.

3:196  On each map: Drawn and printed by Federal Surveys, Lagos, Nigeria.

3:197    On each map: Prepared by Geographic Mapping Division, RTSD.

3:198    On most maps: Collins-Longman Atlases.

3:199    Maps are engraved by Augustine Ryther, Remigius Hogenberg, Leonard Terwoort, Nicholas Reynolds, Cornelius Hogius, and Francis Scatter.

3:200    Maps engraved and printed by U.S. Geological Survey.

3:201    "Lithographed by DMAAC 1-79."

3:202    "Manufactured by Replogle Globes, Chicago, Ill."

3:203    "Reprinted by: Rubinstein's Office Products . . . Kennett Square, Pa."

3:204    Signed by Barber, Thos. Bowen, Flyn, I. Luffman, J. Prockter, S. Pyle, Jn. Roberts, I. Taylor, and G. Terry, as engravers.

3:205    Commemorative book plate signed by R.V. Tooley inserted.

3:206    Map 38 signed by Barriere and Dien as sculpsit and other maps are signed by E. Dussy as engraver.

3:207    Reprint sponsored by the Heritage League of Northwest Illinois, Stockton, Ill.

## EDITION AND HISTORY (3.7B7)

3:208    Ed. statement followed by month and year of publication.

3:209    Ed. statement in left lower margin: June 1964 18th edition-2.

3:210    Ed. statement differs on some sheets: Vorläufige Ausgabe II. 41.

3:211    Differs from other ed. in having large-size symbols and names for state parks.

3:212      Includes various issues of some sheets.

3:213      Revision of: The 1971 atlas of Buena Vista County, Iowa.

3:214      Rev. ed. of: Federal aid highway systems by county. 1977.

3:215      Rev. ed. of: Atlas of Australian resources. 2nd series.
1962.

3:216      Rev. ed. published as: Chart kit BBA, Block Island, R.I.,
to the Canadian border. 1980.

3:217      Eighth ed. published as: U.B.D. complete street directory
of Adelaide city & suburbs.

3:218      Previously published as: Hampton & Newport News, Va.
street map. 1980.

3:219      Previously published as: Atlas of the Borough of Manhat-
tan, city of New York. New York : G.W. Bromley Co.,
1916.

3:220      Earlier ed. does not show hiking routes.

3:221      Original: Cincinnati, from a point west of Covington, Ky.
Cincinnati : Middleton, Wallace & Co., [1856].
      (Facsimile)

3:222      Originally published: London : C. Saxton, 1579.
      (Facsimile)

3:223      Originally published by U.S. Coast and Geodetic Survey.
In upper margin: Printed at the World's Columbian Exposi-
tion 1893. Specially reprinted from the original plate in 1980
by the National Ocean Survey for the Washington Map
Society.
      (Facsimile)

3:224      Originally printed on 2 sheets, 117 x 88 cm.

3:225      Originally printed on 4 sheets, 73 x 111 cm. Also issued
on 4 sheets without plastic covering.

3:226      Based on: United States, Department of the Interior,
Geological Survey, Alaska map E.

3:227        Based on: General highway map, Medina County, Texas, prepared by the Texas State Highway Department, Planning Survey Division, in cooperation with the U.S. Department of Transportation, Federal Highway Administration, Bureau of Public Roads.

3:228        From: Railroad communication between Boston and Canada / Boston City Council. 1852.

3:229        "Base map source: 1970 air photo."

3:230        Supplement to: Atlas de Kinshasa, 1975.

3:231        "Supplement to the National Geographic, February 1981, page 224A, vol. 159, no. 2-West Indies."

3:232        To accompany: Relation historique, 1814-1834 which constitutes pt. 1 of: Voyage de Humboldt . . . 1805-1834.

3:233        "To be used in conjunction with establishment circular B.26 of 1970."

3:234        "Reprint 1981."

3:235a       Reprint (1st work). Originally published: Atlas of Jo Daviess Co., Illinois. Chicago : Warner, Higgins & Beers, 1872.

3:235b       Reprint (2nd work). Originally published: Plat book of Jo Daviess County, Illinois. [Philadelphia] : North West Publishing Co., 1893.

3:235c       Reprint (3rd work). Originally published: Standard atlas of Jo Daviess County, Illinois . . . Chicago : G.A. Ogle & Co., 1913.
             (Notes used for reprint edition of two or three formerly independent works)

3:236        Facsimile.

3:237        Facsim. ed. of 500 copies produced in commemoration of the 400th anniversary of the publication of the atlas.

3:238        Facsimile of 1725? ed.

3:239        Facsim. of bird's-eye view showing military operations in the vicinity of Dôle (France).

3:240    Facsim. of map dated ca. 1895 in the collection of the Alexandria Public Library.

3:241    Facsims. of topographic maps originally issued by the Romanian Military Geographical Institute.

3:242    Reproduced from the author's 1611 atlas: The theatre of the Empire of Great Britaine.

3:243    "Reproduced from the original in the John Carter Brown Library, Brown University."

3:244    Reproduction of hand drawn master.

3:245    This unpublished original map was used as a master to produce 1 of the maps in accompanying text.

3:246    Awarded blue ribbon in 1979 American Congress on Surveying and Mapping Map Design Competition.

3:247    "Checked . . . 1-79." Sheet 6 has "Checked . . . 12-79."

3:248    "Checked, W.A.C., 1976."

3:249    "Date drawn: Aug. 1, 1978."

3:250    "Published with Drift 1920. Reprinted as Solid edition, 1967. Reprinted at 1:50 000 scale 1972."

3:251    "This edition limited to 500 copies."

3:252    Limited ed. of 100 copies bound in vellum.

3:253    Original map discovered in the Chotek Library, chateau of Kačina.

## MATHEMATICAL AND OTHER CARTOGRAPHIC DATA (3.7B8)

3:254    Prime meridian: Paris and Athens.

3:255    Prime meridian: Rome (Monte Mario).

3:256    The General map of England and Wales has degrees and minutes of latitude and longitude in the border.

3:257    Gauss-Boaga grid.

3:258    Irish grid.

3:259    National grid.

3:260    Romanian (Lambert) grid.

3:261    UTM grid.

3:262    Regional and UTM grids.

3:263    "The Universal transverse Mercator (UTM) grid overlay is based on the Everest geodetic system."

3:264    "U.T.M. grid zone 36. Grid lines at 2000 metres."

3:265    "Universal transverse Mercator grid zone 38."

3:266    "10,000 meter universal transverse Mercator grid, zone 16."

3:267    Oriented with north to the bottom.

3:268    Oriented with north to the right.

3:269    Oriented with north toward the lower right.

3:270    Oriented with north toward the upper left.

3:271    Oriented with north toward the upper right.

3:272    "Looking south."

3:273    The atlas contains ca. 30 maps at scale 1:500,000 and ca. 90 maps at scale 1:500,000 to 1:3,500,000.

3:274    Principal maps 1:5,000,000; supplementary maps at various scales.

3:275    Principal maps at scale 1:316,800 or 5 miles to 1 inch.

3:276    Cornwall road map, scale: 10 miles to 1 in.

3:277    Vertical profiles: Horizontal scale ca. 1:3,500,000, vertical scale ca. 1:10,000.

3:278      "This map contains a 20% vertical distortion due to computer line-printer format."

3:279      "All drawings in this folio have been reduced to one-half the original scale"--P. 1 of cover.

3:280      Same map at reduced scale on verso.

3:281      "Map not to exact scale."

3:282      Bar scale incorrect.

3:283      "Relative distances shown for references purposes only."

3:284      Polar sheets: Scale 1:6,000,000; polar stereographic projection.

3:285      Shows sheet outlines of the 17 = 100′ topographical survey.

3:286      Globe gores for shading and 25 cm. globe.

3:287      Globe gores for 30 cm. (12 in.) globe.

## PUBLICATION, DISTRIBUTION, ETC. (3.7B9)

3:288      "Published by the National Museum of Wales in conjunction with Wales Gas."

3:289      "Published by Good Beginnings, Inc. . . . in cooperation with the Lackawanna Chamber of Commerce."

3:290      "Published by the Metropolitan Fort Myers Chamber of Commerce through it's [sic] Fort Myers Lee County News Bureau."

3:291      "Issued by Automobile Club of Southern California and California State Automobile Association."

3:292      Trade ed. simultaneously published by Prentice-Hall as: Prentice-Hall's Great international atlas.

3:293      Printed in Singapore by Singapore Offset Printing Pte. Ltd.

3:294    Printed and bound in Scotland by Wm. Collins Sons & Co. Ltd.

3:295    Distributor's statement stamped on.

3:296    Name and address of distributor stamped on.

3:297    Distributed by Grosset & Dunlap.

3:298    Jointly distributed by Peninsula Motor Club (Bradenton Division) and Southeast National Bank of Bradenton.

3:299    Dates from map 18N and map 39S.

3:300    Date from p. 2 (3rd group).

3:301    "February 1981."

3:302    Date stamped on: 7. Jan. 1980.

3:303    Foreword dated 1976; printed 1978.

3:304    Maps dated 1945; foreword dated 1948.

3:305    Maps dated between 1804 and 1814.

3:306    Plates 6 and 23 dated 1820.

3:307    On recto: December 1980.

3:308    "Published November 1981."

3:309    "Published and issued June 1981."

## PHYSICAL DESCRIPTION (3.7B10)

3:310    Irregularly shaped.

3:311    Annotated before being photographed.

3:312    Annotated in pencil and ink to show roads and country houses as of 1794.

3:313       Annotated in yellow ink and pencil.

3:314       Braille with printed captions.

3:315       Place names handwritten.

3:316       Some street names handwritten.

3:317       Aeronautical information overprinted in red on base map:
            Republic of Zambia / compiled, drawn, and published by
            the Surveyor General, Ministry of Lands, Natural Resources,
            and Tourism, Lusaka, 1975.

3:318       Words "Preliminary" and "November 1978" overprinted
            with x's in title.

3:319       Some sheets printed on both sides.

3:320       Two folded col. maps and duplicate legend inserted.

3:321       Includes ill.

3:322       Coloring differs from other ed.

3:323       Hand colored.

3:324       Some sheets hand col.

3:325       Designed to be folded.

3:326       Designed to be folded to 29 x 17 cm.

3:327       Folded as pocket atlas 22 x 15 cm.

3:328       Designed to be marked and erased in school use.

3:329       Designed to be cut out and folded.

3:330       Designed for use with radial index tape measure.

3:331       Each sheet covers 1 district.

3:332       Each sheet covers 1 or more districts.

3:333       Geographic coverage complete in 12 sheets.

3:334    Geographic coverage complete in 5 sheets. Earlier eds. complete in 6 sheets.

3:335    "Mechanical locator" attached.

3:336    Tape anchored on face of map serves as "mechanical locator" for finding streets as indexed.

3:337    Tape indicator, for use in locating streets, attached to p. [2] of cover.

3:338    Globe features two way interior lighting by means of detachable electric cord and interior light bulb.

3:339    Globe lights up from inside by means of detachable electric cord and interior light bulb.

3:340    Transparent shell represents the sky. The moon and earth can be rotated to see the constellations for any time of year.

3:341    Issued in portfolio.

3:342    Map in 3 strips and 6 sections.

3:343    Four holes punched at top for loose-leaf binder.

3:344    Three-ring binder holes in upper margin.

3:345    Has punch-holes for installation in subway coaches.

3:346    Has punch-holes for hanging.

3:347    Issued with metal grommets for hanging.

3:348    Issued with metal rods for hanging.

3:349    Issued in clear plastic jacket with attached marker flaps.

3:350    Issued with plastic cover for each pair of sheets.

3:351    Also issued with plastic film covering.

3:352    Also issued without plastic covering.

3:353    Also issued with cloth backing or plastic film covering.

3:354    Transparent overlay attached to back fly leaf: v. 2.

3:355     Four maps have transparencies.

3:356     Map 2 is a transparent plastic overlay.

3:357     Some maps preceded by transparent plastic overlay with boundaries shown.

3:358     Label on verso of each sheet.

3:359     Revision label pasted over list of town officers.

3:360     Mounted on cardboard.

3:361     Mounted on cloth backing. Originally folded to 25 x 11 cm.

3:362     Sectioned and mounted on cloth backing.

3:363     Cut and mounted in 8 sections.

3:364     Mounted on spindle with plastic base; height when mounted ca. 46 cm.

3:365     Mounted on metal stand by a metal cradle connected to a circular, moveable metal scale graduated in statute miles and hours of time, which in turn is connected to a 2nd circular metal scale graduated in degrees of latitude.

3:366     Mounted on wooden stand by a brass ring graduated in degrees of latitude.

3:367     Stand contains holder for accompanying atlas.

3:368     Mounted under plastic film.

3:369     Blue line print.

3:370     Blue line print of a manuscript map.

3:371     Blueprint.

3:372     Negative.

3:373     Photocopy of original in the National Archives.

3:374     Consists of separate photocopies of the recto and verso of the original.

3:375      Some sheets are photocopies.

3:376      Proof copy.

## ACCOMPANYING MATERIAL (3.7B11)

3:377      Accompanied by fact sheet (1 leaf ; 28 x 22 cm.).

3:378      Accompanied by text (48 p. : ill. ; 16 cm.).

3:379      Accompanied by typescripts ([2] leaves ; 27 cm.).

3:380      Accompanied by index map (1 leaf ; 46 x 36 cm.) ; supplementary map sheet: 7201.1 (1 leaf : col. maps ; 46 x 36 cm.).

3:381      Accompanied by text photocopied from the Mar. 1959 issue of the Long Island forum: Fire Island map of 1798 (2 leaves : ill. ; 28 x 22 cm.).

3:382      Accompanied by text: Planning considerations, land ownership. (vii, 7 p. : ill. ; 28 cm.).

3:383      Accompanied by text: Pianta-souvenir, Napoli, Pompei-Capri-Ischia = Map (30 p. : col. ill. ; 17 cm.).

3:384      Accompanied by map and text: Some things to see on your image (1 leaf ; 28 x 22 cm.).

3:385      Accompanied by index map: Index / the Maryland National Capital Park & Planning Commission (1 leaf : photocopy ; 86 x 108 cm.).

3:386      Accompanied by sheet of text: The dymaxion airocean world Fuller projective-transformation ; Fluid geography : a primer for the airocean world / Buckminster Fuller ([1] leaf : ill. ; 56 x 87 cm.).

3:387      Accompanied by sheet of text: Edward Wright's map of the then known world, for Hakluyt's Principal navigations [ca. 1600] : a note to accompany the facsimile published by the John Carter Brown Library, Brown University, Providence, Rhode Island, 1978 ([28] p. : 28 x 22 cm.).

3:388      Accompanied by title page sheet: Report of the Governor
           of the Panama Canal, under Public Law 280, 79th Congress,
           1st Session, approved December 28, 1945, plates 1-8 : copy
           no. 38 ([1] leaf ; 26 cm.).

3:389      Accompanied by: United States Champion wall map index
           (14 p. ; 29 cm.).

3:390      Accompanied by: Canton-Massillon metro area map street
           index and Brewster-Navarre area map supplement (15 p. :
           col. map ; 27 cm.).

3:391      Accompanied by: A Champion map index book of East
           Saint Louis, Illinois & vicinity ([10] p. : maps ; 29 cm.).

3:392      Accompanied by: Index to streets (including list of
           hospitals, churches & places of general public interest) :
           1:20,000 map of Dublin (85 p. : ill. ; 22 cm.).

3:393      Accompanied by: Planning considerations, topography
           and slope (vii, 13 p. : ill., maps ; 28 cm.) ; Index to
           topographic maps of Alabama (1 sheet ; 64 cm.).

3:394      Accompanied by: Little Whitestick and Cranberry Creeks
           watershed, floodplain map index, Raleigh County, West
           Virginia : scale 1:24,000 (1 leaf : maps ; 28 x 40 cm.).

3:395      Accompanied by: Floodplain management study area
           vicinity map, Smith Creek, Rockingham County, Virginia :
           scale 1:60,000 : March 1980 (1 leaf : col. map ; 28 x 56
           cm.) ; Floodplain management study area and mosaic sheet
           index, Smith Creek, Rockingham County, Virginia : scale
           1:60,000 : March 1980 (1 leaf : col. map ; 28 x 56 cm.).

3:396      Most volumes include separate folded index map.

3:397      Two folded col. maps in jacket pocket (t. 2): Catalunya,
           Balears, mapa de carreteras. Scale ca. 1:360,000. 1 col. map
           (42 x 76 cm. folded to 21 x 10 cm.); and Barcelona, plano
           guía urbana. Scale ca. 1:16,500. 1 col. map (56 x 7 cm. fold-
           ed to 19 x 10 cm.).

3:398      Issued with pins in various sizes and colors to represent
           planets.

3:399      Plastic index device in pocket.

3:400    Issued with plastic index location finder in pocket.

3:401    Includes plastic time indicator.

3:402    Includes plastic indicator to "Set hour over one city then read time for other cities."

3:403    Includes geometer.

## SERIES (3.7B12)

3:404    Series title from distributor's catalog.

3:405    "Principal maps also published separately in the Australia 1:5,000,000 map series"--Pref.

3:406    Series is a naval air training review series.

3:407    Two sheets have series designation: Glacier map series.

3:408    Sheets 2, 3, 4 annotated: RR-52.

3:409    Supersedes: Special research report ; RR-13.
        (Series number is RR-52)

3:410    Sheet 1 lacks series number.

## AUDIENCE (3.7B14)

3:411    Intended audience: Grades 3-5.

3:412    "Unclassified."

3:413    Stamped on: Restricted.

3:414    Stamped on before being photographed: Limited distribution.

3:415    Stamped on verso: Reproduction rights restricted, contact Neville Public Museum, Green Bay, Wisconsin."

# CONTENTS (3.7B18)

3:416        Bibliographical references.

3:417        Bibliography in accompanying text.

3:418        Bibliography in v. 2 of accompanying text.

3:419        Encomiums and references: leaf [7] (1st group).

3:420        Errata slip tipped in.

3:421        Some maps have errata sheets pasted on.

3:422        Index bound in.

3:423        Indexed.

3:424        Indexed for points of interest.

3:425        Indexed for selected buildings.

3:426        Index map on sheet 1.

3:427        Sheet 1 is title-legend sheet.

3:428        Maps of Hungary annual events, Hungary castles and nature preserves, Budapest, and Lake Balaton, and ill. (some col.) on cover.

3:429        Advertisements on verso.

3:430        Indexed advertisements on verso.

3:431        Business and telephone directories on verso.

3:432        Car rental agency index and advertisement on verso.

3:433        Coat of arms on verso.

3:434        Gazetteer on verso.

3:435        Folding instructions on verso.

3:436        Indexes on verso.

3:437    Indexes, maps of Volusia County and Florida, and ill. on verso.

3:438    Lists of community services on verso.

3:439    Location map on verso.

3:440    Map of Garvin County, important telephone numbers, and advertisements on verso.

3:441    Forty maps of islands, with text, on verso.

3:442    Three maps showing tourist routes, distance chart, chart of road signs, and col. ill. on verso.

3:443    Notes, col. ill., and indexed advertisements on verso.

3:444    Street index, directories, boundary map, and col. ill. on verso.

3:445    Nine subject maps, 6 traffic flow diagrams, 5 graphs, and location map on verso.

3:446    Tourist information on verso.

3:447    Tourist information, distance table, 9 subject maps, and col. ill. on verso.

3:448    Text on verso of some sheets.

3:449    Text and gazetteer on verso.

3:450    Text, bird's-eye view of Pa. State University and vicinity, location map, and ill. on verso.

3:451    Text, ill., and regional map on verso.

3:452    Text, ill., 3 indexed maps, and location map on verso.

3:453    Text, indexes, indexed tables of recreation facilities, and distance table on verso.

3:454    Text, indexes, descriptive list of hiking routes, descriptive index to points of interest with ill., map of city region, and advertisements on verso.

3:455     Text, indexes, telephone directory, civic information, map of "Surrounding area of south Hillsborough, Florida," ill. (some col.), and advertisements on verso.

3:456     Text, indexes, tourist information, col. ill., and indexed maps of Chilecito and La Rioja on verso.

3:457     Text, maps of Wayne County and Mt. Olive, bank directory, and ill. on verso.

3:458     Text, maps of Pike County, Mississippi, and Percy Quin State Park, indexed map of Summit, Mississippi, and distance diagram and advertisements on verso.

3:459     Text includes "Generalized tectonic map of Burma."

3:460     Includes 2 ancillary maps.

3:461     Includes coat of arms and advertisements.

3:462     Includes descriptive index to hiking routes, indexes, and inset of city center.

3:463     Includes 16 detachable outline maps.

3:464     Includes distance chart, location map, and col. ill.

3:465     Includes distance list.

3:466     Includes floodplain profile graph.

3:467     Includes gazetteer and index.

3:468     Includes 3 hypsometric profiles.

3:469     Includes ill. and text.

3:470     Includes annotated ill. of houses in margins.

3:471     Includes illegible indexes.

3:472     Includes index, 2 location maps, distance chart, and 8 insets.

3:473     Includes indexes and advertisements.

3:474    Includes indexes, emergency service numbers, and advertisements.

3:475    Includes indexes, location map, and col. ill.

3:476    Includes indexes, street diagram, and maps of "Downtown Seattle," "Seattle Center," and "Seattle, Tacoma and vicinity."

3:477    Includes indexes to points of interest and advertisements.

3:478    Includes indexed boundary diagram.

3:479    Some sheets include sheet index of 1:25,000 topographic sheets.

3:480    Includes inset of city center.

3:481    Includes inset of Brigantine and indexed advertisements.

3:482    Includes inset of Caernarvon with index to points of interest, inset of Bangor, and coats of arms.

3:483    Includes 2 insets of southern coasts, insets of Oporto and Lisbon, and island insets of Madeira and Porto Santo.

3:484    Some sheets include insets.

3:485    Includes instructions for use and assembly.

3:486    Includes lists of geographical equivalents and abbreviations.

3:487    Includes location maps.

3:488    Includes notes and 2 geological cross-sections.

3:489    Includes notes and indexes.

3:490    Includes notes and interstate highway directory.

3:491    Includes notes and system index.

3:492    Includes notes, indexes, 2 insets, col. ill., coat of arms, and advertisements.

3:493    Some sheets include notes and 1 or more insets.

3:494     Includes quadrant diagram.

3:495     Includes statistical information about sports.

3:496     Includes street indexes and advertisements.

3:497     Includes street index, inset, and city center map.

3:498     Includes table of radio station frequencies and call-letters, graph, and MHSZ insigne.

3:499     Includes text and compilation map.

3:500     Includes text and Mystic Seaport insigne.

3:501     Includes text and population data.

3:502     Includes "Index to USAF aerospace planning charts."

3:503     Includes "Map of Burma showing the status of geological mapping."

3:504     Includes 2 col. maps on 1 folded plate attached to p. 3 of cover: Majorca, scale 1:200,000 (48 x 61 cm.) and Palma, scale 1:10,000 (39 x 48 cm.).

3:505     Included between maps 14 and 15: Carte du Royaume de France / C.F. Delmarche, 1814. 1 folded map (49 x 61 cm.).

3:506     Inserted: A general map of the roads of Scotland / Taylor and Skinner. 1 folded map (35 x 32 cm.).

3:507     Ancillary maps: Main distances -- Geology -- Eruption -- Precipitation (mm. per year) -- Temperature in January -- Temperature in July -- County division -- Metalled road.

3:508     Insets: [Moscow and vicinity] -- [Leningrad and vicinity] -- Donets Basin -- [Southeastern USSR].

3:509     Insets: Key to 1:5,000 tracings, scale 1:100,000 -- Map of the Canal Zone, scale 1:300,000.

3:510     Maps on verso: Perth freeway system -- Six one day tours of Perth's environs -- Perth city centre -- Perth & Fremantle city access -- City clipper free bus service.

3:511    Perspective maps on verso: Philadelphia area, New York to Washington, D.C. -- Philadelphia International Airport : [terminal area] -- Center City Philadelphia.

3:512    Contents: Narbonne -- Narbonne, plan monumental : [pictorial map].

3:513    Contents: [Netherlands] -- [Belgium and Luxemburg].

3:514    Contents: Surrey, Sussex, Kent, and Middlesex / C. Saxton. 1579 -- Strip road map . . . / J. Ogilby. 1675 -- Cantii, Southsexia Surriae et Middlesexiae / P. van den Keere. 1605 -- The ichonography or ground plan of Guldeford / J. Harris. 1739 -- Surrey / J. Lindley and W. Crosley. 1793 -- [Surrey before the railways] O.S. (Old Series). 1811 -- Surrey / Chas. and J. Greenwood. 1823.

3:515    Contents: Easy locator index with instructions (35 p.) -- base 1. Jerusalem -- base 2. Holy Land -- base 3. Old Testament lands -- base 4. New Testament lands -- base 5. Bible world.

3:516    Contents: area 1. Lake Mead area -- area 2. Hoover Dam-Lake Mohave -- area 3. Lake Mohave-Needles -- area 4. Needles-Lake Havasu.

3:517    Contents: plate 1. Principal trade routes -- plate 2. Transisthmian canal routes -- plate 3. Canal Zone and vicinity.

3:518    Contents: sheet no. 1 of 2 : [western part] -- sheet no. 2 of 2 : [eastern part].

3:519    Contents: t. 1. Guía urbana de Barcelona -- t. 2. Guías urbanas, entidad municipal metropolitana y otros municipios.

3:520    Contents: W 45, plate 1. Map showing groundwater yields and related features in the DuBois area, Jefferson, Clearfield, and Elk Counties, Pennsylvania -- W 45, plate 2. Map showing depth to the water table and to the top of salt water in the DuBois area, Jefferson, Clearfield, and Elk Counties, Pennsylvania.

3:521    Partial contents: v. 1. Perth -- v. 2. Adelaide -- v. 3. Brisbane and Gold Coast.

3:522    Partial contents: Niagara sheet / by Ernest H. Muller. 1977.

# NUMBERS (3.7B19)

3:523     "2101808182. 2201808145."

3:524     "R210-R215."

3:525     "S-9-1-11 [remainder not on photocopy]."

3:526     "SCS-ENG-317, Rev. 5-69."

3:527     "Base 504784 (546491) 2-82."

3:528     "Map 2411."

3:529     "Replogle 5466."

3:530     "U.Ed. 80-488."

3:531     "U.S. Pat. 2,393,676."

3:532     Plotting no. ASCXX300A."

3:533     Publisher's no.: 90.

3:534     Sheets numbered 412.1 thru 417.1, 4101.1 thru 4102.1.

3:535     Sheets numbered 1541-1543.

3:536     Sheets individually numbered: 124 HUV and HUV 124 discontinuously to 554 HUV and HUV 554.

3:537     Sheets numbered discontinuously 3679 thru 6564.

3:538     Numbers vary on sheets: 1340, 74-1340, 74-13-40, 7413-40.

3:539     Number stamped on: 01051.

3:540     At head of title: Figure IV-4.

3:541     In lower right corner: JFK/79-81.

3:542     On accompanying map: DG 7107.

3:543     On cover spine: Nr 19 00 11.

3:544     On base of globe: R-1222-19.

## COPY BEING DESCRIBED AND LIBRARY'S HOLDINGS (3.7B20)

3:545    Library's copy soiled.

3:546    Library's copy stained.

3:547    Library's copy darkly stained, cracked, and lacking internal and marginal sections.

3:548    Library's copy imperfect: Brittle.

3:549    Library's copy imperfect: Brittle; index map cut out on sheet 5073-21 A.

3:550    Library's copy imperfect: Brittle; inset in lower right corner and portion of inset in upper right corner missing.

3:551    Library's copy imperfect: Some tears on left edge.

3:552    Library's copy imperfect: Lower left side trimmed off.

3:553    Marginal information cut away from library's copy.

3:554    Library's copy imperfect: Lacks small section at upper margin.

3:555    Library's copy imperfect: A small portion in middle lower margin missing.

3:556    Library's copy imperfect: Parts of lower margin missing.

3:557    Library's copy imperfect: Panel title missing.

3:558    Library's copy imperfect: plates 3, 5, 7-14, 22, 25, 27 wanting.

3:559    Library's copy lacks stand. Library's copy imperfect: Small dent in northern hemisphere.

3:560    Last cipher of date unclear on library's copy.

3:561    Library's copy annotated in blue wax crayon; brittle and torn edges.

3:562    Library's copy annotated in marker ink.

3:563    Library's copy annotated in pencil, red and yellow stripes in lower right section.

3:564    Library's copy annotated in lead and red pencil.

3:565    Library's copy annotated in black ink and correction fluid.

3:566    Library's copy annotated in red pencil to cross out incorrect index to points of interest.

3:567    Library's copy annotated in blue ink to indicate date of revision and signature of the author.

3:568    Library's copy annotated in red pencil and ink to show new streets.

3:569    Library's copy annotated: Donated by city of Madison, Nebraska, Mark F. Arbuthnot, city administrator.

3:570    Library's copy signed.

3:571    Library's copy has title "Cheyenne, OK" typed on.

3:572    Title hand lettered on library's copy.

3:573    Library's copy has price crossed out in ink.

3:574    Library's copy has corrections pasted on.

3:575    Library's copy has piece of boundary pasted on.

3:576    Library's copy has "Map Studio" pasted over "Instructa" at head of title.

3:577    Library's copy has mailing address label affixed on verso.

3:578    Library's copy has a label mounted over distributor and 1 other label.

3:579    Stamped on library's copy: Complimentary copy.

3:580    Stamped on library's copy: Produced under contract printing.

3:581    Stamped on library's copy: Judi Kelsey, Duane B. Dillard Realtor . . .

3:582      Library's copy has sheets taped together.

3:583      Library's copy has typescripts attached to the upper left corner.

3:584      Library's copy unassembled.

3:585      Library's copy perforated, with instruction for assembly as dymaxion globe; unassembled.

3:586      Library has no. 198.

3:587      Library's copy lacking sheet no. 3.


## "WITH" NOTES (3.7B21)

3:588      With a separate map on same sheet: Little Whitestick Creek.
           (Examples 3:588-589 illustrate AACR 2 rule 3.1G4)

3:589      With (on verso): The city of Crystal Lake.

3:590      Mounted on a wooden stand to form a pair with: The Trippensee transparent celestial globe.

3:591      Issued in a slip case with 4 other maps of Pennsylvania.
           (Other four maps cataloged separately, with same note)

3:592a     With: Atlas of Canada. New York : Grosset & Dunlap, 1980. Bound together subsequent to publication.
           (Title proper: World atlas; note on first item)
           *For LC's interpretation on the use of "With" notes see Cataloging Service Bulletin, no. 22, fall 1983, p. 20*

3:592b     With: World atlas / by Bill Willett. Glenview, Ill., 1982. Bound together subsequent to publication.
           (Note on second item)

3:593      Issued with: Virginia peninsula atlas / compiled and published by Robert Saxton. Alexandria, Va. : Alexandria Drafting Co., 1980 -- Potomac River basin / Thomas A. Smith. Alexandria, Va. : Alexandria Drafting Co., 1980.
           (One of three bibliographic works issued together in one physical volume without collective title; example illustrates AACR 2 rule 3.1G4)

# 4

# Manuscripts (Including Manuscript Collections)*

## RELATIONSHIP COMPLEXITY (4.7B1)

4:1        Forms part of: Clifton Waller Barrett Library.

4:2        Forms part of: Lincoln Kirsten collection.

4:3        Forms part of: Stefansson collection on the polar regions.

4:4        Forms part of: Guymon detective and mystery fiction collection.

4:5        Forms part of: American Medical Women's Association historical collection.

4:6        Forms part of: Sara Payson Willis Parton (Fanny Fern) papers, 1828-1950.

4:7        Forms part of: Central Files Section 65, Interior Department collection of Indian treaty records.

---

*The examples in this chapter follow the cataloging rules set forth in Steven L. Hensen, *Archives, Personal Papers, and Manuscripts: A Cataloging Manual for Archival Repositories, Historical Societies, and Manuscript Libraries.* (Washington, D.C.: Library of Congress, Manuscript Division, 1983).

4:8        Addition to: George Sarton papers, ca. 1903-1956.

4:9        Addition to: Haxall family papers, 1832-1895; and Haxall family papers, 1835-1920.

4:10       Addition to: Civil War papers, 1852-1892.

4:11       Addition to: Martha Groves McKelvie scrapbooks, 1908-1920.

4:12       Addition to: Foreign Service officers and Dept. of State officials oral history interviews, 1972-1975.

4:13       In: Kimball Flaccus papers, 1932-1969.

4:14       From: David E. Finley papers.

4:15       Formerly cataloged as part of the repository's Joseph Labadie collection.

## COPY/REPOSITORY (4.7B2)

4:16       Facsimile of original in: Pennsylvania State University Libraries' Rare Books Room.

4:17       Photocopy.

4:18       Chiefly photocopies.

4:19       Photocopies of privately owned mss.

4:20       Photocopies of originals which have been lost.

4:21       Photocopies of originals in the offices of the law firm.

4:22       Photocopies of originals at Bethlehem Steel Corporation, Sparrows Point Shipyard, Baltimore, Md.

4:23       Photocopies made from originals in: Kongelige Bibliotek, Copenhagen, Denmark, annotated by Lillian Moore.

4:24       Photocopies made in 1978 from originals retained by Mrs. Evelyn Griffin, church clerk.

4:25     Photocopy made in 1979 from originals loaned to the respository.

4:26     In part, photocopies.

4:27     In part, photocopies and transcripts.

4:28     In part, photocopies of newsclippings.

4:29     In part, photocopies of newspaper clippings.

4:30     In part, photocopies of Davis' writings.

4:31     In part, photocopy of Herbert Hoover letter.

4:32     In part, mimeographed copies of letters of Thomas Burrowes.

4:33     In part, photocopies of Neal papers in other collections.

4:34     In part, photocopies of letters to John Swalop. Locations of originals unknown.

4:35     In part, photocopies of annotated transcripts (typewritten) of originals of business correspondence since destroyed.

4:36     In part, photocopies of Bukowski letters made from originals returned at Bukowski's request.

4:37     In part, photocopies made of Benjamin Harrison's (1726?-1791) will in: Virginia Historical Society collections (Richmond), and other papers of unknown origin.

4:38     In part, photocopies made from originals loaned by founder Elizabeth Boyer, before being sent to Radcliffe College, Schlesinger Library on the History of Women in America, Cambridge, Mass.

4:39     In part, copies and photocopies of originals in: Library of Congress (Washington, D.C.), Ohio Historical Society (Columbus), and Ross County Historical Society (Chillicothe, Ohio).

4:40     In part, photocopies made in 1981 from originals in: Memphis Room, Memphis and Shelby County Public Library and Information Center, and Memphis and Shelby County Office of Planning and Development.

4:41    In part, photocopies made in 1968 of originals then in the possession of Mrs. A.M. Franklin, Mineral Springs Community, Ruston, La., acquired through Mrs. Eugenia Dawson.

4:42    In part, photocopies of correspondence from Nicholas Trist papers in: Library of Congress, Manuscript Division, and of Mumford family scrapbook in private ownership.

4:43    In part, photocopies of James Elliott letters at Indiana State Library and John W. Foster letters at Indiana University, Lilly Library; transcripts (typewritten) of certain correspondence; and microfilm of Thrall family correspondence at Trinity College, Hartford, Conn.

4:44    In part, copies of Foreign Broadcast Intelligence Service reports (1943-1944) at Federal Communications Commission, Washington, D.C.

4:45    Microfiche of original.

4:46    Microfilm of mss. in British Museum, London.

4:47    Microfilm made from originals privately owned.

4:48    Microfilm of originals at Mystic Seaport Museum (Conn.).

4:49    Microfilm and photocopies of originals returned to the Serpan Family.

4:50    Microfilm made in 1977 from originals loaned by T.B. Martin, Omaha, Neb.

4:51    Microfilm made in 1978 from originals which were not retained.

4:52    Microfilm made in 1976 from bound volumes held by International Union of Electrical, Radio and Machine Workers.

4:53    Microfilm made in 1978 of originals loaned by Mrs. Lillian Dereckter, daughter of Israel and Bella Unterberg, Scarsdale, N.Y. Microfilm (master negative) at: University Microfilms, Ann Arbor, Mich.

4:54    Microfilm made from originals deposited in 1960 by the Saumarez family in: Ipswich and East Suffolk Record Office (England).

4:55     Microfilm of original deposited in the repository until 1999 by Urban P. Van Susteren, Appleton, Wis., McCarthy's 1946 campaign manager.

4:56     Microfilm (negative and positive) made from originals loaned by Nebraska Conference of United Church of Christ.

4:57     Microfilm made in 1979 from originals loaned by Rev. I.C.G. Campbell, conference archivist of United Church of Christ.

4:58     Microfilm (negative and positive) made in 1978 from microfilm loaned by Louise Baumann on behalf of Forest Lawn Cemetery Association.

4:59     In part, microfilm of deteriorating scrapbooks.

4:60     In part, microfilm of press scrapbooks which were destroyed.

4:61     In part, microfilm of Melville letters in the collection of Sir John Murray, purchased in 1950.

4:62     In part, microfilm made in 1980 of the letterpress book (1905) owned by Don Coburn, Helena, Mont.

4:63     In part, microfilm (2 reels, negative and positive) made in 1978 of minute book, owned by Bowsher family trust, National Bank & Trust Company, South Bend, Ind.

4:64     In part, microfilm (7 reels) made in 1976 and 1980 from originals in the secretary's office, Louisville, Ky., and in private hands.

4:65     In part, microfilm (14.5 reels : negative ; 35 mm.) made from originals of minutes of Monon Railroad and its predecessors retained by Louisville & Nashville Railroad Company, Louisville, Ky.; and microfilm (2 reels) and photocopies made in 1978 of annual reports, corporate legal records, and sheet music of railroad songs, owned by Frank Van Bree, attorney for Monon Railroad.

4:66     In part, microfilm (6 reels) purchased in 1976 from Vermont Public Records Office. Originals destroyed by State of Vermont.

4:67     In part, microfilm (1 reel : negative ; 35 mm.) of originals of minutes of board of directors meetings retained by the orchestra.

4:68        Transcripts (typewritten) and photocopies.

4:69        Transcripts (typewritten) of 60 letters; location of originals unknown.

4:70        Transcripts (typewritten) made in 1925 and 1943 by Will A. Woldert and Charles B. Wallace, from copies in the possession of Mrs. S.A. Thompson, Dallas, Tex., and other Ashcraft descendants.

4:71        Transcripts and photocopies made from originals in: AAHPER Archives, Washington, D.C.

4:72        Transcripts (typewritten) and photocopies (negative and positive) made from published material, and originals in: North Carolina State Archives, East Carolina University Manuscript Collection, Duke University Manuscript Collection, Southern Historical Collection at the University of North Carolina at Chapel Hill, and in private hands.

4:73        In part, transcripts (typewritten) and photocopies.

4:74        In part, transcripts of original letters and translations from German.

4:75        In part, transcripts (handwritten) of 18th century legal papers made by Parsons and his son.

4:76        In part, transcripts (handwritten) of outgoing correspondence. Location of originals unknown.

4:77        The repository also has photocopy of the Neely diary.

4:78        The repository also has ca. 4 cu. ft. of photocopies of the collection.

4:79        The repository also has microfilm of letter book for 1882-1884.

4:80        The repository also has 1 reel of microfilm of the collection made in 1978.

4:81        The repository also has 3 reels of microfilm (negative and positive) of the collection.

4:82        The repository also has 3 microfilm reels (negative ; 35 mm.).

4:83        The repository also has transcripts (typewritten) of the Masefield-Florence Lamont correspondence.

4:84        The respository also has transcripts (typewritten) of many of the 17th-19th century papers.

4:85        The repository also has transcripts of most of the letters made by members of the Bryan family.

4:86        The repository also has transcripts (typewritten) of 2/3 of the letters provided by the donor.

4:87        The repository also has transcripts (typewritten) made in 1938 by Margaret H. Wood, of Dr. Wood's notes and extracts.

4:88        The repository also has transcripts (typewritten) of the letters with introduction and notes by Wolcott D. Street.

4:89        The repository also holds tapes and transcripts of interviews with Tillow.

4:90        The repository also holds a collection of books, periodicals, and other printed matter relating to President Kennedy, donated by Mr. Tinker.

4:91        The repository has retained the original cassettes.

4:92        The repository has retained the tape-recorded interviews.

4:93        The repository has retained those parts of the microfilmed collection (7 ft.) that were not in deteriorating condition.

4:94        Original collection destroyed.

4:95        For some cases, this is the only extant record.
                (Studybook of law cases)

4:96        Microfilm copies (10 reels) also at: California Historical Society Library (San Francisco) and Iowa State University Library (Ames).

4:97        Wheaton College, Billy Graham Center Archives (Ill.) also has 19 reels of microfilm of the collection and ca. 2000 negatives of photos, made in 1978.

4:98        Columbia University Libraries, New York, N.Y., has copies of many of the letters.

4:99        Copies of each interview transcript have been deposited in: National Library of Medicine, Bethesda, Md., and in libraries at Northwestern University, Chicago, Ill., Radcliffe College, Cambridge, Mass., University of California, Berkeley, and University of Kansas, Lawrence.

4:100       Some of the earlier volumes were microfilmed in 1952 by Church of the Latter-Day Saints and are available at South Carolina Historical Society (Charleston).

## BIOGRAPHICAL/HISTORICAL (4.7B3)

4:101       Architect and local historian, of Bel Air, Md.

4:102       Author and translator; full name, Beatrice Reynolds Kinkead, also known as Beatrice Kincead.

4:103       Born Dorothea or Dorothy Payne; married 1st John Todd, Jr., 2nd James Madison.

4:104       Dancer, known as the Fairy of Light.

4:105       Dancer and teacher; b. Dorette Henriette Ehrich-Grimme, married Sherman S. Rogers.

4:106       Explorer; b. Paul Belloni Du Chaillu.

4:107       German-American family, of Philadelphia, Pa.

4:108       Jewelry designer of New York, N.Y., and Little Silver, N.J.

4:109       Manufacturer of transportation vehicles, both horsedrawn and motorized, including wagons, carriages, and auto-mobiles, founded 1852, as C. & H. Studebaker, then C. & J.M. Studebaker, Studebaker Brothers Manufacturing Company, and Studebaker Packard; ceased making automobiles, 1966.

4:110       Merchant, judge, Revolutionary officer, and State legislator, of Windsor County, Vt.

4:111      Mystery writer, whose real name is Charles H. Huff.

4:112      Philosophic anarchist and author; b. Max Nacht, also
used pseudonyms Stephen Naft and Max Norton.

4:113      Professor of comparative literature, Dartmouth College,
author, bookseller, and founder of Westholm Publications.

4:114      Professor of anatomy, Dartmouth Medical School
(1911-1947) and medical director, YMCA in France
(1918-1919).

4:115      Resident of Memphis, Tenn.; b. Annie Pope Smith.

4:116      Wife of Henry Morrison Flagler; b. Mary Lily Kenan;
later married to Robert Worth Bingham.

4:117      Chapter founded in 1929.

4:118      Chartered 1941 as Negro Public Library; name changed in
1961.

4:119      Established in 1875 and closed in 1974.

4:120      Formed in early 1970s to oppose Iowa legislation
establishing deposits on bottles and cans.

4:121      Founded in 1951; national headquarters in Rockville, Md.

4:122      Founded in 1869 as Augsburg Seminary in Marshall, Wis.;
moved to Minneapolis, Minn., in 1872; reorganized as
Augsburg College in 1963 when the theological seminary
separated from the college.

4:123      Literary society formed in 1919 by writers, musicians, and
artists who met at Ina Coolbrith's home, to study the history
and literature of California, discuss members' works, and
assemble and present their personal and literary
reminiscences. After Coolbrith's death, the circle was continued by her niece and grandniece, Mrs. Finlay Cook and
Ina Cook Craig, respectively.

4:124      Medical school located in Chicago, Ill.; founded as
Woman's Hospital Medical College in 1870; name changed
to Woman's Medical College of Chicago; became part of
Northwestern University in 1892 and closed in 1902.

4:125    Organized in 1852; also known as St. Louis Typographical Union No. 8.

4:126    Press publishing surrealist poetry, woodcuts, lithographs, and other literary and artistic works, chiefly in its literary magazine, Kayak.

4:127    Railroad running between Washington, D.C., and Chesapeake Beach, Md.

4:128    Women's organization which has met since 1883 to read papers on history and other topics.

## SCOPE AND CONTENT/ABSTRACT (4.7B4)

4:129    Handwritten ms. with corrections made by Miller.

4:130    Holograph, in ink, with additions in pencil by the publisher.

4:131    Ms. and printed documents.

4:132    Handwritten and typewritten mss. of Pollock's biography of Billy Graham, published in 1966; and letter (1973) from Pollock.

4:133    Ms., paste-up dummies, page proofs, and book jacket, for Bawden's The peppermint pig (1975), a book for children.

4:134    Holograph ms. with corrections in the hand of the author and printer's marks of Ludewig's work (published New York, 1846); together with letters of presentation (1846) from Ludewig to Peter Force.

4:135    Literary mss., some with annotations by Sir William Rothenstein and William Butler Yeats. Includes versions of Gitanjali (1912) and writings of Snehalata Sen and others.

4:136    Preliminary draft and copy-edited ms. of Keiler's The art of teaching art.

4:137    Audio tapes of major addresses, study papers, and area briefs presented at the congress; transcripts of major study papers; minutes of the planning committee; documents recording public reaction to the congress; and drafts of the Wheaton Declaration, the congress' final report. Most participants were from Interdenomination Foreign Mission Association and Evangelical Foreign Missions Association.

4:138     Autograph collection of clerical correspondence and signed documents by bishops of the Protestant Episcopal Church in the U.S.A. The correspondence deals entirely with church matters. Many of the letters have portraits of the bishops accompanying them.

4:139     Chiefly autographs of statesmen, foreign naval officers, and others who visited the Naval War College.

4:140     Photocopies of 5 autograph albums and the letters of Moriz Rosenthal.

4:141     Burial cards for individuals interred at the cemetery, recording residence, marital status, race, age, cause and date of death, nearest relative, and other information.

4:142     Business papers, reports, ledgers (1919-1946), and 112 maps (1876-1947), chiefly relating to the mine's later period of operation, 1919-1955. Maps cover other mines of the Comstock Lode in Nevada.

4:143     Card files, printed and ms. maps, census data, photos, and other research material, compiled by Williamson/ Awsumb, Architects, Memphis, Tenn., commissioned by the association to do historical research necessary to prepare a National Register nomination form for the neighborhood as an historic district. Includes The Central Gardens handbook (1981), published by the firm as the result of their work.

4:144     Chiefly weekly church bulletins (1932-1944) of a Scandinavian-language congregation; together with history of the church, list of pastors, and copies of Moravian catechisms (1898).

4:145     Clippings from Lincoln, Neb., newspapers relating to murders by Charles Raymond Starkweather (1938-1959) and Caril Ann Fugate, their trials, Starkweather's execution, and Fugate's applications for parole.

4:146     Constitution and bylaws (1888), records of stockholder shares, financial statements (1898-1899), stock certificates (1888-ca. 1894), receipts (1888-1893), and material relating to the association's receivership and dissolution.

4:147    Arithmetic and penmanship copybooks, primarily of early 19th century Ohio and Pennsylvania school children.

4:148    Correspondence and other papers of the family of Dr. Chillion Packard. Includes letters from the doctor's son at school and after 1861, at war; together with 19th century valentines.

4:149    Correspondence (1968-1973), diary (1969), scrapbook (1968-1969), newspaper clippings, and other papers, relating to Voegler's experience in Washington, D.C., as a Congressional page, 1969, and as a White House summer intern, 1971-1973. Includes manuals and material from Capitol Page School.

4:150    Correspondence, receipts, bills of lading, and advertisements, relating to boots and shoes. Firms represented include Charles Warren, New York and Boston, and Fogg & Holmes and J.H. Lester, both of Boston, Mass.

4:151    Daybook of Smoot's store at Northwest Fork Bridge, Talbot County, Md., a stronghold of the Nicholites (New Quakers), many of whom are mentioned in the book.

4:152    Daily diary (ca. 50,000 p. in 63 v.), with index; together with poetry by Van Bibber, monograph about Bel Air, Md., photocopies of letters and newspaper clippings, and other papers.

4:153    Diary reflecting Droddy's experiences as a soldier in Texas and Mexico during the Mexican War, describing camp life. Persons mentioned include Albert Sidney Johnston, Ephraim McLean, and Zachary Taylor. Includes genealogical material.

4:154    Drawings and prints, some on verso of correspondence and clipped from newspapers and periodicals.

4:155    Designs for household articles, furniture, and home interiors; together with articles on Lott's work (1955) and obituary (1978).

4:156    Fragment of an ethical work in dialogue form, evidently unpublished.

4:157  Jewelry designs, mostly in pencil or watercolors.

4:158  Journal by an unknown person recording a trip by packet from New York to Providence, R.I., with a stop at Newport, and then by sleigh through Attleboro and Dedham, Mass., to Boston.

4:159  Journals (1906-1941, 1948-1955) and pocket agenda notebooks (47 v., 1916-1956).

4:160  Letter (1785) from George Washington to David Stuart; 2 letters (1865 and undated) of Ralph Waldo Emerson; single letters of Charles Sumner and John Greenleaf Whittier; poem (1880) of Samuel Longfellow; receipt signed by Washington Irving; and logbook (1749) of sloop Three Brothers on a voyage from Rhode Island to the West Indies.

4:161  Letter, suppressed chapter of Twain's Life on the Mississippi (1883), scrapbook, guest book (1908-1910), and portrait (photo).

4:162  Letters from Rome to Antonio Marcheggiani with observations on the course of the Risorgimento in Italy; together with packet of official documents (ms. and printed).

4:163  Letters from Watson to his mother, describing events and activities as British Headquarters Officer in India during the Sepoy Rebellion.

4:164  Letters of VanderHoof written while a student at Dartmouth College, primarily to his parents, Emma Frances Douglas VanderHoof (1858-1937) and Hervey Brundage VanderHoof (1858-1901), who resided in Chicago and San Francisco.

4:165  Letters to Brown from friends upon the death of his son, Oliver.

4:166  Letters, mostly to Hunt, including 140 from Sir John Everett Millais, cofounder with Hunt of Pre-Raphaelite movement.

4:167  Chiefly personal letters from John, Isaac, and Rebecca Murrell, relating to plantation life and Civil War in Claiborne Parish, La., together with excerpts from Isaac's daybook of business transactions (1840s). Correspondents include Lou Eddins.

4:168     Fifty-eight letters (1891-1892) from Addison to her mother, Ann de Wolf (Lovett) Gibbs, forming a journal of a tour of Europe; ms. (345 p.) of an unpublished work, Fables and gables of Brittany; mss. of 18 children's books; musical compositions (2 v.), mostly unpublished; and watercolor drawings and other artwork.

4:169     Ca. 300 letters from Masefield to Florence Lamont are published in: Letters of John Masefield to Florence Lamont / edited by Corliss Lamont and Lansing Lamont. 1979.

4:170     Logbook, documents, and other papers, belonging to Kane and his family, together with Margaret Elder Dow's unpublished biography, Elisha Kent Kane, additional research material gathered by Dow, and writings by Dow and others on Kane's ships and voyages.

4:171     Material from the time capsule placed under the Benjamin Franklin statue in Washington Square, San Francisco, Calif., in 1879 and opened in 1979. The bulk of the collection consists of papers of Henry Daniel Cogswell (1820-1900), dentist, of San Francisco, including papers concerning the proposed Cogswell Dental College, inventory of his property, copies of his will, papers concerning his proposition to erect a drinking fountain and establish the Women's Pioneer Hotel. Contributions from others include Sarah B. Cooper and Charles Otto.

4:172     Memoirs of Dillon's childhood in Claiborne Parish, La., including biographical material on her father, William Henry Pace, farmer and sawmill operator, of New Athens, La., and her mother, Rebecca Frances (Pate) Pace; genealogical notes on the Pace and Pate families; and copies of poems, homilies, and prayer. Includes material on Mt. Lebanon, La., details on Claiborne Parish families, and farm, recreational, religious, and school activities there.

4:173     Minutes of annual church conferences, constitution, covenant, rules of decorum, treasurer's report, church rolls, and yearbooks.

4:174     Minutes (4 v., 1883-1920) and financial ledger (1883-1907), all in Danish.

4:175     Notes, lecture notes, reports, and class lists, relating to Lord's career. Includes lecture notes (1908-1911) from University of Iowa.

4:176        Ordnance forms, lists, and orders, relating chiefly to Bowen's Civil War service in 52nd Illinois Infantry and Sherman's Georgia campaigns; and Pikes Peak diaries (1859) relating to his gold prospecting adventures in eastern Colorado.

4:177        Photo and film files include television news footage.

4:178        Mostly photos of Labrador and Texas.

4:179        Project of the Memphis Search for Meaning Committee in cooperation with Reader's Digest, National Endowment for the Humanities, and Memphis State University, to collect material concerning the sanitation workers' strike and assassination of Dr. Martin Luther King, Jr., and the effect of these events on the city of Memphis, Tenn., and race relations there.

4:180        Scattered records chiefly of various Waterbury organizations, including library records, record book (1827-1839) of Temperance Society of Waterbury, and records from charitable organizations.

4:181        Chiefly 13 scrapbooks documenting McKelvie's life as author, ranch owner, and wife of Gov. Samuel R. McKelvie. Includes her interviews with actors and actresses and 11 letters from Hollywood cowboy star William S. Hart.

4:182        Souvenir artifacts, deeds, periodicals, publications, posters, phonodiscs, and photos, relating to the career of singer Elvis Presley (1935-1977).

4:183        Speeches, citations, booklets and programs by Mann, and photos; and biographical sketch entitled The Mann Brothers of Lincoln, Neb.

4:184        Survey forms (ca. 1700 items) providing personal, family, and military information on men who served in World War I, and letters and photos collected from interviewees. Questionnaires also list relatives who served in the war or previous wars.

4:185        Transcripts of tape-recorded interviews with 39 women physicians and others, relating to women in medicine, most conducted by Regina Morantz.

4:186        Typescripts of early poems, some with ms. revisions.

4:187     Name, rank, state, and other information about 1600
          Confederate dead, copied from wooden headboards by Col.
          G.T. Parker, U.S. Army officer in charge of burial at
          Vicksburg National Cemetery.

4:188     Refrain only, remainder lost.

4:189     Early version of The thin man and letter from Hammett.

# ARRANGEMENT (4.7B5)

4:190     Arranged alphabetically by signer.
          (Collection of promissory notes)

4:191     Calendar in alphabetical order of the journals of the
          House of Lords.

4:192     Bird notes arranged alphabetically by type of birds;
          miscellaneous material arranged alphabetically by subject of
          folders.

4:193     Letters arranged chronologically, 1938-1958; lectures
          arranged chronologically, 1947-1951, and alphabetically by
          topic; miscellaneous pieces relating to Beecher's career as a
          consul arranged alphabetically by country of consulate.

4:194     Arranged in 5 series as follows: Crayon drawings and
          india ink drawings of gestures and poses (2 boxes); 200
          drawings for the poetics of gestures (10 boxes); notes for
          "the state of grace" (1 box); clippings and small scrapbooks
          (18 boxes); and commentaries on the exercises of Odic-
          Kintzel's system numbered in various sequences (1 box).

# LANGUAGE(S) (4.7B6)

4:195     Partly in cipher.

4:196     In English Fraktur.

4:197     In Latin calligraphy.

4:198      In cursive Greek.

4:199      In Hebrew longhand.

4:200      In French, Hebrew, and other languages.

4:201      Chiefly in Norwegian.

4:202      Primarily in Polish, also Hebrew, German, Yiddish, and English.

4:203      Many of the papers are in Russian.

4:204      Much of the collection is in Dutch.

4:205      Most of the collection is in Ukrainian. Portions have been translated into English.

4:206      Part of the collection is in Latvian.

4:207      Diary in Spanish, printed by hand.

4:208      Letter in incorrect Italian and phonetically spelled English.

4:209      Sermons in Danish.

4:210      All poems are in Czech.

4:211      Latin documents are accompanied by English translations.

4:212      Gaelic mss., together with non-Gaelic material.

4:213      Includes English translations of the original Welsh letters.


## PROVENANCE (4.7B7)

4:214      Collection originally begun by Carl Jackson and completed by Stuart Forth.

4:215      Originally collected by Peter Sinkler and arranged by his granddaughter, Emily Breckenridge, after Sinkler's disappearance. Purchased by Thomas Reed in 1918 who added to the collection with materials purchased from dealers in London and Zurich, 1924-1932.

4:216    Formerly part of the collection of Lord Braye, Stanford Hall, Rugby, Eng.

4:217    In part, formerly deposited in South Carolina Historical Society (Charleston).

4:218    Gift of Southern California Historical Society, 1974; in part, formerly owned by Horace Bell.

4:219    Gift of Mr. and Mrs. Jilton, 1980; previously discarded by Johnson City City Hall; formerly part of Johnson City Engineering Dept. records.

4:220    Gift of Mr. and Mrs. James M.E. Mixter, 1979. Mrs. Mixter (formerly Phebe Baker Perry) collected the papers.

4:221    Gift of Paul Tillich, Cambridge, Mass., 1946; transferred from the Widener Library, 1960.

4:222    Gift of Maria C. Lanzar-Carpio, 1928, who acquired much of the collection from Welsh for use in researching her doctoral dissertation.

4:223    Gift of Studebaker Corporation to George Arents Research Library, Syracuse University, ca. 1967, and transferred to Discovery Hall Museum, 1978.

4:224    Separated from the repository's Valders Canning Company records, which were gifts of Charles C. Christel, Manitowoc, Wis., 1974, and Ruth Glasgow, Pasadena, Calif., 1976.

4:225    Gift, in part, of James Strobridge, 1977; provenance of bulk of the collection is unknown.

4:226    Purchased from Mrs. Winfield Partridge, Bay St. Louis, Miss., 1976. The collection was in the possession of Col. Kammerling's descendants.

4:227    Transferred from Harvard University Archives, which received the collection as a gift from Dr. Lichtenstein.

4:228    Willed to Smith College and Radcliffe College; the Radcliffe portion was later given to Smith.

# SOURCE/DONOR (4.7B8)

4:229     Acquired with records from Buffalo County, Neb., court-house.

4:230     Acquired from Alexander Laing, Evelyn Nef, and Vilhjalmur Stefansson.

4:231     Acquired from Sotheby's.

4:232     Acquired prior to 1953.

4:233     Acquired from Mary Augusta (Hoover) Aiken, 1975.

4:234     Acquired from Ms. Bissell's estate, via Pasadena Art Museum, 1963.

4:235     Acquired from Mrs. Dillon through Thadeus T. Pardue, 1969.

4:236     Acquired from family and friends, 1943-1948.

4:237     Acquired from various sources, including Mrs. Yeats, 1950.

4:238     Bulk of the collection acquired from the division in 1963; later material received as gift of Betty Boslaugh, Lincoln, Neb., 1980.

4:239     In part, acquired through Dr. Philip Cook, and Lincoln Parish Library, Ruston, La.

4:240     Bequest of Dayton C. Miller, Jan. 19, 1942.

4:241     Chiefly bequest of Oswald Garrison Villard, 1949.

4:242     Deposits and purchases, 1959-1977.

4:243     Deposit by Mr. Aiken; purchased from Mrs. Aiken; gifts of James N.B. Hill, Howard Mumford Jones, and Alfred Claghorn Potter; and other acquisitions.

4:244     Deposits by Edward Hartshorne, 1931, and Lawrence Stabler, date unknown; and bequest of Mary Hartshorne Nonnan, Locust, N.J., 1978-1979.

4:245    Deposited by Mr. Guild's great-granddaughter, Nancy G. DeCesare, 1969; converted to gift, 1976.

4:246    Deposited by Marion B. Abbot, Elinor R. Abbot, and Henry Dehon Abbot, 1955.

4:247    Permanent deposit by the repository's oral history project, 1979-1982.

4:248    Gift, 1940.

4:249    Anonymous gift.

4:250    Gifts of various donors.

4:251    Gift, ca. 1910, and purchase, 1978.

4:252    Gifts and deposits, 1977-1979.

4:253    Gift of trustees of the observatory, 1970, 1974.

4:254    Gift of the association through Anita Terauds, secretary, 1975.

4:255    Gift of American Missionary Association.

4:256    Gift of University of Washington Library, Archives and Manuscripts Division, Seattle, 1979.

4:257    Gift of Miss Brice, 1972 and 1978.

4:258    Gift of Mr. Lord, 1955-1970.

4:259    Gift of Lady Edris Allan, Kingston, Jamaica, 1975.

4:260    Gift of Sara Roberta Church, 1976. Additions to the collection are expected.

4:261    Gift of Mr. Tureaud's widow, Lucille DeJoie Tureaud, 1974 and 1977.

4:262    Gift of Henry S. Roane, church clerk and part-time pastor.

4:263    Gift of Mr. Harlow's son-in-law and daughter, Mr. and Mrs. Harold J. Berman, 1978.

4:264      Gift of Ralph Lowell, James Hale Lowell, and their sons, in memory of John Lowell (1856-1922), 1943.

4:265      Gifts of Donald E.H. Frear and Svend Pedersen, College of Agriculture, 1964, 1966.

4:266      Gifts of Senator and Mrs. Aiken and other sources.

4:267      Gift of Henry L. Abbott and others, 1951.

4:268      Gift, probably from a descendant of the Billings family, 1941.

4:269      Gift of the estate of Gerhard Gade, 1958.

4:270      Gift of Mr. West's estate, 1977, received 1979.

4:271      Gift of Mr. Hubert, 1973, and of C.L. Reynolds, executor of his estate, 1977 and 1978.

4:272      Gift of the heirs of the estate of Mary Anne (Mason) Anderson, 1976 and 1978.

4:273      Probably gift of an heir of Charles Butler Rogers.

4:274      In part, gift of the estate of Mrs. Alfred Aldrich through John Neff, 1956.

4:275      Chiefly gift of Julian Magarey Barclay after the death of Mrs. Barclay, 1951.

4:276      Chiefly gift of Mrs. Joseph M. Edinburg, 1972-1974, and purchased from Malcolm Ferguson, 1948.

4:277      Bound volumes were gift of W.A. Jackson, Cambridge, Mass., 1962; Swann letters were gift of Ifan Kyrle Fletcher, London, Eng., 1960.

4:278      Continuing gift of E.T. Guymon, Jr., San Diego, Calif.

4:279      Loan from Mr. McGrath, Moorhead, Minn., through Dr. Catherine Cater, 1971.

4:280      Permanent loan of Dr. Stone's grandson, John S. Stone, ca. 1955.

4:281    Placed on loan in the library by the composer, May 9, 1962.

4:282    Purchase, ca. 1940.

4:283    Purchases and gifts, 1977-1981.

4:284    Purchased at auction, 1977.

4:285    Purchased at Sotheby's, London, Eng., through Martin Breslauer, 1972.

4:286    Purchase from In Our Time, Cambridge, Mass., upon recommendation of Dr. Roger Esson, Memphis State University Dept. of English, 1977.

4:287    Purchased from Elkin Mathews Ltd., Bishops Stortford, Eng., 1943-1949; Hamil & Baker, Chicago, Ill., 1953; and from other sources.

4:288    Letters purchased from Richard Macnutt, Tunbridge Wells, Eng., 1970; and music purchased from Giorgio Careri, Rome, Italy, 1950.

4:289    Purchased with the Elkan N. Adler library, 1923.

4:290    Placed in the repository by Harvey Dean, director of libraries, 1978.

4:291    Probably placed in the library by institute trustees after Dr. Murphy's death.

4:292    Presented by Ms. Adams, New York, N.Y., 1968-1972.

4:293    Received as part of National Broadcasting Company records, 1970.

4:294    Received from Melba (Mrs. Edward) Kirkpatric, 1978.

4:295    Received from Newburyport Public Library, Mass., and continuous gift of James Parton.

4:296    Received from the estate of Nadia Boulanger, July 18, 1980.

4:297    Received with the records of Nebraska Division, American Association of University Women, 1970.

4:298  Archival transfer, 1950.

4:299  Transfer from Smithsonian Institution, 1976.

4:300  Transferred from the collection of the Canal Zone Library-Museum, 1979.

4:301  Transferred from the university administration building, 1979, where a portion (1973-1977) of Dr. Culp's papers remains.

4:302  Mimeographed and print and near-print material from various organizations has been transferred to the repository's Contemporary Social Action File.

4:303  Photos and architectural drawings of buildings designed by Cleaveland have been removed from the collection and transferred to other depts. in the repository.

4:304  Related blueprints have been transferred to the repository's audiovisual collection. Related maps have been transferred to the repository's map collection.

4:305  Related photos have been transferred to the repository's photographic collection. Several costumes are in the museum collection.

4:306  Chiefly transferred from Harvard University, Museum of Comparative Zoology.

4:307  Chiefly transfers from U.S. Dept. of State, 1904, and U.S. Treasury Dept., 1917; and various gifts and purchases, 1930-1981.

4:308  Possibly removed from Beaufort County Court House, S.C., by William Henry Trescott in 1851.

4:309  Additions to the collection are expected.

## RESTRICTIONS AND ACCESS (4.7B9)

4:310  Open to qualified researchers.

4:311  Open to researchers under library restrictions.

4:312    Research access restricted until 1995.

4:313    Records less than 10 years old are closed to investigators.

4:314    Access restricted.

4:315    Access restricted to those with written permission of Agnes de Mille.

4:316    Permission to consult may be obtained from Mrs. Maxine Wills or Miss Maxine Wills.

4:317    Access restricted until April 1999.

4:318    Access restricted until 1988 except with written permission of Sara Roberta Church or Dr. Charles W. Crawford, Memphis State University. Miss Church may extend the term of restriction during her lifetime.

4:319    Access restricted in part.

4:320    Access restricted, in part; Ms. Hardwick's permission required to examine her correspondence.

4:321    Access to 9 Beerbohm letters restricted until 1984.

4:322    Access to certain student records (2 ft. of material) restricted.

4:323    Access to original diary restricted; only photocopy may be used.

4:324    Access to originals restricted. Microfilm copy available for research.

4:325    Access to vital records dated 1900 or later restricted.

4:326    Autobiography is restricted to reference use only.

4:327    Use of case files restricted for 75 years from date of their creation.

## LITERARY RIGHTS AND COPYRIGHT (4.7B10)

4:328    Copyright interests have been reserved.

4:329    Information on literary rights available in the library.

4:330    Literary rights of Robert Lamb have been dedicated to the public.

## FINDING AIDS (4.7B11)

4:331    Finding aid published by the repository.

4:332    Described in: Medical College of Pennsylvania : oral history collection on women in medicine catalogue. Philadelphia, 1978.

4:333    Described in: The LaFollette family collection. Washington, D.C. : Library of Congress, Manuscript Division, 1981.

4:334    Card catalog and microfilm index in the repository.

4:335    Item index in the repository.

4:336    Register of reels in the repository, and inventory of collection on reel 12.

4:337    Subject index cards in the repository.

4:338    Indexed by architect and location.

4:339    Many of the transcripts are indexed.

4:340    Collection has been analyzed by the repository.

4:341    A composite collection consisting of small groups of papers or single items listed and described separately in the repository.

4:342    Cataloged and indexed individually in the repository, where most of the original tapes are retained.

4:343        Unpublished preliminary box list in the repository.

4:344        Unpublished calendar in the repository.

4:345        Unpublished checklist in the repository.

4:346        Unpublished description in the repository.

4:347        Unpublished finding aid and index in the repository.

4:348        Unpublished inventory in the repository.

4:349        Unpublished shelf-list in the repository.

4:350        Unpublished finding aids available for the Senn, Frank, and Murphy papers.

4:351        Unpublished lists of cases in the repository.

4:352        Card index to correspondence in the repository. University of Florida Library, Gainesville, also has microfilm (5 reels) of the index.

4:353        Larger collections of Bellini, Puccini, Rossini, and Verdi material that were acquired as part of the purchase have been entered separately in this catalog.

4:354        Portions of the collection have been cataloged separately.


## OTHER SOURCES OF DESCRIPTION (4.7B12)

4:355        NUCMC MS 72-1942.

4:356        Formerly cataloged as part of NUCMC MS 60-1735.

4:357        Described in: University South Caroliniana Society Program.

4:358        Described in: Inventory of the corporate records of Studebaker Automotive Division / George Arents Research Library at Syracuse University. 1971.

4:359    Described in: Guide to the microfilm edition of
temperance and prohibition papers / edited by Randall C.
Jimerson, Francis X. Blouin, Charles A. Isetts. Ann Arbor :
University of Michigan, 1977. p. 196-204.

4:360    Described in: The Robert R. Church family of Memphis /
Pamela Palmer, editor. Memphis, Tenn. : Memphis State
University Press [1979] (Mississippi Valley collection
bulletin ; no. 10).

4:361    Described in: The Memphis Multi-Media Archival Project
: the 1968 sanitation workers strike : final report to the
National Endowment for the Humanities / prepared by
David G. Yellin and Carol Lynn Yellin. Memphis State
University, 1974. (J.W. Brister Library monograph series ;
no. 2).

4:362    Described in: Robinson Jeffers at Occidental College : a
checklist of the collection in the Mary Norton Clapp
Library. Los Angeles, 1955; and Theodore Lilienthal, Robinson Jeffers and the Quercus Press / by Ward Ritchie ; with
a Checklist of the Lilienthal-Jeffers collection / by Tyrus G.
Harmsen. Los Angeles : Occidental College, 1974.

4:363    Also described in: Catalog of the manuscript and archival
collections and index to the correspondence of John Torrey /
compiled by Sara Lenley . . . [et al.]. Boston : G.K. Hall,
1973. p. 232-233.

4:364    Described more fully in: Bulletin of the New York
Academy of Medicine. Vol. 15, 1969. p. 761-766.

4:365    More fully described in: South Carolina historical
magazine. Vol. 82, no. 2 (April 1981) p. 187-190.

4:366    Partially described in: Library of Congress quarterly journal. Vol. 25, no. 1 (Jan. 1968) p. 63-65.

4:367    Some are described in: Preliminary listing of the San Francisco manuscript collections in the library of the California
Historical Society / by Diana Lachatanere. San Francisco :
California Historical Society, 1980, entry nos. 53, 161, 162,
229.

## PUBLISHED VERSIONS (4.7B13)

4:368    Published by EP Microfilm Ltd., 1974.

4:369    A microfilm (38 reels) of the papers has been published by: Center for Western Studies, Augustana College, Sioux Falls, S.D., with an accompanying guide entitled: Guide to the microfilm edition of the Richard F. Pettigrew papers at the Pettigrew Museum, Sioux Falls, South Dakota / edited by Gary D. Olson. 1978.

4:370    Adlum's memoirs of his Revolutionary War service were microfilmed for James S. Schoff and published as: Memoirs of the life of John Adlum in the Revolutionary War / edited by Howard H. Peckham. Chicago : Caxton Club, 1968.

4:371    Published in: Nantucket Historical Association bulletin. Vol. 1, no. 2 (1898).

4:372    Entire collection, with Heindel letters from the American Library, American Embassy, London and elsewhere, is being published in: Letters of Richard H. Heindel / edited by Ruth Noble Heindel. 1984-

4:373    In part, published in: Quinze ans de ma vie / Loie Fuller. Paris : F. Juven, 1908 and Fifteen years of a dancer's life / Loie Fuller. London : H. Jenkins, 1913.

4:374    Melville's journals and much of his correspondence have been published.

4:375    Mrs. Webster's journal was published in 1942 under the title: Mr. W. & I.

4:376    Vol. 1 of Col. Bouquet's orderly books was published as: Bouquet's march to the Ohio : the Forbes Road . . . / edited . . . by Edward G. Williams. Pittsburgh : Historical Society of Western Pennsylvania, 1975. Vol. 2 was published in: Western Pennsylvania Historical magazine. Vol. 2, 1959.

4:377    Williams' journal was published by the repository as: The New Zealand journal, 1842-1844, of John B. Williams, of Salem, Massachusetts . . . / edited by Robert W. Kenny. 1956.

4:378    Grimké and DuBose's papers published in: South Carolina historical and genealogical magazine. Vol. 12-19; Elliott's papers published in: Yearbook, 1889 : City of Charleston.

4:379    Many of the letters from Beerbohm to Turner are published in: Letters to Reggie Turner / edited by Rupert Hart-Davis. 1964.

4:380    Edited typescripts of many of the letters were published in: Letters from Dartmouth / by Douglas VanderHoof. 1940.

4:381    Most letters from the period 1750-1754 have been published in: South Carolina historical and genealogical magazine. Vol. 31-33, 1930-1932.

4:382    Parts of the reminiscences were published in: Pioneers in Dakota Territory, 1879-1889, edited by Grimstad's son-in-law, Henry Bakken.

4:383    Parts of the collection are published in: The letter book of Esek Hopkins, Commander-in-Chief of the United States Navy, 1775-1777 (1932) and The correspondence of Esek Hopkins, Commander-in-Chief of the United States Navy (1933), both published by the repository.

4:384    A portion of Vredenburgh's correspondence was privately published in the 19th century.

4:385    Portions of the collection have been published in: Tyler's quarterly historical and genealogical magazine, Vol. 27 (April 1946) p. 255-273.

4:386    Portions of the collection have been published, notably in: Life of Arthur Lee / by R.H. Lee. 1829 (2 v.), and in: The diplomatic correspondence of the American Revolution / edited by Jared Sparks.

# PHYSICAL DESCRIPTION/CONDITION (4.7B14)

4:387    Partially printed.

4:388        Pen-and-ink and pencil.

4:389        Pen-and-ink, charcoal, and chalk drawings.

4:390        Manuscript in pen-and-ink and watercolor superimposed on blue line print base map.

4:391        Ink on transparencies.

4:392        In pencil.

4:393        Principally in pencil, 2 p. in ink.

4:394        Pencil, pen-and-ink, and watercolor on tracing paper.

4:395        Watercolor and ink.

4:396        Annotations on verso.

4:397        Annotated in pencil, on verso, with Canal Zone Library map checklist number: 249.

4:398        Additions and corrections annotated in pencil.

4:399        Stamp and annotations in black and red ink and pencil on verso.

4:400        Includes notations in pencil for added orchestral doubling.

4:401        Includes pencilled ornamentation in the composer's hand, presumably for violin.

4:402        Title in pencil on matte board.

4:403        At head of title on photocopy in red ink: Revised version.

4:404        Signed "With kindest regards of Fritz Kreisler"--P. [2].

4:405        Contains 2 complete wax seals and a partial seal directly on the vellum.

4:406        Envelope included.

4:407        The map sheet is attached, as an insert, to the folded leaf of text, and the combined piece has been refolded to 21 x 9 cm.

4:408    Watermark: W. Morris.

4:409    Imperfect: A few ink smears, annotations in pencil, and some holes.

4:410    Imperfect: Not colored and small sections missing.

4:411    Imperfect: Brittle along fold lines; some patches.

4:412    Imperfect: Many letters deteriorated along fold lines and edges.

4:413    Imperfect: Deterioration along margins and index missing from lower right corner.

4:414    Imperfect: Stained by water.

4:415    Diary for 1901 faded and mostly illegible.

4:416    Imperfect: Mildewed and partially foxed.


## TITLE TRANSCRIPTION/SOURCE (4.7B15)

4:417    Title transcribed.

4:418    Ms. cover title transcribed.

4:419    Title transcribed from caption.

4:420    Title transcribed from Canal Zone Library map checklist.

4:421    Title transcribed from piano part; in caption, original title crossed out and replaced by: Troisième duo brilliant.


## VARIATIONS IN TITLE (4.7B16)

4:422    Also known as: The Seven days war briefings.

4:423    Title on spine: First lady of Amherst.

# 5

# Music

## FORM OF COMPOSITION AND MEDIUM OF PERFORMANCE (5.7B1)

5:1      Chance composition.

5:2      Children's opera.

5:3      "Compilation of instrumental music from Gluck's opera . . . put together for a recording"--Pref.

5:4      Excerpts from the motion-picture score: An ideal husband.

5:5      Incidental music for the play by Ken Hill.

5:6      Opera.

5:7      Opera excerpt.

5:8      Opera in 3 acts.

5:9      Operetta excerpts ; English and German words.

5:10      Pieces put together by the editor to form a suite ; originally published in Recueil des pièces de guitare, Brussels, 1729.

5:11    Reconstruction of portions of Acts 3 and 5 of the opera from the ms. (Mus. E 120) which contains excerpts from all acts with continuo acc.

5:12    Sacred and secular choruses.

5:13    School songbook ; without music.

5:14    Song cycle.

5:15    Song, in part folk, associated with the Hudson River and the sloop Clearwater.

5:16    Suite.

5:17    Principally hymn tunes and Scottish folk-songs, without words ; unacc. melodies.

5:18    Principally unacc. melodies.

5:19    School songbook ; principally unacc. melodies.

5:20    Unacc. melodies.

5:21    Unacc. melodies, transcribed by Higinio Anglés.

5:22    Unacc. melodies ; words printed as text.

5:23    Folk songs, principally for varying choruses.

5:24    Principally ballate and madrigals for 2-3 voices.

5:25    Folk dance tunes and hymn tunes, the latter with words.

5:26    Folk music for voices and/or instruments ; Russian and Uzbek words.

5:27    Songs for soprano, flute, and piano.

5:28    Song arrangements, for guitar.

5:29    Teaching pieces for 2 violins.

5:30    Hymnal ; chord symbols included.

5:31    Hymns, with music.

5:32        Melodies, in part with words ; those without words may be vocalized according to instructions on p. xi.

5:33        Melodies, with chord symbols.

5:34        For medium voice.

5:35        For voices.

5:36        SATB.

5:37        SATBSATB.

5:38        For chorus (SATB).

5:39        For 4-5 voices, unacc.

5:40        For high voice and piano.

5:41        For voice and lute.

5:42        For voice and piano, with chord symbols.

5:43        For voices and piano, with chord symbols.

5:44        For chorus (SATB) and organ ; words also in Greek romanized.

5:45        For chorus (SATB) and piano, 4 hands.

5:46        For chorus (SSAATTB) and piano or organ.

5:47        For women's voices, speaking; men's voices, chanting the Psalm; percussion; and organ.

5:48        For baritone and percussion (5 players) ; with stage action and costume.

5:49        For piano, violin, and optional soprano or tenor.

5:50        For congregation in unison (or baritone solo), chorus (SATB), flute, and string orchestra.

5:51        For 2-4 voices and/or instruments.

5:52        For wordless mixed chorus and orchestra.

5:53        For wordless soprano and wind quintet.

5:54        "For concert or stage presentation. Unison voices and piano with optional percussion and guitar"--Cover.

5:55        For solo voices (ST) and chorus (SSAATTBB) ; includes piano reduction for rehearsal.

5:56        For soprano, double mixed chorus, 4 instruments (bassoons, trombones, or violin, 2 violas, and violoncello), and continuo ; figured bass realized for organ.

5:57        For band.

5:58        For organ.

5:59        For string orchestra.

5:60        For string quartet.

5:61        For piano, with words.

5:62        For piano, with interlinear words.

5:63        For piano, with Ukrainian and English words.

5:64        For flute and magnetic tape.

5:65        "For flute (oboe/recorder in C/violin) and basso continuo"--Cover.

5:66        For oboe and string orchestra.

5:67        For recorder and piano.

5:68        Fragments of incomplete works for horn and orchestra.

5:69        For recorder or flute and continuo.

5:70        For solo violin and string orchestra, with organ, piano, and percussion.

5:71        For vibraphone and marimba (1 player) and piano.
            (Title proper: Percussion duo)

5:72        For 4 players, 3 tom toms each graduated in pitch.
            (Title proper: Quartet, twelve tom toms)

5:73      For percussion (6 players).

5:74      For 1 or 2 viols and continuo.

5:75      For 4 trumpets, 2 horns, 2 trombones, and 2 tubas (or 2 trumpets, horn, trombone, tuba, and organ).

5:76      For 6 trumpets.

5:77      For 8 violins, 3 violas, 2 violoncellos, and 2 double basses.

5:78      For 8 unspecified instruments.

5:79      Arr. for 8 unspecified instruments with optional percussion ; includes chord symbols.

5:80      Arrangements for piano or organ, with chord symbols.

5:81      Arr. principally from keyboard works.

5:82      Original works and arrangements.

5:83      Arrangements, possibly by Lewis Ramondon, were originally published in London, 1711.

5:84      Arrangements.

5:85      Piano reduction by the composer.

5:86      Acc. arr. for piano.

5:87      Acc. arr. for 2 pianos in part with percussion.

5:88      Principally with keyboard acc.

5:89      "Instrumental accompaniment for flute, oboe, clarinet and string . . . "--Caption.

5:90      "Despite the precise allocation [in ms.] of the (unfigured accompaniment) to a violoncello, the piece is written like a sonata with figured-bass accompaniment . . . nowhere does the work resemble a string duet"--Pref.

5:91      Acc. originally for orchestra.

5:92      Unacc.

5:93        Harp part added to voices originally unacc.

5:94        The 2nd, 4th-5th works unacc. ; keyboard reduction included for rehearsal only.

5:95        Children's chorus: SSAA SSAA ; acc. arr. for piano.

5:96        Chorus: TTBB.

5:97        Keyboards: Piano/celesta.

5:98        The 1st work is for organ, 4 hands ; the 2nd for organ (2 persons, 3 hands, and pedal) or for flute and organ (2 hands and pedal) ; includes part for flute.

5:99        The 3rd movement is for harpsichord solo.

5:100       Folgen 3-4 for organ and 1 wind instrument.

5:101       Figured bass realized by John Madden ; includes continuo part for bassoon, violoncello, or viola da gamba.

5:102       Figured bass realized for harpsichord by John Madden ; includes part for violoncello, viola da gamba, or bassoon.

5:103       Figured bass realized for keyboard instrument ; includes part for melodic bass instrument by Robert Paul Block.

5:104       Figured bass realized for organ ; "the continuo instrument should be the organ though Castello suggests that harpsichord will serve"--Pref.

5:105       Figured bass realized for piano or harpsichord and violoncello.

5:106       Unfigured bass realized by Robert Paul Block.

5:107       Unfigured bass realized for piano or harpsichord.

5:108       Realization may be adapted for theorbo.

5:109       Includes keyboard reduction.

5:110       With keyboard reduction of the instrumental and vocal parts.

5:111       Score includes piano reduction of the orchestral parts.

5:112    Contains studies and exercises, music arr. for flute, complete 1st flute parts from orchestral works, and flute parts from solos for flute and piano.

5:113    The 1st-6th works include keyboard reduction for rehearsal only ; the 7th-8th works include optional continuo (basso seguente) added by the editor.

5:114    Originally for orchestra.

5:115    Originally for piano 4 hands.

5:116    Originally for 4 voices.

5:117    Originally for 8 voices and orchestra.

5:118    Originally for soprano and instrumental ensemble.

5:119    Originally for high voice and harp.

5:120    Originally for violin and continuo.

5:121    Originally for flute, violin, and continuo; the original violin line has been "assigned to the harpsichord."

5:122    Originally an incomplete fragment for violoncello and piano ; completed and arr. for horn and piano by the editors.

5:123    "Since descant recorders are rarely played today, the recorder part has here been notated at sounding pitch and also transposed down a step to make it suitable for a descant recorder in C . . . thus, the concerto was originally in A major but in the present edition is in G major"--Pref.

5:124    Includes part for bass instrument.

5:125    Part for solo violin.

5:126    Parts for trumpet in D and B*b*.

5:127    Parts for woodwinds and strings in score format.

5:128    Parts in score format for violin and voice.

5:129    Parts in score format (4 for choir 1, 4 for choir 2) ; includes part for basso generale added by the editor.

5:130    With solo voices (SATB) and chorus (SATB).

5:131    With narrator.

5:132    Final variation for soprano with text from Romeo and
         Juliet by Shakespeare.

5:133    May be performed in various combinations of or ex-
         clusively with 3 solo voices and/or instruments.

5:134    Chorus part, omitted from final dance, must be supplied
         from another edition for complete performance.

5:135    Needed for performance: 2 slide projectors, 2 mono tape
         playback systems.

5:136    Tape of electronic portion available from publisher.

5:137    "To facilitate turning over, a separate violin 1 part for no.
         12 is inserted."


## TEXT (5.7B2)

5:138    Kikuyu words.

5:139    Principally Italian words.

5:140    Without the words.
         (Statement of responsibility reads: music by Richard
         Rodgers ; & [words by] Hart)

5:141    In part French words ; in part wordless.

5:142    English words ; without the dialogue.
         (Statement of responsibility reads: [music by] Franz
         Léhar ; original book and lyrics by Victor Leon and
         Leo Stein)

5:143    English words taken from Luke 6:20-23.

5:144    Latin words, from Virgil's Georgica, book 4 (221-227).

5:145    Latin words from Psalms 76 and 101 also printed as text,
         p. [4].

5:146      German words, also printed as text: p. [70]-[71].

5:147      German words, also printed as text on p. 2.

5:148      Latin words, also printed as text preceding each work.

5:149      English words printed as text: p. [2-3].

5:150      Norwegian words printed as texts ; includes melodies with chord symbols.

5:151      Greek words with romanization.

5:152      Japanese words, in characters and romanized.

5:153      Performance notes in Italian.

5:154      Texts and prefatory material in Galecian.

5:155      The 5th and 6th songs include Welsh words.

5:156      Chinese words, with prefatory matter and explanatory notes also in English.

5:157      English words, most include original German texts.

5:158      Italian words ; English translations printed at bottom of each page.

5:159      Italian words ; printed also as text with German translations on p. 58-59.

5:160      Latin words, also printed as text with German translation: p. [4].

5:161      Latin words from Medieval hymns and the Bible ; English translation on p. [i].

5:162      Catalan or Latin words.

5:163      English and German words.

5:164      Maori and, in part, English words.

5:165      English and Yoruba words ; instructions for the games in English.

5:166    Japanese (romanized) and English words, from Botan kuroku by Shiki Masaoka, English translation by Earl Miner.

5:167    Concluding commentary in English and German.

5:168    Instructions for performance in English and Japanese.

5:169    Pref. in English and French by the composer.

5:170    Pref. in English and German: p. [iii]-viii.

5:171    Words from Ecclesiastes and 1. Corinthians printed as text in German and Russian (p. 4-5).

5:172    Instructions for dancing given in Ukrainian, with Russian translation, preceding the music arr. for piano.

5:173    Critical notes in English, French, and German.

5:174    Foreword by Shin-Ichiro Ichikawa in German, with English translation by E.D. Echols and French translation by François Brulhart.

5:175    Words in English, German, French, and other languages.

5:176    In part with Latin, French, Italian, or Spanish words.

5:177    Romanian and English words for all songs ; many also have German and/or Hungarian words.

5:178    Notes in Czech, English, French, German, and Russian (xii p.).

5:179    Words by various authors, in English, French, Latin, Polish, or Spanish ; partially printed as text with Polish translations (p. [4-5]).

5:180    Words printed as text (p. 6-7).

5:181    Words printed also as text on p. iii.

5:182    Words printed also as text on p. [2].

5:183    Words printed as text with translation in English, French, and Hungarian (p. [2-7]).

5:184        Text from: The Jesuit relations / St. Jean de Brébeuf.

5:185        "Text from [the first play of] the Chester Mystery plays"--T.p. verso.

5:186        Title from Lyrisches Intermezzo LXI / Heinrich Heine ; printed as text: p. 15.

5:187        The carol: God rest ye merry, gentlemen.
             (Subtitle reads: Variations on a Christmas carol for orchestra)

5:188        Translation of: Harpsichord method.

5:189        Title is translation of a line from a ballade by François Villon.

## SOURCE OF TITLE PROPER (5.7B3)

5:190        Caption title.

5:191        Colophon title.

5:192        Cover title.

5:193        Title from accompanying material.

5:194        Title from caption.

## VARIATIONS IN TITLE (5.7B4)

5:195        Added t.p.: The notes of a madman.

5:196        Added t.p.: I believe in this earth! : Fifteenth symphony.
             (Title proper in Russian transliterated)

5:197        Added t.p.: Kompositionen. B. Konzerte, Band 10, 2. Supplement / Karl Friedrich Abel.

5:198        Caption title: Sonata, D XII 5, for tromba (trumpet), strings & continuo.

5:199    Colophon title also in English: The Collection of Chinese folk songs.

5:200    Cover title: Fanfare, pavan & fughetta.

5:201    Spine title: Musikalische Gestaltung.

5:202    Title in caption: Kiku : a ragtime piece for flute and piano.

5:203    First line of text: Painters all of ev'ry station.
         (Title by which commonly known; title proper: A Song on St. Luke's night)

## PARALLEL TITLES AND OTHER TITLE INFORMATION (5.7B5)

5:204    Parallel title in Japanese.

5:205    Added t.p.: Dodenklacht voor Salvador Allende = Complainte pour Salvador Allende = Complaint for Salvador Allende.

5:206    Caption title: Wariacje w formie ronda = Variationen in Rondoform = Variations in rondo form.

5:207    "An ecumenical hymn book."

5:208    "Op. 14."

5:209    "Op. 8 (1976)"--Caption.

5:210    "Piano-conductor"--Prelim. p. 3.

## STATEMENTS OF RESPONSIBILITY (5.7B6)

5:211    Arr. by the composer from his vaudeville-opera The Eatanswill election.

5:212    Contains works by Francesco da Firenze and others.

5:213    Words compiled by the composer.

5:214    The works are anonymous.

5:215    At end: Daniel Ingalis.

5:216    Composed in part by L. Beaulieu and J. Salmon. Cf. Fétis. Biog. univ. des musiciens. 2. ed., p. 232.

5:217    "Created by Joybug Teaching Aids, inc."--T.p. verso.

5:218    Edited by Bernard Thomas.

5:219    "Issued by the Berlioz Centenary Committee, London, in association with the Calouste Gulbenkian Foundation, Lisbon"--P. [2] of cover.

5:220    "A masque written by David Mallet and James Thomson"--P. xi.

5:221    Revised and fingered by R. Sheetz.

5:222    "Story adapted from the Icelandic myth as told by Snorri Sturluson in the Prose Edda"--4th prelim. p.

5:223    Folge 4 edited by Wolfgang Karius.

5:224    "The editor's commentary was translated by Stanley Appelbaum specially for the present edition"--T.p. verso.

5:225    English translation of words by Donald Sutherland.

5:226    Includes libretto by Antonio Ghislanzoni, with English translation by Edmund Tracey, and commentaries.

5:227    Italian libretto by Giovan Gualberto Bottarelli.

5:228    Latin words, by Ovid.

5:229    Libretto by the composer, based on Shakespeare's Much ado about nothing.

5:230    Libretto from the play by Oscar Wilde, translated into German by Hedwig Lachmann.

5:231    Words by La Chesnaye.

5:232    Words by John Milton (Paradise lost XI 799-805) and Wm. Shakespeare (Ulysses' speech, Troilus and Cressida, Act 1, Scene 3).

5:233    With engravings from designs by Jacques Patin.

5:234    Based on Ancelot's Elisabeth d'Angleterre.

5:235    Based on themes from: I puritani / Bellini.

## EDITION AND HISTORY (5.7B7)

5:236    English version published in 2 v.

5:237    Originally composed as a separate work ; later incorporated into Patria IV.

5:238    Composed in 1959.

5:239    "[Composed] 1960, redone and revised 1979"--P. [3].

5:240    Composed Dec. 1970, revised 1971.

5:241    First work composed 1969, revised 1977 ; 2nd work composed 1977.

5:242    "Edition Peters"--Cover.

5:243    Edition Eulenberg: no. 1601.

5:244    Edited from the 1st ed. (London : Walsh & Hare, [ca. 1726]).

5:245    Edited from the 1st ed. published: London : Printed for Harrison & Co., 1793.

5:246    Ed. from 1st ed. parts in the Cloister Library, Einsiedeln, Switzerland, and the Library of Congress, Washington, D.C. (Zurich : G. Naigueli, [18--?]).

5:247    Edited from a copy of the 1707 ed. published by Walsh, Hare, and Randall, in the library of Durham Cathedral (Mus C 98).

5:248      Edited from the only known copy (in the Auckland Public Library, Auckland, N.Z.) of the 1st ed. published by J. Walsh and J. Hare, London.

5:249      Edited from a copy of the 1644 reprint of the original ed. in the Bodleian Library (Ms. Mus. Sch. c155a-e).

5:250      Edited from copies in the Schleswig-Holstein State Library, Kiel (1st work) and the Central Library, Zurich (2nd work).

5:251      Edited from untitled, unfinished draft and some additional sketches in the Parry Room Library, Royal College of Music, London.

5:252      Edited from: Ms. in the Bavarian State Library (Mus. Ms 2872).

5:253      Edited from: Ms. in the British Library, London (Add MS 53723).

5:254      Edited from: Ms. parts, Westdeutschen Bibliothek, Marburg (MUS Ms 4356, 4355).

5:255      Edited from: Ms. parts in the Archivio Musicale of the Basilica of San Petronio, Bologna (D XII 5).

5:256      Edited from a ms. in the Fürstlich. Oettingen-Wallerstein'sche Bibliothek.

5:257      Edited from the holograph ms. in the Deutsche Staatsbibliothek, Berlin.

5:258      Edited from holograph parts in the collection of Count Gabriel Mörner, Esplunda, Sweden.

5:259      From a collection of 36 canzoni by various composers originally published in Venice in 1608 by A. Rauerij.

5:260      Originally published in the 9th and 10th lesson of Der getreue Musikmeister.

5:261      Reprint. Originally published: Paris, 1733-1748.

5:262      Reprint. Originally published: Berlin : Fürstner, 1905.

5:263    Reprint. Originally published: Warsaw : Fryderyk Chopin Institute, 1949-1950.

5:264    Reprint. Originally published: Paris : Schonenberger, [1840?]. With new introd.

5:265    Reprint. Originally published: Braunschweig : G.M. Meyer, [185-?]. Pl. no.: 950.

5:266    Reprint. Originally published: Braunschweig : H. Litolff's Verlag, [ca. 1890]. Pl. no.: 12558.

5:267    Reprint. Originally published: A first sett of six sonatas spirituale or voluntarys. London : Printed & sold by Jno. Preston, [ca. 1782].

5:268    Reprint (3rd work). Originally published: Sinfonie G Moll für grosses Orchester, op. 43. Leipzig : Fr. Kistner, [1872].

5:269    Reprinted from various 19th century eds.

5:270    "Musical text reprinted from the Complete critical edition of the works of Leoš Janáček, series F/volume 1."

5:271    Reproduced from a ms. written and originally owned by Branwell Brontë ; written ca. Nov. 1831-Jan. 1832.

5:272    Photoreproduction of copy located in the Fonds musical, Bibliothèque nationale, Paris.

5:273    Photoreproduction of edition published by Bolvin et al. located in the Fonds musical, Bibliothèque nationale, Paris.

5:274    Photoreproduction of a ms. in the Conservatoire royal de musique, Brussels (2039).

5:275    Songs are reproduced directly from editions of the sheet music.

5:276    The 1st and 2nd works reproduced from ms. copies made by the composer's son and owned by Barry Sterndale-Bennett.

5:277    To accompany the sound tape set with the same title.

5:278    May be performed separately, or simultaneously with the

composer's Engramme, Circuits intégrés, and/or Eon under
the title: ROT : (Random organized time).

# NOTATION (5.7B8)

5:279      Songs in number notation with chord symbols and guitar
chord diagrams.

5:280      Melodies ; staff and number notation.

5:281      Staff and tablature notation ; includes chord symbols.

5:282      Tablature notation ; in part with words.

5:283      Vol. 1 includes lute tablature.

5:284      Includes chord symbols.

5:285      Includes music in letter notations.

5:286      Includes tonic sol-fa notation.

5:287      Transposed from D$b$ to D major.

# PUBLICATION, DISTRIBUTION, ETC. (5.7B9)

5:288      Imprint from label on p. [2] of cover.

5:289      Imprint from label on p. 1 of music.

5:290      Label on t.p.: Frankfurt ; New York : Peters.

5:291      Additional imprint on label on t.p.: Frankfurt ; New
York : C.F. Peters.

5:292      "1973 rev. 76"--P. 1 of 1st violin part.

5:293      Distributor from label on t.p.

5:294      Rental material.

## DURATION OF PERFORMANCE AND PHYSICAL DESCRIPTION (5.7B10)

5:295      Duration: 5 min.

5:296      Duration: 17 min., 47 sec.

5:297      Duration: 15:16, 18:31, or 22:22 (depending on performance method chosen).

5:298      Duration: 16-17 min.

5:299      Duration: ca. 7 min.

5:300      Duration: ca. 15:00.

5:301      Duration of the 2nd excerpt: 1:20 without repeats.

5:302      Bound at top, 5 pages in each group split into 4 parts of 2 measures each to allow for melodic permutations.

5:303      Each page contains 6 p. of the full-sized vocal score.

5:304      Issued in parts.

5:305      Each symphony also paged separately.

5:306      Each work also separately paged.

5:307      On double leaves.

5:308      Printed on double leaves.

5:309      Principally in choirbook format.

5:310      Original version is superimposed in smaller notes below the piano orchestral score.

5:311      Reproduced from holograph.

5:312      Reproduced from Davies holograph.

## ACCOMPANYING MATERIAL (5.7B11)

5:313    Accompanied by instructions for performance (15 p. : ill. ; 32 cm.).

5:314    Instructions for gong player (1 leaf) laid in.

5:315    Musical examples also included as musical supplement ([8] p. ; 22 cm.) in pocket.

## AUDIENCE (5.7B14)

5:316    Intended audience: Ages 8-13.

5:317    Intended audience: Kindergarten through intermediate grades.

5:318    Intended audience: Young performers.

5:319    "Audience level: intermediate/junior."

5:320    For children.

## CONTENTS (5.7B18)

5:321    Discography: p. 114-115.

5:322    The rollography and discography are the same in each volume.
   (Title proper: The complete works of Scott Joplin : in two volumes)

5:323    Libretto: p. xiii-xxi.

5:324    Each part also includes the score.

5:325    Includes bibliographical references, discography, and index.

5:326    Includes facsim. of original lute tablatures on p. 2-3.

5:327    Includes instructions for performance.

5:328    Includes instructions for performance in German and English.

5:329    Includes notes and suggestions for teachers.

5:330    Includes the texts for the lost portions of the work.

5:331    Vol. 4 includes "Chord dictionary in all the scales" and v. 5 includes "Scales and arpeg[g]ios."

5:332    Two copies of piano/electric piano part included.

5:333    In part with tune indications or tunes.

5:334    Comprises no. 8, 13-16 of op. 52.

5:335    Contents: Prelude -- Fantasy -- Divertimento.

5:336    Contents: Sinfonia in C -- Sinfonia in B -- Sinfonia in A.

5:337    Contents: All my loving (I) -- I feel fine -- Things we said today -- It's only love -- All my loving (II) -- I'm looking through you -- I should have known better -- Julia -- Maxwell's silver hammer -- Hey Jude.

5:338    Contents: Little ring of love = Pipsi, holde Pipsi -- The spirit of Montmartre = Um zwölfe in der Nacht -- Wonderland for two = Nur das eine Wort sprich es aus!

5:339    Contents: El cóndor pasa / Daniel Alomía Robles -- Estrella hermosa / Ignacio Arbulú Pineda -- Muliza y Chimayche / [Anonymous] -- La huanuqueña / Mariano Ignacio Prado -- Selva selva / [Anonymous].

5:340    Contents: Trumpet air / Telemann -- Andante from Flute sonata, op. 1, no. 9 / Handel -- Pastorale / Stravinsky -- Fairy-tale, op. 113, no. 4 / Schumann -- Largo from Flute sonata / Bach.

5:341    Contents: Light o' love / anon. -- Fortune my foe / anon. -- Loth to depart / anon. -- Bonny sweet robin : Margaret Board lute book -- Romanesca : Bottegari lute book -- Fantasia 31 / Francesco da Milano.

5:342   Contents: Upon Julia's clothes / text by Robert Herrick --
The turtle / text by Ogden Nash -- Une allée du Luxem-
bourg / text by Aloysius Bertrand -- The ancient mariner
(Verse 1) / text by Samuel Taylor Coleridge.

5:343   Contents: v. 1. In youthly years / Robert (?) Parsons.
Most men do love the Spanish wine. If floods of tears -- v.
2. How now, shepherd, what means that? Sweet, stay
awhile! why do you rise? Shall I weep, or shall I sing? The
marigold of golden hue / Leonard Woodson.

## PLATE NUMBERS AND PUBLISHERS' NUMBERS (5.7B19)

5:344   Publisher's no.: 19 2024 03.

5:345   Publisher's no.: 66752a.

5:346   Publisher's no.: B & B 22 564 (1246).

5:347   Publisher's no.: JWC 55186-55190.
     (Inclusive consecutive numbering; beginning letters
     precede first number only)

5:348   Publisher's no.: 6893-6896 E.D.
     (Ending letters follow last number only)

5:349   Publisher's no.: 523, 570, 612 GM.
     (Nonconsecutive numbering)

5:350   Publisher's no.: N.M. 123/549.
     (Nonconsecutive numbering with more than three
     numbers)

5:351   Publisher's no.: M.R.1962A-M.R.1965A.
     (Give letters which precede and follow numbers in
     conjunction with each number)

5:352   Publisher's no.: Edition 10888.

5:353   Publisher's no.: Wilhelm Hansen edition no. 4347 A.

5:354      Pl. no.: 1.2882.7.

5:355      Pl. no.: L.G. Co. 52140.

5:356      Pl. no.: UE 16535 C.

5:357      Reissued from Breitkopf & Härtel plates. Pl. no.: B. & H. 1224.

## COPY BEING DESCRIBED AND LIBRARY'S HOLDINGS (5.7B20)

5:358      Library's copy has 8 parts.
           (Physical description area reads: 1 score (43 p.) + 7 parts ; 30 cm.)

5:359      Library's copy: Folded and bound in case (18 cm.) A few words of 3rd stanza text torn away at lower margin.

5:360      Library's copy imperfect: Brittle and torn; some tears are taped.

5:361      Library's copy imperfect: Cover missing.

5:362      Library's copy autographed: Sarah Caldwell.

5:363      Gift of Leo Allen Whitehill and Sarah Ruth Whitehill in honor of Mr. Whitehill's father Samuel Weiselberg, 1977.

# 6

# Sound Recordings

## NATURE OR ARTISTIC FORM AND MEDIUM OF PERFORMANCE (6.7B1)

6:1        Comedy monologues.

6:2        Interview.

6:3        Lectures.

6:4        Radio comedies.

6:5        Play for child actors.

6:6        Inspirational poems, read by the author.

6:7        Lecture, given by the author.

6:8        Novel, read by the author.

6:9        Two stories, read by the author.

6:10      Radio drama, produced and directed by Yuri Rasovsky.

6:11      Radio reports, presented by the American Chemical Society.

6:12      Selections of American and English poets and writers.

6:13      Bluegrass music.

6:14      Blues.

6:15      Blues from the Baton Rouge, La. area.

6:16      Chance compositions.

6:17      Country music.

6:18      Dramatic symphony.

6:19      Field recording of marsh life sounds.

6:20      Gospel quartets.

6:21      Harpsichord music from: Pièces de clavecin / D'Anglebert.

6:22      Excerpts from a television production.

6:23      Highlights from a CEB program presented in San Francisco in Mar., 1980.

6:24      Irish music.

6:25      Jazz ensembles.

6:26      Jazz quintets (sides 1-2) and sextets (sides 3-4).

6:27      Jazz quintets with occasional vocals.

6:28      Jazz sextets.

6:29      Musical comedy excerpts.

6:30      Opera.

6:31      Opera arias and ensembles.

6:32      Opera in 3 acts, sung in Italian.

6:33      Opera in 2 acts, sung in German and performed in the composer's 1814 revision.

6:34        Piano music.

6:35        Portuguese songs are villancicos ; Laudate pueri and songs are unacc.

6:36        Principally musical numbers from the sound track of the picture starring the Marx Brothers.

6:37        Principally opera excerpts ; various soloists, principally with unnamed orchestras.

6:38        Principally orchestra music.

6:39        Principally sacred quartets with organ.

6:40        Principally songs.

6:41        Principally traditional songs.

6:42        Probably overtures to lost operas.

6:43        "Protest songs of our time"--Container.

6:44        Rock music.

6:45        Songs, composed by members of the band.

6:46        Soul music.

6:47        Spontaneous improvisations of Lennon-McCartney songs reinterpreted in the styles of various composers.

6:48        Symphonic poems.

6:49        Venezuelan folk songs.

6:50        The 1st work is a symphonic poem.

6:51        Original works and arrangements.

6:52        Arr. by Udo Unger for string quartet, solo harpsichord, and 2 harpsichords.

6:53        Arrangements for flute and guitar by Almeida, except the 2nd and 4th works, originally for flute and guitar ; the final work originally for violin and guitar.

6:54        Arr. for synthesizers.

6:55        All except the 3rd work arr. for trumpet and orchestra ; various original media.

6:56        Created principally on a Roland computer, model MC-8. (Recording of electronic music)

6:57        Electronic music (without words).
            (Statement of responsibility reads: music [composed, arranged, and played] by Dave Greenslade ; words by Patrick Woodroffe)

6:58        For 4-12 performers.

6:59        For string orchestra with harpsichord ; no. 6, 8, 10, and 12 with solo violin, no. 2-4 are concerti grossi.

6:60        Principally for unspecified instruments.

6:61        Jazz duets, except the 5th work a vibraharp solo and the 6th work a piano solo.

6:62        Violin and piano music, except the 2nd work which is unacc.

6:63        Originally an open score, without instrumental specification, but probably intended to be played on a keyboard instrument. Cf. Grove, 5th ed.

6:64        Originally for piano quintet, arr. by the composer.

6:65        Originally for voice and bass (figured or unfigured).

6:66        Originally notated in open score, probably for keyboard instrument.

6:67        The 1st and 2nd works, taken from incidental music for the play by Alphonse Daudet, collected and arr. for large orchestra by the composer and E. Guiraud (respectively) ; 3rd work, originally for piano, 4 hands, orchestrated by the composer.

6:68        The 1st and 4th-7th works originally for organ.

6:69        The 1st and 6th works originally for orchestra, the 3rd for instrumental ensemble, and the 4th for piano.

6:70    The 1st work a wind quintet ; the 2nd a string quartet ; the 3rd for winds and strings.

6:71    The 1st work for women's chorus and speaking group ; the 2nd for women's chorus, 2 horns, and harp ; the 3rd for women's chorus.

6:72    The 1st work originally for string quartet, the 3rd originally for viola and piano, arr. by the composers.

6:73    The 2nd work originally for piano.

6:74    The 2nd work originally for vocal quartet and piano, 4 hands.

6:75    The 3rd work for string orchestra.

6:76    The 6th work, originally for string orchestra, is an excerpt from a suite.

6:77    The last work originally with string orchestra.

6:78    BWV. 1060 reconstructed by Franz Giegling from the composer's version for 2 harpsichords and string orchestra.

6:79    The Holst march originally for band, the Grainger for band or piano.

6:80    The sonatas for clarinet and piano, op. 120, transcribed by the composer for violin and piano.

6:81    Played by the composer on saxophones, clarinets, and bamboo flutes.

6:82    Performed on period instruments.


## LANGUAGE (6.7B2)

6:83    In French.

6:84    In Italian, introduced in English.

6:85    Read in Latin.

6:86        Sung in English.
            (Title proper: Lustige Witwe)

6:87        Sung in German and Latin respectively.

6:88        Lieder sung in English.

6:89        Operetta in 3 acts, sung in German.

6:90        Song sung on the recording by Matthew Sakowsky in
            Ukrainian and English, with chorus and instrumental
            ensemble.

6:91        The 1st work sung in German.

6:92        The 1st work sung in Norwegian ; the 4th sung in
            German, text translated from the Japanese.

6:93        The 1st 2 works sung in German ; the 3rd in Italian.


## SOURCE OF TITLE PROPER (6.7B3)

6:94        Title from container.

6:95        Title from container ; additional title on container: Dame
            Janet Baker sings Schubert popular songs.

6:96        Title from container spine.

6:97        Title from publisher's catalog.

6:98        Title from script (3 p.) inserted.

6:99        Title from spine of container.

6:100       Title from syllabus.

6:101       Title from verso of container.

6:102       Titles from containers.

## VARIATIONS IN TITLE (6.7B4)

6:103      Another title on container: Carolyn Heafner sings American songs.

6:104      Title in notes on container: Birds, beasts, and flowers.

6:105      Title on container: Highlights from Scottish Opera's production of The merry widow.

6:106      Title on container: Requiem : Grande messe des morts.

6:107      Title on container (26 x 18 cm.): Jim Anderson's How to live rent free in the 1980's.

6:108      Title on container verso: Thomas Brown presents The sounds of digital percussion.

6:109      Title on outline: Evidence with Irving Younger.

6:110      Titles in booklet: American Indian stories and songs ; The building blocks of language--the word, the story, the book.

6:111      Titles on container: Till Eulenspiegel ; Death and transfiguration.

6:112      The 1st-7th works originally issued with title Here's Jaki (New Jazz 8256) ; the 8th work originally issued on Out front! (Prestige 7397) ; the 9th-16th works originally issued with title Hi fly (New Jazz 8273).

6:113      Title of 2nd work on container: Danse sacrée et danse profane.

6:114      Vol. 2 has title: Lord I wish I could see.

## PARALLEL TITLES AND OTHER TITLE INFORMATION (6.7B5)

6:115      Added titles on container: Sacred songs from Schmelli's song book = Chants sacrés du recueil de Schmelli.

6:116    Additional titles on containers: Gregorian chant = Chant grégorien.

6:117    Parallel titles on container: Songs of the Synagogue of Florence = Manginot Bet ha-keneset ha-gadol shel Firentsi = Chants de la Synagogue de Florence = Canticos de la Sinagoga de Florencia.

6:118    "A heart play"--Inner sleeve.

6:119    Subtitle on container: 32 original songs and poems from My weekly reader.

6:120    Subtitle on container: Songs made famous by Fred Astaire.

6:121    Subtitles on container: In celebration of the winter solstice : traditional and ritual carols, dances, and processionals.

## STATEMENTS OF RESPONSIBILITY (6.7B6)

6:122    Cast: Freeman F. Gosden, Charles J. Correll.

6:123    David McCallum, Carole Shelley, readers.

6:124    Dramatic readings performed by Sarah Bernhardt, Constant Coquelin, and Ernest Coquelin.

6:125    Moderator: Melvin I. Friedman.

6:126    Narrator: Stuart Finley.

6:127    Read by Irene Worth ; directed and abridged by Ward Botsford.

6:128    Read by Maureen Stapleton ; directed by Paul Kresh.

6:129    Read by Princess Grace of Monaco and Richard Pasco ; devised and directed by John Carroll.

6:130    Read by Serge Cassel.

6:131    Read in Middle English by Prunella Scales and Richard Bebb ; directed by Derek Brewer.

6:132        Starring Freeman F. Gosden and Charles J. Correll.

6:133        The 1st work with Eugene Hamm, narrator.

6:134        Lonnie Brooks Band.

6:135        Melos Quartett Stuttgart.

6:136        Performed by the Brothers 'n Bluegrass.

6:137        Percussions de Strasbourg.

6:138        Wren Consort.

6:139        S.E.M. Ensemble (2 sopranos, countertenor, tenor, baritone, bass, 2 flutes, 2 clarinets, and 2 trombones).

6:140        London Philharmonic Orchestra or (in Vaughan Williams and Delius marches) New Philharmonia Orchestra.

6:141        Harpsichord: Wm. Neil Roberts.

6:142        Organ: Heinz Markus Göttsche.

6:143        Piano: Michel Béroff, Jean-Philippe Collard.

6:144        Harpsichord: Trevor Pinnock (instrument built by Andreas Ruckers, Antwerp, 1646).

6:145        Piano (Bösendorfer): Bernard Ringeissen.

6:146        Piano (Steinway): Yasuo Watanabe.

6:147        Pamela Pyle Resch, piano ; recorded 3 times.

6:148        Paul Zukofsky, violin.

6:149        With Barry Snyder, piano (except in the Bach Sarabande).

6:150        J.C. Burris, vocals, harmonica, and bones.

6:151        Performed on a Philip Belt copy of Mozart's Walter fortepiano, Vienna, 1786.

6:152        Jos van Immerseel, piano (Michael Rosenberger, Vienna, ca. 1795).

6:153    Franz Haselböck, playing the Gabler organ of Benedictine Abbey.

6:154    Franz Haselböck, playing the Bielfeldt organ, St. Willehadl-Kirche, Osterholz-Scharmbeck.

6:155    Daniel Chorzempa, playing the organ in De Bovenkerk, Kampen, The Netherlands.

6:156    Anton Heiller, organ (St. Mary Church, Hälsingborg, Sweden).

6:157    Art Blakey, drums ; Jazz Messengers (tenor saxophone, trumpet, piano, and bass).

6:158    Carole Bogard, soprano ; John Moriarty, piano.

6:159    Chet Atkins, Doc Watson, vocals and guitars, with electric bass, percussion, and rhythm guitars.

6:160    The composer, piano, horn, guitar, principally in various combinations with Pepper Adams and Jerry Dodgion, saxophones, Candido, drums, Jack Elliot, guitar, Georgè Mrgdichian, oud, and Ali Hafid, dumbeg and vocal.

6:161    The composer, horn, piano, Pakistani flutes, penny whistles, twin shepherd flute, shanai, percussion, with assisting instrumentalists and vocals in varying combinations.

6:162    Contains performances by the Golden Leaf Quartette, Birmingham Jubilee Singers, Four Great Wonders, Famous Blue Jay Singers, Dunham Jubilee Singers, Ravizee Singers, Bessemer Sunset Four, Heavenly Gospel Singers, Kings of Harmony, and the C.I.O. Singers.

6:163    Electronic realizations and performances by Wendy Carlos on synthesizer.

6:164    Henri Albers, baritone, with orchestra.

6:165    In quintets: Eric Dolphy, flute, bass clarinet, and alto sax ; Ken McIntyre, flute and alto sax ; Walter Bishop, Jr., piano ; Sam Jones, bass ; Art Taylor, drums. In sextets: Eric Dolphy, clarinet and alto sax ; Booker Ervin, tenor sax ; Mal Waldron, piano ; Ron Carter, violoncello ; Joe Benjamin, bass ; Charlie Persip, drums.

6:166        Jaki Byrd, piano and alto sax ; Ron Carter, bass ; Roy Haynes, drums (1st-8th works) ; Pete LaRoca, drums (9th-16th works).

6:167        Jean Martin, piano (Chopin and Liszt works) ; Juliette Greco, narrator (Sand texts).

6:168        Jessye Norman, mezzo-soprano ; Geoffrey Parsons, piano ; Ulrich von Wrochem, viola (in op. 91).

6:169        Jon Bartlett and Rika Ruebsaat with ensemble.

6:170        Judy Holliday, Sydney Chaplin (Bells are ringing) ; Ethel Merman, Jack Klugman (Gypsy) ; Barbra Streisand, Sydney Chaplin (Funny girl).

6:171        Laurindo Almeida, guitar ; Bob Magnusson, bass ; Jeff Hamilton, drums.

6:172        Sheila Jordan, voice ; Steve Kuhn, piano ; David Liebman, saxophones ; Lyle Mays, synthesizer ; Bob Moses, drums ; Steve Swallow, bass.

6:173        Yehuda Hanani, violoncello ; Edward Auer, piano.

6:174        1st and 2nd works: Norwegian Wind Quintet (1st work for flute, oboe, and clarinet). 3rd work: Astri Herseth, soprano, with ensemble (piano, organ, saxophone, double bass, and percussion) ; Sverre Bruland, conductor. 4th work: Bjarne Larsen, violin ; Arne Sletsjøe, viola.

6:175        In the 1st work: Ensemble of organ and percussion (2 performers and 2 assistants). In the 2nd work: Oslo Wind Soloists. In the 3rd work: Jan Henrik Kayser, piano. In the 4th work: Frøydis Ree Werke, horn. In the 5th work: Brynjar Hoff, oboe.

6:176        Edda Moser, Helen Donath, sopranos ; Siegfried Jerusalem, tenor ; Hermann Prey, baritone ; Benno Kusche, bass-baritone, and others ; Bavarian Radio Chorus ; Munich Radio Orchestra ; Heinz Wallberg, conductor.

6:177        Erna Berger, soprano, with various other soloists, orchestras, and conductors.

6:178    Evelyne [sic] Brunner, Helena Vieira, sopranos ; Naoko Ihara, alto ; Alain Zaepffel, countertenor ; Alejandro Ramírez, tenor ; Philippe Huttenlocher, bass ; Choeur symphonique et Orch. de la Fondation Gulbenkian de Lisbonne ; Michel Corboz, conductor.

6:179    Exsultate [sic] Singers ; Garret [sic] O'Brien, conductor or organist-conductor ; sung in English.

6:180    Geoffrey Brown, English horn ; Osian Ellis, harp ; London Philharmonic Orchestra ; conducted by the composer.

6:181    James Galway, flute ; principally with the National Philharmonic Orchestra, Charles Gerhardt, conductor.

6:182    Joana Silva, soprano ; Margarida d'Almeida, alto ; Orlando Worm, bass ; organ ; Chorus of the Gulbenkian Foundation of Lisbon ; Fernando Eldoro, conductor.

6:183    Los Angeles Chamber Orchestra ; Gerard Schwarz, conductor.

6:184    Miwako Matsumoto as Violetta ; Maria Parazzini as Teodora ; William Johns as Il Bravo ; Antonio Savastano as Pisani ; Paolo Washington as Foscari ; orchestra e coro del Teatro dell'opera di Roma ; Gabriele Ferro, conductor.

6:185    New York Philharmonic, Pierre Boulez, conductor (1st work) ; Susan Davenny Wyner, soprano, Speculum Musicae, Richard Fitz, conductor (2nd work).

6:186    Performed by the group Musica Ibérica (with accompaniment on period instruments) ; Nelly van Ree Bernard, director.

6:187    Philadelphia Orchestra ; Eugene Ormandy, conductor.

6:188    Prague Chamber Orchestra ; without conductor.

6:189    Richard Adeney, flute ; Bournemouth Sinfonietta ; Ronald Thomas, conductor.

6:190    Schenectady County Community College Percussion Ensemble ; Thomas A. Brown, conductor.

6:191      Soloists ; Chorus ; Orchestra ; Robinson, conductor.

6:192      St. Antony Singers ; Margaret Phillips, organ ; Nilo Alves, conductor.

6:193      Walter Gieseking, piano ; Orchestra filarmonica di New York ; Guido Cantelli, conductor.

6:194      With chorus, Leo Kopf, conductor, Paul Mania, organ (v. 1).

6:195      Jazz ensembles, featuring Betty Carter, vocals, with various assisting instrumentalists.

6:196      John Lennon, vocals, guitar ; Yoko Ono, vocals ; assisting instrumentalists and vocals.

6:197      Marie-Claire Alain, playing various organs.

6:198      Performed by Do'a (the composers) on various instruments.

6:199      Performed by Do'a (the composers) on various instruments; with assisting instrumentalists and background vocals.

6:200      Played by the composer.

6:201      Sung and played by the composer, in part with other instrumentalists and vocalists.

6:202      Sung and played by the composer, with other singers and instrumentalists.

6:203      Sung by the composer and others as specified below. (Performers are specified in the contents note)

6:204      Sung, recited, and played (guitar) by the composer, with rhythm instruments.

6:205      Sung variously by Clementina de Jesus, Doca, and Geraldo Filme, with percussion ensemble.

6:206      Various cantors, organists, choruses, orchestras, and conductors.

6:207     Various ensembles under the auspices of Revels, Inc. ; John Langstaff, director.

6:208     Various male gospel quartets from Birmingham and surrounding Jefferson Co., Ala.

6:209     Various orchestras and conductors.

6:210     Various performers.

6:211     Various performers ; original instruments.

6:212     Various performers with orchestra acc.

6:213     Vocals, fiddle, guitar, and banjo variously by Oscar and Eugene Wright.

6:214     William Ackerman, guitar, playing original solos and duets with various instruments.

6:215     General editor: Peter W. Schroth.
          (Recording of a symposium)

6:216     Author's name from narration.

6:217     Author's name from publisher's catalog.

6:218     Condensed by the author.
          (Spoken record)

6:219     Compiled and annotated by John Edward Hasse and Frank J. Gillis.
          (Annotations in program notes)

6:220     Principally by John Burstein ; sung by him with instrumental ensemble.

6:221     The libretto is by Andrea Leone Tottola.

6:222     Words by Hart ; music by Rodgers.
          (Statement of responsibility reads: composed by Rodgers & Hart)

6:223     Arrangements by Frederic Mills, Eugene Watts, Ralph Sauer, Ronald Romm, and Neil Balm.

6:224    Arr. and sung by Soledad Bravo accompanying herself on the guitar.

6:225    From the author's: Foundation and empire.

6:226    Based on a theme by Frederick the Great.

6:227    Based on a 3-program series produced by French-Swiss Television on the folk music instruments of Switzerland.

6:228    Based on: Léonore, ou, L'amour conjugal / J.N. Bouilly.

6:229    Based on the author's book: How to live rent free. [Rev. world ed.] [c1978].

6:230    Based on the book: Philadelphia : Lippincott, c1965. Text abridged by Margaret Albrecht.

6:231    Based on the songs collected in: O negro e o garimpo em Minas Gerals / de Aires da Mata Machado Filho. Rio de Janeiro : J. Olympio, 1943.

6:232    The 1st work is based on the composer's Solo for voice 2.

6:233    The 1st work, taken from orchestral suites collected and arr. by Bizct and E. Guiraud, originally written as incidental music for the play by Alphonse Daudet ; the 2nd work opera excerpts.

6:234    Libretto by John Oxenford, based on: The Colleen Bawn / Dion Boucicault.

6:235    Words by Emile Deschamps, based on Shakespeare.

6:236    Words principally from Polydora by G.F. Daumer.

6:237    The 2nd work, usually ascribed to Wagner, may be by Heinrich Baermann ; originally for clarinet and 5 strings ; here performed without double bass.

6:238    Presented by the Center for Peaceful Change, Kent State University ; written, engineered, and produced by Corey H. Deitz.

6:239    Presented by the School of International Affairs, Columbia University ; interviewer, Margot Adler ; announcer, Allen Lewicki.

6:240    Recorded in association with the British Council.

6:241    "Recorded in co-production with Supraphon."

## EDITION AND HISTORY (6.7B7)

6:242    First recited at St. James's Palace, London, in Nov. 1978.

6:243    An abridgement of the translation by Lowell Bair,
published: New York : Bantam Books, c1972.

6:244    Published in: Medieval music / edited by W. Thomas
Marrocco and Nicholas Sandon.

6:245    Overture to 1st work appropriated from another work.

6:246    Based on the program held Oct. 8-9, 1979.

6:247    Text of the 1st work adapted from the Bible
(Deuteronomy 32 and Matthew) ; text of the 2nd,
Psalm 112.

6:248    "All tunes previously issued on various Pacific Jazz
albums."

6:249    "All selections previously released"--Containers.

6:250    Previously released as 2531 279.

6:251    Reissue of: 139 003.

6:252    Reissue of: BGS 70674-BGS 70675.

6:253    Reissue of: Deutsche Grammophon 136 451.

6:254    Reissue of radio transcription recordings broadcast by
Mexican border radio stations, 1938-1942.

6:255    Original cast recordings by Decca, Columbia, and RCA
Victor.

6:256    Originally issued in France on Isabel Records.

6:257     Originally issued on Columbia (Bells are ringing, Gypsy) and Capitol (Funny girl) labels.

6:258     The 1st-6th works originally issued on Epic LN 3202.

6:259     "Substantial portions of this album are contained in the soundtrack of the motion picture, The Secret life of plants"--Container.

6:260     Principally from film soundtracks, 1927-1958.

6:261     Recorded from Duo-Art reproducing-piano rolls.

6:262     Recorded from a broadcast by Rádio MEC in May 1962.

6:263     Recorded from 12 episodes of the program of the same title, Feb.-May 1945.

6:264     Recorded from the Television Española ; Federico Moreno Torroba, conductor.

6:265     Recorded during a performance.

6:266     Recorded at Variety Sound, New York, N.Y.

6:267     Recorded at the Northeast Community Center, San Francisco, and at West Dakota, Berkeley, Calif.

6:268     Recorded at the Eastman School of Music (Downey and Johnston works) and at the Gasparo Studios, Nashville (Seeger).

6:269     Recorded during concerts in Concord, Calif., and at the Hillside Club, Berkeley, Calif.

6:270     Recorded in Switzerland.

6:271     Recorded in the auditorium of the University of Maryland University College's Center of Adult Education.

6:272     Recorded in the field by Patrick Sky.

6:273     "Recorded in the Masonic Auditorium, Cleveland" --Container.

6:274     "Recorded live at the Laff Stop, Encino, California"--Container.

6:275     Recorded principally at Peregrine's Rest, Perkinsville, Vt.

6:276     The 2nd work recorded at CBS Recording Studios, New York.

6:277     "Recorded at Coast Recorders, San Francisco, CA, August 1978"--Container.

6:278     Recorded at Earth Audio Techniques, N. Ferrisburg, May-June 1977.

6:279     Recorded at Howard Schwartz Recording Studio, New York, May 28-29, 1980.

6:280     Principally recorded at the Wright's home in Princetown, W. Va., summer and fall 1975.

6:281     Recorded during performances in Europe in the fall of 1962.

6:282     Recorded in the Paris Conservatoire, Apr. 1-3, 1980.

6:283     Recorded Aug. 1980 at Coast Recorders, San Francisco, Calif.

6:284     Recorded May 28 and June 21, 1962, at Hola Penthouse Studios, New York City.

6:285     Recorded Feb.-Nov. 1979 at Studios West, North Vancouver, B.C.

6:286     Recorded July 21, 1980, at the ATLA Annual Convention in Montreal.

6:287     Recorded 1972-1975 at various locations in Paris.

6:288     Recorded Apr. 10-11 and July 1, 1979, Guildhall, Southampton.

6:289     Recorded during performances: Jan. 27, 1952, Musikvereinssaal, Vienna (op. 102) ; June 20, 1950, Titania Palast, Berlin (op. 56).

6:290 Principally recorded during performances Sept. 20, 1979, at the Berklee Center for the Performing Arts, Boston.

6:291 Recorded 1950-1959 in EMI Studio No. 1, Abbey Road, London.

6:292 Recorded in performance, June 1977, New York, and May 18, 1977, Havana, Cuba.

6:293 Recorded Sept. 29, 1980, in Scottish Rite Cathedral, Philadelphia.

6:294 Recorded May 31, 1979, in the Concert Hall, Göteborg (1st-2nd works) and Oct. 15, 1979, at Studio 2, Swedish Radio, Stockholm (3rd work).

6:295 The 1st work recorded May 29, 1980, at the Sacred Heart Church, University of Notre Dame, Notre Dame, Ind. ; 2nd-3rd works recorded Jan. 25, 1978, at Herrick Memorial Chapel, Occidental College, Los Angeles.

6:296 Recorded May 1978-

6:297 Recorded Mar. 1979.

6:298 Recorded Aug. 1925 (v. 1).

6:299 Recorded Mar. 16, 1980.

6:300 Recorded Dec. 15-16, 21, 1979.

6:301 Recorded live Mar. 25, 1956.

6:302 Recorded 1932-1959.

6:303 Recorded 1903-1918 ; originally issued on wax cylinders by Gramophone and Typewriter Co., Zon-o-phone, Edison Wax Cylinder, and Aeolian Vocation.

6:304 Recorded in the 1940s and 50s.

6:305 Vol. 2 recorded 1925-1928.

6:306 Recorded June 28, 1960 (quintets) and June 27, 1961 (sextets).

6:307    Recorded Sept. 1978 (no. 1 and 6) and May 1978 (no. 2-5).

6:308    Recorded Mar. 14, 1961 (1st-8th works) and Jan. 30, 1962 (9th-16th works).

6:309    Recorded from live performances on Feb. 2, 1936 (1st work) and Apr. 9, 1933 (2nd work).

6:310    The 1st-6th works recorded May 13 and 16, 1955 ; the remainder Apr. 25, 1956.

6:311    Eds. recorded: Boosey & Hawkes ; Universal Edition.

6:312    Eds. recorded: Emerson ; Novello.

6:313    Eds. recorded: Salabert (1st work) ; Mills Music (2nd-3rd works) ; Peters (4th work).

6:314    Eds. recorded: Studio P/R (1st and 3rd works) ; Volkwein Brothers (2nd and 4th works) ; Jenson (5th work).

6:315    Recorded from the ed. by Kenneth Gilbert (Paris : Heugel).

6:316    Eds. recorded: New York : C.F. Peters.

6:317    Eds. recorded: New York : Henmar Press ; Bryn Mawr : Elkan-Vogel (2nd-3rd works).

6:318    Ed. recorded: New York : Doubleday, c1930.

6:319    Ed. recorded: Paris : Salabert, 1980 (Kenneth Gilbert).

6:320    Ed. recorded: Leipzig : Breitkopf & Härtel, 1874. (Werke / Johann Sebastian Bach ; v. 21).

6:321    Eds. recorded: New York : Ballantine Books, c1964 ; New York : Ballantine Books, c1960.

## PUBLICATION, DISTRIBUTION, ETC. (6.7B9)

6:322    Distributor from label on container.

6:323     Distributor from label mounted on container.

6:324     Imprint from superimposed label.

6:325     Imprint on container covered by label: Odeon.

6:326     Imprint under label reads: EMI Vox de su Amo.

6:327     Label name from labels covering original label name: His Master's Voice.

6:328     Label on container: Distribution, WEA, Filipacchi Music.

6:329     Distributed in the U.S. by: Edcorp.

6:330     Licensed from: Seon.

6:331     Licensed from: Erato 70954.

6:332     Private record ; not for sale.

6:333     "Private record, not for sale."


## PHYSICAL DESCRIPTION (6.7B10)

6:334     In container (29 cm.).
          (Sound cassette)

6:335     In container ; manual sequence.
          (Sound disc)

6:336     In 3 containers ; manual sequence.
          (Sound disc)

6:337     In          containers.
          (Sound disc)

6:338     Vols. 1 and 2 in one container.
          (Sound disc)

6:339     In loose-leaf binder (29 cm.).
          (Sound cassette)

6:340          Set in container (25 cm.).
                  (Sound cassette)

6:341          Set in loose-leaf container (30 cm.).
                  (Sound cassette)

6:342          Set in loose-leaf binder with printed materials (29 cm.).
                  (Sound cassette)

6:343          Set in loose-leaf binder with reference materials (29 cm.).
                  (Sound cassette)

6:344          Set in loose-leaf binder with script (29 cm.).
                  (Sound cassette)

6:345          Includes 2 additional cassettes: 1980 updates of titles 2 and
               3.

6:346          Digital recording.

6:347          Digital recording ; automatic sequence.

6:348          Direct-to-disc recording.

6:349          Direct to disc recording ; Ambisonic UIIJ--stereo
               compatible.

6:350          "Direct cutting."

6:351          Half speed mastered.

6:352          "Newly retransferred on 2 LPs"--Container.

6:353          "Mono/stereo."

6:354          Bells are ringing is a mono. recording.

6:355          The 1st-2nd works are mono.

6:356          The 3rd and 4th works originally mono. ; electronically
               reprocessed to simulate stereo.

6:357          "Artphone transcription system 2 channel re-recording
               from originally monaural source"--Labels.

6:358          Automatic sequence.

6:359    Manual sequence.

6:360    Manual sequence ; in 3 containers.

6:361    Durations on labels.

6:362    Durations on labels and containers.

6:363    Durations: 15 min. each.

6:364    Durations: 4 min., 4 sec. each side.

6:365    Duration: 1:25:08.

6:366    Durations: 16:13 ; 19:00 ; 14:21 ; :48.

6:367    Durations: 15 min., 57 sec. ; 5 min., 41 sec. ; 21 min., 56 sec.

6:368    Durations: ca. 16 min. ; ca. 6 min. ; ca. 12 min.


## ACCOMPANYING MATERIAL (6.7B11)

6:369    Accompanied by study guide (120 p. ; 29 cm.).

6:370    Biographical notes by Edward J. Smith ([4] p.) laid in container.

6:371    Biographical notes in German by Clemens Höslinger and discographical information on containers.

6:372    Biographical notes, notes on the sessions, and discography, by Dan Morgenstern (15 p. : ill.) bound in container.

6:373    Biographical notes on container ; texts and notes on the instruments ([8] p. : ill. ; 28 cm.) inserted.

6:374    Biographical notes on the pianist on container.

6:375    Biographical sketches (2 p.) inserted in container.

6:376    Booklet by Woodroffe (47 p. : col. ill.) bound in container.

6:377        Booklet containing program notes by Archie Green, William H. Koon, and Norm Cohen, words of the songs, bibliography, and discography (18 p. : ill.) inserted in container.

6:378        Descriptive and biographical notes on container.

6:379        Descriptive leaflet in pocket of container.

6:380        Durations and program notes by James Durant on container.

6:381        Durations and program notes in Russian on container.

6:382        Durations included on card laid in.

6:383        Durations on booklet.

6:384        Durations, personnel, discographical information, and program notes on containers.

6:385        Durations with program notes by Didier C. Deutsch on container.

6:386        "Furtwängler and Strauss" by Dennis Dobson on container.

6:387        Guide laid in container (30 cm.).

6:388        In container with background essays by J.M. Llorens and others.

6:389        In container (30 cm.) with bibliography and biographical information on the author.

6:390        The libretto includes an English translation by Brian Thornton and Jeremy Commons (26 p.) and program notes by Don White (20 p. : ill.) laid in container.

6:391        Libretto includes English translation, program notes by Eberhard von Lewinsky, and biographical notes on the artists.

6:392        Lyrics on inner liner.

6:393        Lyrics printed as text on inner sleeve.

6:394   Notes by Janet Jeppson (Asimov) on container.

6:395   Notes on container.

6:396   Notes on the guitarist by Jim Crockett on container.

6:397   Notes on the organs, specifications, and registrations on container.

6:398   Notes on the recording processes and program notes on container.

6:399   Notes on Toscanini's interpretations of the recorded works by Harvey Sachs in English with French, German, and Italian translations on container.

6:400   Personnel and program notes on containers.

6:401   Program notes on container ; words ([4] p.) inserted.

6:402   Program notes on inner containers ; notes on the performers ([4] p. : ports. ; 30 x 11 cm.) laid in outer container.

6:403   Program notes and specifications of the organs on container.

6:404   Program notes with texts (48 p. : ill. (some col.)) laid in container.

6:405   Program notes and texts of the 1st 2 works with English translations on container.

6:406   Program notes in French on container ; booklet (4 p.) by Raymond Saint-Gilles inserted.

6:407   Program notes in Italian and English on container ; texts, with English translations (7 p.) inserted.

6:408   Program notes in Japanese (1 sheet : ill.) inserted in container.

6:409   Program notes, principally in German, laid in containers.

6:410   Program notes by the flutist on container.

6:411   Program notes by the composer in English and Portuguese on container.

6:412    Program notes by the composer and biographical notes on him on container.

6:413    Program notes by the composer and text of the 2nd work on container.

6:414    Program notes by the organist and organ specifications ( v. (16 p. each) ; 29 cm.) in containers.

6:415    Program notes by Leonard Feather on container.

6:416    Program notes by Barry Serota on container of v. 1.

6:417    Program notes, in part by William Livingstone, on container.

6:418    Program notes, principally by Stephen Carlton, on container.

6:419    Program notes by Stephan Calt (v. 1) and Don Kent (v. 2) on containers.

6:420    Program notes by John McDonough (6 p.) bound in and on container.

6:421    Program notes by Terence Rees ([1] leaf ; 28 cm.) inserted.

6:422    Program notes by Françoise Vincent-Malettra in French, English, and German on container.

6:423    Program notes by Alain Perier in English and French (8 p. : ill.) bound in container.

6:424    Program notes by Paolo Petazzi in German, English, French, and Italian, and durations (8 p. : ill.) laid in container.

6:425    Program notes by Stefan Kunze in German, French, and Italian and by Robert Simpson in English on container.

6:426    Program notes by Julian Rushton in English and French and by Wolfgang Dömling in German and Italian, with Latin text and English, French, and German translations (2 p.) inserted in container.

6:427      Program notes by André Tubeuf in English and French, and libretto, with English translation, ([11] p.) laid in container.

6:428      Program notes by Lothar Hoffmann-Erbrecht in English, French, and German on container, with texts in English, French, and German (2 p.) inserted.

6:429      Program notes by Antony Ransome on container ; texts with English translations (1 sheet ; 23 x 28 cm.) inserted.

6:430      Program notes by Rita Rack on container ; texts of the songs, with English translations (1 sheet) inserted.

6:431      Program notes by David W. Eagle and text by Schiller, with English translation on container.

6:432      Program notes by Leonard Burkat and notes on the recording process on inner sleeve.

6:433      Program notes by Michael Keeley and notes on the organ on container.

6:434      Program notes by Amram and biographical notes on him on container.

6:435      Program notes by Gregory Sandow and biographical notes on the performers (6 p. : ill.) on verso of accompanying poster.

6:436      Program notes by Patrick Szersnovicz and notes on the performers in French on container.

6:437      Program notes by Doug Seroff and words of the quartets (10 p. : ill.) bound in container ; program of the Jefferson County Quartet Reunion, Oct. 12, 1980 (20 p. : ill.) inserted.

6:438      Program notes by Frédéric Robert, biographical notes on the pianist, and notes on the recording process in French on container.

6:439      Program notes by Roswita Borschel and the performer and notes on the instrument in German, French, English, and Italian on container.

6:440    Program notes by Sergio Segalini, translated by A. McIntyre, on container.

6:441    Program notes by Eric Mason and Suvi Raj Grubb and text, with English translation, on container.

6:442    Program notes by Francine Mallet, with English translation by Charles Whitfield (8 p. : ill.) bound in container.

6:443    Program notes by Carl de Nys, translated into English by A. Laude, on container ; text, with English translation, on sheet inserted in container.

6:444    Program notes in Portuguese by Luiz Paulo Horta and Airton Barbosa ([2] p.) inserted in container.

6:445    Program notes in German by Knut Franke, with French and Italian translations, and in English by Christopher Headington on container.

6:446    Program notes in German by Karl Schumann, with English and French translations, on container and German texts, with English and French translations ([4] p. : port.) inserted in container.

6:447    Program notes in French by Rémi Jacobs, with English translation, on container and recording (1 sound disc : 45 rpm, stereo. ; 7 in.) of the performers discussing Bartók inserted.

6:448    Program notes in English and German by Karl Schumann and miniature score (47 p. : ill.) laid in container.

6:449    Reminiscences in Italian and English by Di Stefano on container.

6:450    Reminiscences by Berger in English, French, and German on container.

6:451    Specifications of the organ and program notes on container.

6:452    Synopsis by N. Pirella and program notes by Dan François (10 p. ; 28 cm.) in container.

6:453    Synopsis in Spanish on container.

6:454     A talk with Charles Gerhardt, by Christopher Palmer, begun on container and concluded on insertion ([4] p. : ill.).

6:455     Texts of the songs on inner sleeve.

6:456     With booklet (14 p.), verse ([7] leaves), and photographs ([7] leaves) inserted in container.

6:457     Words of the songs on container ; essays in Portuguese by Tárik de Souza and Paulo Mendes Campos (8 p. : ill.) bound in.

6:458     Words on inner liner.

## SERIES (6.7B12)

6:459     "PCM recording"--Label.

6:460     "Limited edition collector's series"--Label on container of v. 1.

6:461     "Abbey Road 50th anniversary album"--Container.

## AUDIENCE (6.7B14)

6:462     Intended audience: Ages 16 through adult.

6:463     Intended audience: Lawyers.

6:464     Intended audience: Religious.

6:465     Intended audience: Scientists who have not had formal training in the field.

6:466     Designed to be used with an annual report of a major company whose business involves manufacturing or commerce.

## OTHER FORMATS AVAILABLE (6.7B16)

6:467    All selections previously issued in various formats.

6:468    Conference proceedings (10 sound cassettes) also issued under same title.

6:469    Issued also as transcripts no. 1,000 and 997.

6:470    Issued also in cartridge (ARS1-3061) and cassette (ARK1-3061).

6:471    Issued also in cassette: 3301 317.

6:472    Issued also on reel.

6:473    Lecture issued also as videorecording.

6:474    Pre-conference tapes (2 sound cassettes) also issued under same title.

## SUMMARY (6.7B17)

6:475    Summary: Chronicles the wars between the forces of the Mule and the planets controlled by the Foundation.

6:476    Summary: Discusses ethical considerations and key definitions, elements of a valid revocable trust, planning the trust, drafting and implementing the trust, etc.

6:477    Summary: Preparation for future participants in the Workshop on Business Crime--Pre-indictment Advocacy to be held in 1981 at the New York University School of Law. Tells listeners what to review and read in order to enhance their participation in the conference.

6:478    Summary: A story about a lawyer in a small Alabama town in the 1930s whose defense of a Black man arouses the town's prejudice and hostility.

6:479    Summary: An abridged version of the author's work, read by Tom Conti.

6:480    Summary: The author discusses the collecting of autographs, the language of autograph catalogs, and the features which make a particular autograph rare or desirable.

6:481    Summary: In a report on weather forecasting, Dr. Somerville discusses the history, advances, and problems of predicting climate changes. In a report on deep-water organisms, Dr. Hessler describes the discovery and types of strange creatures that scientists found on the floor of the Pacific Ocean in the late 1970s.

6:482    Summary: Lon Ashe nostalgically reminisces about his professional life of five decades as a trial lawyer and as a member of ATLA.

## CONTENTS (6.7B18)

6:483    Contains dance pieces, principally of the 17th century, from Germany, Bohemia, France, England, the Netherlands, Italy, and Spain.

6:484    Includes between the 2 scenes of the 2nd act the composer's Leonora overture no. 3 (not no. 2 as stated on item).

6:485    Includes the composer's chorale prelude Vor deinin Thron tret ich hiermit (California Boys Choir ; Douglas Neslund, director) (2 min., 20 sec.).

6:486    The largo of the Sonata, BWV 529, is inserted between the Prelude and fugue, BWV 545.

6:487    The performance of the 10th symphony contains only the 1st movement (adagio).

6:488    Side 4 is a test record.

6:489    Side 6 includes 2 arias and a duet from the 1828 version featuring Della Jones and Eiddwen Harrhy, sopranos.

6:490    On container: Notes on the composer / Peter Wolf. Notes on music / Sonya Monosoff. Notes on the instruments / Laurence Libin.

6:491          Partial contents: Four songs: Liebeshymnus : op. 32, no. 3 ; Verführung : op. 33, no. 1 ; Winterliebe : op. 48, no. 5 ; Waldseligkeit : op. 49, no. 1.

6:492          Partial contents: Portuguese songs: A la villa voy (1 min., 15 sec.) ; Mil vezes llamo la muerte (3 min., 10 sec.) ; Ojuelos graciosos (1 min., 30 sec.) ; Ay mi Dios / Pedro de Cristo (2 min., 48 sec.).

6:493          Partial contents: A mirror on which to dwell: Anaphora (3 min., 51 sec.) ; Argument (2 min., 54 sec.) ; Sandpiper (2 min., 30 sec.) ; Insomnia (3 min., 19 sec.) ; View of the Capitol from the Library of Congress (3 min., 4 sec.) ; O breath (4 min., 1 sec.).

6:494          Contents: Idiophones -- Membranophones -- Cordophones -- Aérophones.

6:495          Contents: A rattletrap automobile -- Sapphire is cheating? -- A new house for $500.00! -- The $20,000.00 inheritance -- The 10,000th broadcast show -- The 25th anniversary program.

6:496          Contents: No. 1 in F major, BWV 1046 -- No. 3 in G major, BWV 1048 -- No. 4 in G major, BWV 1049 -- No. 5 in D major, BWV 1050 -- No. 2 in F major, BWV 1047 -- No. 6 in B-flat major, BWV 1051.

6:497          Contents: 16 different songs on several older coin-operated disc music boxes -- 2 selections of tunes played on the Wheelbarrow Piano of Ghent, Belgium -- 4 selections of tunes scored in the late 1800s for a concert player piano -- Itona crank organ (parlor model) -- 3 selections of the sound of the Photo Player, a suction activated calliope.

6:498          Contents: Overture -- When my dreams come true (vocal) -- Groucho's love scene (with Margaret Dumont) -- When my dreams come true (Harpo, harp) -- Groucho & Chico pun around -- Monkey doodle do (vocal) -- Groucho & Chico play auction -- Dance number -- I want my shirt (Toreador song) -- Gypsy love song (Chico, piano) -- Finale.

6:499          Contents: Sonata no. 23 in F minor, op. 57 (ca. 24 min.) -- Sonata no. 26 in E-flat, op. 81a (ca. 16 min.) -- Polonaise in C, op. 89 (5 min., 30 sec.).

6:500    Contents: Remedios (5:06) -- Processional (3:46) -- The impending death of the virgin spirit (6:02) -- The bricklayer's beautiful daughter (3:49).

6:501    Contents: At home: Travelling blues (4 min., 56 sec.) ; Birds of Montparnasse ( 2 min., 32 sec.) ; Splendor in the grass (4 min., 23 sec.) ; Sioux rabbit song (1 min., 47 sec.) ; Home on the range (4 min., 17 sec.) -- Around the world: Kwahare (Kenya) (3 min., 33 sec.) ; Pescau (Panama) (2 min., 38 sec.) ; From the Khyber Pass (Pakistan, Afghanistan) (1 min., 38 sec.).

6:502    Contents: Zenith -- Crystal streams -- Song of the dove / R. Armstrong -- Oneness / K. LaRoche -- Village Earth -- Ornament of hope -- Dance of the children -- The valley of search.

6:503    Contents: Quartet for piano and strings in E-flat major, op. 47 / Robert Schumann (Jamie Laredo, violin ; Walter Trampler, viola ; Leslie Parnas, violoncello ; Richard Goode, piano) -- Variations for flute and piano, D. 802 : (On Trockne Blumen from Die schöne Müllerin, D. 795) / Franz Schubert (Paula Robison, flute ; Richard Goode, piano).

6:504    Contents: Concerto no. 1 in D major, op. 6 / Paganini (with Royal Philharmonic Orchestra ; Lawrence Foster, conductor) -- Suite italienne / Stravinsky (with Bruno Canino, piano. Originally for violoncello and piano) -- Winter from The four seasons / Vivaldi (with London Philharmonic Orchestra) -- Caprice no. 24, op. 1 / Paganini (for solo violin).

6:505    Contents: Roman carnival overture / Berlioz ; arr. Frank Wright -- Carnival. Burlesque / Helen Perkin -- Suite from The carnival of the animals / Saint-Saëns ; arr. Gordon Langford -- Iberia. Carnival in Seville / Albéniz ; arr. Roy Newsome -- Lisbon carnival / Gilbert Vinter -- Carnival overture / Dvořák ; arr. Roy Newsome.

6:506    Contents: Six études, op. 16 ; Sonatina no. 3 ; Chorale prelude, Meine Seele bangt und hofft zu Dir / Ferruccio Busoni -- Eleven children's pieces ; Six studies for piano, op. 70 ; Two ricercari on the name B.A.C.H. / Alfredo Casella.

6:507    Contents: Humus : the life exploring force / Don Cherry
(18:36) -- Sita Rama encores / traditional ; arr. and adapted
by Don Cherry (4:17) -- Actions : for free jazz orchestra /
Krzysztof Penderecki (conducted by the composer) (16:33).

6:508    Contents: I'm afraid the masquerade is over / Herbert
Magidson, Allie Wrubel (4 min., 6 sec.) -- You call it
madness, I call it love / Gladys DuBois . . . [et al.] (3 min.,
52 sec.) -- Put your little foot right out (5 min., 57 sec.) --
Captain Bill / Monty Alexander, Ray Brown, Herb Ellis (3
min., 8 sec.) -- Sister Sadie / Horace Silver (4 min., 4 sec.).

6:509    Contents: Dingue le bangue / J.D. San-Macdony (4 min.,
14 sec.) -- Unaccustomed Bach / J.S. Bach (7 min., 17 sec.)
-- You and I / Vinicius de Morais, Norman Gimbel, Carlos
Lyra (5 min., 12 sec.) -- Claire de lune samba / Claude
Debussy (4 min., 50 sec.).

6:510    Contents: The legend of Wooley Swamp / C. Daniels . . .
[et al.] (4 min., 14 sec.) -- Carolina (I remember you) / C.
Daniels . . . [et al.] (5 min., 11 sec.) -- Lonesome boy from
Dixie / T. Crain, J. Williams (4 min., 43 sec.) -- No potion
for the pain / T. DiGregorio, G. Wohlgemuth (4 min., 24
sec.).

6:511    Contents: v. 1. The '60s -- v. 2. The '70s.

6:512    Contents: 1-2. Products liability overview -- 3. Punitive
damages. Damages -- 4. Legal innovation and imagination --
5. Psychic injuries -- 6-7. A tort law update -- 8. Whither the
civil jury?

6:513    Contents: 1-2. Current issues in special education law (2
cassettes) -- 3. Analyzing educational services -- 4. Individualized education program plan -- 5. Individualized education
program plan (cont.). Impartial due process hearing.

6:514    Contents: [1] Meeting the defenses in products liability
cases / Herman B. Glaser -- [2] Trial tactics & techniques in
products liability cases / Edward M. Swartz.

6:515    Contents: 1. Discovery in products cases / Reese J. Joye,
Jr. Discovery against the U.S. / Michael Pangia. Admis-
sability [sic] of government reports / Richard Schaden -- 2.
Richard Schaden (cont.). Product or service / Tom H.
Davis. Terrorist activities / Larry Goldhursh. Prejudgment

interest / Susan E. Loggans -- 3. Susan E. Loggans (cont.). Aviation admiralty law / Alan J. Konigsberg.

6:516      Contents: Act 1. Introduction/Duet: A highly respectable wife ; Entry of widow ; Solo: I'm off to Chez Maxime ; Duet: All's one to all men where there's gold ; Duet: Red as the rose in Maytime ; Finale -- Act 2. Introduction, dance, and villa-song ; Duet: Jogging in a one-horse gig ; March-septet: You're back where you first began ; Finale -- Act 3. The cake walk ; Can can ; Duet: Love unspoken ; Encore.

6:517      Contents: reel 1. Phonetic alphabet/Japanese. Brooklyn/ American southern -- reel 2. Standard English/Cockney. Irish/Scots -- reel 3. French/Italian. German/Russian.
     (Stage dialects)

6:518      Contents: tape 1-2. The tempest -- tape 3-5. Hamlet.


# NOTES ON PUBLISHERS' NUMBERS (6.7B19)

6:519      Original matrix and serial numbers on labels.

6:520      Laff Records: A-215.

6:521      Audio Lab. Record: ALC-1043.

6:522      Musical Heritage Society: MHS 4374.

6:523      Canadian Folk Workshop: CFW 001 (RR-28525).

6:524      Columbia: M2X 35895 (AL 35950-AL 35951).

6:525      Hollcraft Recordings: LRS-RT-6516 (on container: LRS-RT-6513).

6:526      Philips: 6747 444 (6598 783-6598 784).

6:527      Rubini Collection: GV 47, GV 80.

6:528      Lebendige Vergangenhelt: LV 63-LV 64, LV 108, LV 286.

6:529      Interchord: INT 185.750-INT 185.752.

6:530        Miller-Brody Productions: L515-L516, L518X.

6:531        Sonic Arts: LS 1 I (matrix)-LS 1 IV (matrix).

## COPY BEING DESCRIBED AND LIBRARY'S HOLDINGS (6.7B20)

6:532        Library's copy lacks program note insert.

6:533        Library's copy lacks v. 1: GV 47.

6:534        Library's set incomplete: MHS 3825 lacking.

6:535        "This edition limited to 10,000 copies. This is no. 2884"--T.p. of program notes.

## "WITH" NOTES (6.7B21)

6:536        With: Preparing trial and deposition witnesses / Charles F. Brega.
             (Examples 6:536-539 illustrate AACR 2 rule 6.1G4)

6:537        With: Laudate pueri / E.L. Morago -- Chansons portugaises.

6:538        With: Concerto, trumpet, 2 oboes and continuo solo, D major / G.P. Telemann -- Concerto, trumpet, woodwinds and continuo solo, C major / Tomaso Albinoni.

6:539        With: [Sonatas, violin, piano, no. 5, op. 24, F major] / Beethoven.

# 7

# Motion Pictures and Videorecordings

## NATURE OR FORM (7.7B1)

7:1     An AMCEE videotape conference, recorded live at the 1980 National Conference on Safety, Health, and Loss Control.

7:2     An episode from the television program entitled: The Great space coaster.

7:3     Horror film.

7:4     Musical.

7:5     Parody of the motion picture: Close encounters of the third kind.

7:6     A segment from the television program: Non-fiction television.

7:7     A segment of CBS reports, hosted by Harry Reasoner.

7:8     Staged especially for television.

7:9     Travelog.

7:10    Western.

# LANGUAGE (7.7B2)

7:11    In English.
        (Title proper: Kino pravda)

7:12    In German.

7:13    Dialogue in French.

7:14    Spanish dialogue, English subtitles.

7:15    In French with English subtitles.

7:16    In Spanish with English narration.

7:17    In Armenian and Russian with English subtitles.

7:18    Dubbed into English.

7:19    Issued also in Chinese (Mandarin).

7:20    Issued also in French, German, Japanese, Spanish, and Swedish.

7:21    Issued also in Spanish, with narration by N. Pérez González.

7:22    Issued also in Spanish under title: Isla de Pascua, with narration by Felicia Montealegre.

7:23    Issued also in English dubbed version.

7:24    Issued also with German subtitles.

7:25    Issued also with Spanish subtitles and with French transcript.

# SOURCE OF TITLE PROPER (7.7B3)

7:26    Title at end of film.

7:27    Title from accompanying booklet.

7:28        Title from container.

7:29        Title from distributor's catalog.

7:30        Title from script.

7:31        Title supplied from speaker's notes.


## VARIATIONS IN TITLE (7.7B4)

7:32        Title in publisher's catalog: Rediscovering herbs.

7:33        Title on booklet: The Rules of soccer, simplified.

7:34        Title on container: Profile in courage, Thomas Hart Benton.

7:35        Title on guide: Sedatives & hypnotics.

7:36        Title on leader's guide: Working smarter, not harder.


## PARALLEL TITLES AND OTHER TITLE INFORMATION (7.7B5)

7:37        On p. 4 of publisher's catalog: The 400 blows = Les quatre cents coup.

7:38        Parallel title on press release: Cabane de rondins.

7:39        Subtitle: Featuring Jim Henson's Sesame Street Muppets, Burr Tillstrom's Kukla, Fran and Ollie, Mister Rogers' Neighborhood, and Captain Kangaroo.


## STATEMENTS OF RESPONSIBILITY (7.7B6)

7:40        Cast: Charles McCallum (Bert), Jack Kirwan (Jack), Patti Crocker (Mrs. Potts).

7:41        Cast: Kate Reid (Auntie), Christian Slater (Charlie).

7:42        Commentator: David Attenborough.

7:43        Correspondent: Bill Redeker.

7:44        Host: Meryl Streep.

7:45        Moderator: Dave Moore.

7:46        Moderator: Edwin D. Kilbourne ; panelists: Stuart D. Cook, R. Gordon Douglas, Jr., Walter R. Dowdle, David S. Fedson, Gordon W. Howe.

7:47        Presenter: Joseph P. Earley.

7:48        Credits: Adapter, Paul Gagne.

7:49        Credits: Advisers, Gorm Rasmussen, Ib Emler, Gabriel Sorensen.

7:50        Credits: Animator, Don Duga ; editor, Bert Feldman ; voices, Anne Costello, Corinne Orr.

7:51        Credits: Camera, Steve Luhring ; voices, Margaret Mitchell, Charlie Glaize, Pam Manner ; music, Chuck Loucka, David March.

7:52        Credits: Camera, editor, Donald J. Hoeg ; adviser, Loren Cocking.

7:53        Credits: Cameraman and editor, David A. Silverman ; music, Evan M. Greenspan.

7:54        Credits: Cameraman, Steve Uzzell ; editor, Fred Burnham ; narrator, Diane Page.

7:55        Credits: Cameraman, William Heffner ; special effects, S.S. Wilson ; editor, Vince Matsudaira.

7:56        Credits: Cameramen, Henry Lynk, Ray Wirlin, David Watts, O.S. Pettingill, Jr. ; narrator, Doug Jeffers.

7:57        Credits: Cinematographer, Marsha Kahm ; graphic design, Sara Bouwsma ; narrator, Janeal Quinnell.

7:58     Credits: Editor, Linda Jassim.

7:59     Credits: Educational consultants, Barbara M. Newman, Philip R. Newman.

7:60     Credits: Music, Bill Brennan.

7:61     Credits: Photographers, Tom McDonough . . . [et al.] ; editors, David Peoples, Ralph Wikke ; narrator, Paul Frees ; music, Martin Bresnick.

7:62     English sound track prepared by International Film Bureau.

7:63     Developed at the University of Kansas.

7:64     Developed by a consortium of U.S. and Canadian education agencies as part of the Secondary School Television Project.

7:65     Researched and developed by Drs. Dorothy G. and Jerome L. Singer.

7:66     Made in cooperation with the Knock Out Graffiti in Glendale Committee.

7:67     Produced in cooperation with the New Jersey College of Medicine and Dentistry.

7:68     "Produced under the direction of the Chemistry ETV Committee: Charles F. Wilcox, James M. Burlitch, and Stanley T. Marcus"--Booklet.

7:69     "Produced with the cooperation of the Suicide Prevention and Crisis Center of San Mateo County"--Guide.

7:70     Funded by Texas Education Agency, Texas Dept. of Human Resources, and Texas Dept. of Community Affairs.

## EDITION AND HISTORY (7.7B7)

7:71     Recorded at Caesar's Palace, Las Vegas, Nev., on July 4, 1976.

7:72    Filmed on location in London and Paris from November 1982 through February 1983.

7:73    Shown in an exhibit at the President's Committee on Employment of the Handicapped.

7:74    An adaptation of a portion of the book: Winnie-the-Pooh / A.A. Milne.

7:75    An adaptation of the 19th-century Russian novel: Oblomov / by Ivan Goncharov.

7:76    Adapted from: The trouble with Miss Switch / Barbara Brooks Wallace.

7:77    Adapted from the book: The Virginian / Owen Wister.

7:78    Adapted from an ABC News television documentary.

7:79    Adapted from the 1960 motion picture of the same title.

7:80    Adapted from the book of the same name by Alyse Newman.

7:81    Adapted from the book of the same title by S.E. Hinton.

7:82    Adapted from the play: The belle of Amherst / by William Luce.

7:83    Adapted from the short story of the same name by Tennessee Williams.

7:84    Based on: What Katy did / Susan Coolidge. What Katy did at school / Susan Coolidge.

7:85    Based on: Quinkins / by Percy Trezise and Dick Roughsey.

7:86    Based on: Beauty and the beast / retold by Marianna Mayer.

7:87    Based on: John Brown, Rose, and the midnight cat / story by Jenny Wagner ; ill. by Ron Brooks.

7:88    Based on: A field guide to the birds / text and ill. Roger Tory Peterson.

7:89        Based on: The clown of God / told and illustrated by Tomie de Paola.

7:90        Based on: Angus lost / told and pictured by Marjorie Flack.

7:91        Based on the ballad: Tam Lin.

7:92        Based on the book: William's doll / Charlotte Zolotow.

7:93        Based on the play: The swamp-dwellers / Wole Soyinka.

7:94        Based on the plays: Als de dood and Je moet ermee leren leven.

7:95        Based on Aesop's fable: The boy who cried wolf.

7:96        Based on the Grimm brothers' fairy tale: King Thrushbeard.

7:97        Based on a poem by Crosbie Garstin.

7:98        Based on the book of the same name by Janice May Udry.

7:99        Based on the book of the same title by Rosemary Wells.

7:100       Based on the cartoons of Gerard Hoffnung.

7:101       Based on the poem of the same name by Edward Lear.

7:102       Based on the short story of the same name by O. Henry.

7:103       Based on the story of the same title by Damon Runyon.

7:104       Based on the tale by Karel Čapek.

7:105       Edited, English version of the German film: Eisenstaedt--Deutschland (45 min.).

7:106       Edited from a longer version produced by Shanghai Animation Film Studio.

7:107       Edited from the motion picture: Gorilla. 1981.

7:108       Edited from the Paramount Pictures feature film of the same name.

7:109    Music and sound effects added to the edited version of the 1914 silent film first released by Biograph.

7:110    First of 40 programs.

7:111    Originally filmed in 70 mm. Omnimax.

7:112    Originally broadcast on PBS.

7:113    Originally issued as motion picture in 1947.

7:114    Originally produced for showing at the Fourth International Conference on the Peaceful Uses of Atomic Energy, held in Geneva, Switzerland, in the fall of 1971.

7:115    Originally shown on television.

7:116    Originally aired on the television program entitled: CBS library.

7:117    Originally broadcast on the CBS television program entitled: 60 minutes.

7:118    Originally broadcast on the television program entitled: 30 minutes.

7:119    Originally released in Germany under title: Oh, wie schön ist Panama.

7:120    Originally released as a 35 mm. Charlie Chaplin comedy in 1925 by United Artists.

7:121    Originally shown in Canada on the television program entitled: Portraits of power.

7:122    Originally shown on the ABC News television program: Close-up.

7:123    Originally shown on the educational television program entitled: The Baxters.

7:124    Originally shown on the television program: 60 minutes.

7:125    Originally shown on the television program entitled: Wildlife on one.

7:126    Previous version, issued as motion picture in 1963, has title: Laws of heredity.

7:127    Previously issued as filmstrip in 1979.

7:128    Previously issued as motion picture and filmstrip in 1945.

7:129    Previously issued in less complete version under title: Thunder over Mexico.

7:130    Previously released as motion picture in 1946.

7:131    Previously released in 1974.

7:132    Rev. ed. of: The Magic book. 1963.

7:133    Rev. version of: From mountains to microns. 1959.

7:134    Rev. version of the motion picture: Policeman--day and night. 1963.

7:135    Rev. version of the motion pictures issued under their individual titles in the series: Simple machines. 1968.

7:136    Issued also in longer version (46 min.).

7:137    Longer version issued in 16 mm.

7:138    Longer version (88 min.) issued under same title.

7:139    Longer version (59 min.) issued by Opus Films.

7:140    Shorter version subsequently issued by Wombat Productions.

7:141    Updated version of the 1975 motion picture entitled: Up with teachers.

7:142    Updated version of the 1975 motion picture of the same name.

7:143    Issued also in edited version (30 min.).

7:144    French version entitled: Mer mère.

7:145    Spanish version of the motion picture: When fire starts. 1979.

7:146    English version by Judy Duris.

7:147    English version of the film of the same title.

7:148    Uses documentary footage from: Joan Robinson, one woman's story.

7:149    Correlated with: A guide to physical examination / Barbara Bates.

7:150    Correlated with the book: Economics exchange / Willard M. Kniep.

7:151    Sequel: Learn not to burn.

7:152    Sequel to: An Act of Congress.


## PUBLICATION, DISTRIBUTION, ETC., AND DATE (7.7B9)

7:153    Made in 1949.

7:154    First released in Canada.

7:155    First released in England in 1980.

7:156    First released in Czechoslovakia by Československý film-export under title: Muž, který dovedl létat.

7:157    First released in Australia under title: Mates, martyrs, and masters.

7:158    First released in U.S.S.R. in 1980 under title: Moskva sljesam nje jerit.

7:159    Simultaneously released in Canada.

7:160    A foreign film (United Arab Emirates).

7:161    A foreign film (U.S.S.R.).

7:162    A foreign videorecording (Canada).

7:163     A foreign videorecording (England) originally issued as motion picture in 1956.

7:164     Distributed in the U.S. by: Lawrence, KS : Centron Films.

7:165     Also distributed in Great Britain by the Centre for Instructional Television.

## PHYSICAL DESCRIPTION (7.7B10)

7:166     Optical sound track.

7:167     Cinemascope and quadraphonic sound.

7:168     Double system sound.

7:169     Sound accompaniment for automatic operation only.

7:170     Sound accompaniment for manual operation only.

7:171     Sound recorded on Channel 1 only, Channel 2 for learner response.

7:172     Film: 14,150 ft.

7:173     Sepia print.

7:174     Technicolor.

7:175     Negative print.

7:176     U-matic.

7:177     U standard.

7:178     Issued as 1/2 in. or U-matic 3/4 in.

7:179     Issued as Beta or VHS.

7:180     Issued as cassette (Beta 1/2 in. or VHS 1/2 in.) or reel (Type C 1 in.).

7:181    Issued as cassette (U-matic 3/4 in. or Beta 1/2 in. or VHS 1/2 in.) or reel (1 in. or 2 in.).

7:182    Issued as cassette (U-matic 3/4 in. or Beta 1/2 in. or VHS 1/2 in.) or reel (Quadruplex 2 in.) ; issued also as motion picture.

7:183    Issued as U-matic 3/4 in. or Beta 1/2 in. or VHS 1/2 in.

7:184    Issued as U-matic 3/4 in. or VHS 1/2 in.

7:185    Extended play tape.

7:186    Silent film at the speed for sound, 24 fr. per sec.

7:187    Cinema 360 ; made for dome projection.

7:188    Loop films.

7:189    Three-dimensional film.

7:190    Designed for use with the Beseler CUE/SEE projector.

7:191    Widescreen (1:85).

7:192    With captions.

7:193    Captioned for the deaf.

7:194    Closed captioned for the hearing impaired.

7:195    Issued also without captions.


## ACCOMPANYING MATERIAL (7.7B11)

7:196    With interview critique sheet.

7:197    With script.

7:198    List of cast and credits on container.

7:199    Sound cassettes contain sample interviews.

7:200     Includes bibliography in teacher's guide.

7:201     With facilitator's guide "Active listening" (22 p. ; 29 cm.).

## SERIES (7.7B12)

7:202     "ABC News special."

7:203     "A National Geographic special."

7:204     "NBC white paper."

7:205     Episode 4 in a series for allied health personnel.

7:206     Part 1 in a series.

7:207     Selections reissued from the series entitled: Special delivery.

7:208     From: Be a better shopper series.

## AUDIENCE (7.7B14)

7:209     Intended audience: Ages 16 through adult.

7:210     Intended audience: Kindergarten and primary grades.

7:211     Intended audience: Grades 3-8.

7:212     Intended audience: Grades 7-12.

7:213     Intended audience: Junior high school through college students and adults.

7:214     Intended audience: Junior high school through college and adult and medical personnel.

7:215     Intended audience: Senior high school through college and adult and teachers of regular and special education.

7:216    Intended audience: College and adult.

7:217    Intended audience: College through adult and local, state, and federal government officials.

7:218    Intended audience: Adults.

7:219    Intended audience: Carbon Products Division employees, customers, and community groups.

7:220    Intended audience: Hearing impaired students, teachers, and students of English as a second language.

7:221    Intended audience: Medical personnel.

7:222    Intended audience: Nurses.

7:223    Intended audience: Supervisors and middle managers.

## OTHER FORMATS AVAILABLE (7.7B16)

7:224    Issued also in 35 mm.

7:225    Issued also as super 8 mm. cartridge.

7:226    Issued also as super 8 mm. and as videorecording.

7:227    Issued also as super 8 mm. on reel or in cassette.

7:228    Issued also as filmstrip.

7:229    Issued also as filmstrip and as slide set.

7:230    Issued also as motion picture.

7:231    Issued also as motion picture and as sound recording.

7:232    Issued also as slide set.

7:233    Issued also as videorecording.

7:234     Issued also as videorecording (27 min.).

7:235     Issued also as 3 separate videorecordings: Creole, The Reluctant dragon, and Beauty and the beast. 1981.

7:236     Issued also as videorecording and as filmstrip.

7:237     Issued also as videorecording and as sound recording.

7:238     Issued also as motion picture by: Indiana University Audio-Visual Center.

7:239     Issued also as videorecording by: PBS Video.

7:240     Issued also on reel with: Creole and The Reluctant dragon, under title Misunderstood monsters. 1981.

7:241     Issued also in cassette with: Creole and The Reluctant dragon, under title Misunderstood monsters. 1981.

7:242     Also issued in b&w and as videorecording.

7:243     Issued also in longer version (40 min.) and as video-recording.

7:244     Issued also, in part, as 3 separate motion pictures: Hug me, The Man who had no dream, and The Silver pony.
          (Motion picture; title proper: A Tale of four wishes)

7:245     Issued also, in part, as 3 separate videorecordings: Hug me, The Man who had no dream, and The Silver pony.
          (Videorecording; title proper: A Tale of four wishes)

7:246     Issued also in other videorecording formats.

7:247     Teaching kit also available.

7:248     Companion slide set also available: Making an impact--community decision-making.

7:249     Corresponding text available.

7:250     Book, based on the series, published as: The body in question / Jonathan Miller. New York : Random House, c1978.

# SUMMARY (7.7B17)

7:251        Summary: Shows the aftermath of the massive eruption of Mount St. Helens in May 1980, as well as subsequent eruptions and volcanic activity.

7:252        Summary: An animated film in which a little boy learns the value of teachers.

7:253        Summary: Five minifilms designed to improve communication in group situations: discussion groups, training sessions, briefing sessions, and meetings. Highlights difficulties encountered by group leaders and participants. Although designed as discussion starters, the films can be shown without discussion.

7:254        Summary: In the first film Nora reaches her twentieth birthday and nothing happens. She reminisces over her past birthdays when, once a year, she could feel she was "Queen for a day." In the second film two teenage-age girls, observing a couple in the park, wish they were old enough to have boyfriends and pretend, each one playing a role.

7:255        Summary: In part one, educator Dr. Madeline Hunter outlines how teachers can plan and sequence their instructional material. In part two, she shows how to minimize the need for practice and, in part three, she considers the question of practice or drill and reviews the principles of the series.

7:256        Summary: With Jason Robards as host, follows actor, director, and producer John Houseman as he rehearses the repertory company which he founded in a production of Shakespeare's King Lear.

7:257        Summary: Focuses on the life, career, and legacy of Franklin Delano Roosevelt, marking the 100th anniversary of his birth. Features interviews with his allies, critics, and observers in the United States and abroad, as well as President Reagan and former Presidents Nixon, Ford, and Carter. Hosted by David Brinkley and featuring correspondents Peter Jennings and Richard Threlkeld.

7:258        Summary: Shows how improvised drama, based on the experiences of the participants, is what fuels the Hodson

Drama Group at the William Hodson Senior Center in the Bronx, N.Y. The mainly Black women's cast dramatizes their reminiscences over the past seventy-five years.

7:259        Summary: Based on a poem by Ogden Nash, tells the story of Mr. and Mrs. Donnybrook, and demonstrates that all things should be taken in moderation.


## CONTENTS (7.7B18)

7:260        Contents: Little Red Riding Hood -- Goldilocks -- The Three little pigs.

7:261        Contents: Just one more thing (3 min.) -- Be prepared (3 min., 30 sec.) -- The decision makers (4 min.) -- Any questions? (3 min.) -- Well, if you ask me (2 min., 30 sec.).

7:262        Contents: film A. Large business -- film B. Small business.

7:263        Contents: lesson 1. General operation -- lesson 2. Sweep alignment of FM-IF strip, pts. 1-2 -- lesson 3. Front-end alignment / Robert French.

7:264        Contents: module 1. Extracellular fluid -- module 2. Intracellular fluid -- module 3. pH -- module 4. Acidosis and alkalosis.

7:265        Contents: module 1. An overview (19 min., 31 sec.) -- module 2. Narcotics (31 min., 57 sec.) -- module 3. Alcohol (31 min., 30 sec.) -- module 4. Hallucinogens and inhalants (38 min.).

7:266        Contents: pt. 1, module 1. Introduction to coma (28 min.) -- pt. 1, modules 2-3. Intracranial causes of coma, pts. A-B (28 min., 20 min.) -- pt. 2, module 1. Metabolic coma, an overview (24 min.) -- pt. 2, module 2. Psychological aspects of coma (22 min.).

7:267        Contents: program 1. Rural youth -- program 2. Urban youth -- program 3. Disabled youth -- program 4. Young single parents.

7:268        Partial contents: session 1. Giving positive feedback --
             session 2. Giving negative feedback -- session 3. Accepting
             negative feedback.

7:269        Contents: tape 1. Control cable splicing -- tape 2.
             Shielding, grounding, cable fault location -- [tape 3] Gaskets,
             O-rings, diaphragms -- [tape 4] Bezel, switch plate fabrica-
             tion.

7:270        Shots: LS of full-rigged brigantine (127 ft.). MS of deck
             scene (20 ft.). CU captain at wheel (80 ft.).
                 (Stock shots)


## NUMBERS BORNE BY THE ITEM (7.7B19)

7:271        E 1.70/2:V 26.

7:272        Supt. of Docs. no.: FEM 1.101.

7:273        "Program no. 1402"--Publisher's catalog.


## COPY BEING DESCRIBED AND LIBRARY'S
## HOLDINGS (7.7B20)

7:274        Library's copy imperfect: Brittle.

7:275        Library's copy imperfect: Image degraded.

7:276        Library's copy imperfect: 500 ft. of film scratched.

7:277        Library's copy imperfect: Scratches on 10 scattered
             frames.

7:278        Library has archival copy only.

## "WITH" NOTES (7.7B21)

7:279        With: The Real world of TV.
            (Examples 7:279-280 illustrate AACR 2 rule 7.1G4)

7:280        With: Paddington weighs in -- Paddington bakes a cake --
            Paddington hits the jackpot.

# 8

# Graphic Materials

## NATURE OR ARTISTIC FORM (8.7B1)

8:1      "News-in-depth filmstrip"--Guide.

8:2      Flipatran overhead projector system.

8:3      "A program of 33 transparencies for the overhead projector."

8:4      Cubist painting.

8:5      "This is a canvas transfer art print."

8:6      Shows anterior view and lateral view.
            (Radiograph)

8:7      Shows side and front views.
            (Radiograph)

8:8      Photographic reproduction of X ray.
            (Slide)

8:9      A 3-image, 25 minute lecture presentation.
            (Slide)

# LANGUAGE (8.7B2)

8:10        Booklet in English, French, German, Russian, and Spanish.

8:11        Captions in Danish, Finnish, and Swedish.
              (Chart)

8:12        One cassette is in English, 1 in Spanish.

8:13        Descriptive text on the back of each picture in English, French, German, and Spanish.

8:14        Manual in English and French.

8:15        Teacher's manual in Russian and English.

8:16        With teacher's guide in German and English.

8:17        With catalog in English and French ([23], [23] p. ; 28 cm.).

8:18        With English and Spanish scripts.

8:19        Issued also in French under title: La France dans l'Amérique du Nord, Saint Pierre et Miquelon.

# SOURCE OF TITLE PROPER (8.7B3)

8:20        Title from cover sheet.
              (Wall chart)

8:21        Title from earlier reproductions.

8:22        Title from instructor's guide.

8:23        Title from label inserted in container.

8:24        Title from printed t.p. accompanying slide set.

8:25        Title supplied by cataloger.

## VARIATIONS IN TITLE (8.7B4)

8:26    Filmstrips 6-10 issued under title: Diesel mechanics III, engine assembly.

8:27    Titles on booklet: Historical monuments in Yugoslavia, etc.

8:28    Title on container: Auto body--paint, materials, and preparation.

8:29    Title on guide: Peru--Cusco, Andean city.

8:30    Title on instruction booklet: Vis-ed Spanish vocabulary cards.

8:31    Title on script: Santo Domingo, Museo de las Casas Reales.

8:32    Title on side of box: Spell it right.
        (Flash card)

8:33    Title on teacher's manual: Ancient Egyptian art and architecture.

8:34    Also called St. Jerome and the lion.

8:35    Also entitled: Mont Sainte-Victoire seen from Gardanne.


## STATEMENTS OF RESPONSIBILITY (8.7B6)

8:36    Narrator: J. Kristopher.

8:37    Narrators: Margaret Diamond, Lillian Dubsky, Erika Hyde, and other survivors of the Holocaust.

8:38    Credits: Animator, Susan Fort ; education consultant and field test manager, Deborah Wemette.

8:39    Credits: Art, Ann Rankin.

8:40    Credits: Artist, Vernon McKissack.

8:41      Credits: Consultant, Dan Irvin.

8:42      Credits: Editor, Carolyn Vanderslice.

8:43      Credits: Illustrators, Alice and Martin Provensen.

8:44      Credits: Photo editor, Nancy Kaye.

8:45      Credits: Photographer, Christine Trufaut ; graphics, Bonnie Acker ; consultants, Robert DeGrasse . . . [et al.].

8:46      Credits: Photographs, Bruce Coleman Limited ; diagrams, Hamlyn Publishing Group Limited.

8:47      Credits: Photography, Phil Atkinson, J. Steven Dick ; art, Jennith Moncrief, John Cruncleton ; consultants, Elizabeth Maggi, Charles K. Harmon, Mary McGarry.

8:48      Credits: Photography, Richard E. Kucera . . . [et al.] ; narration, Lee Duncan.

8:49      Credits: Visuals, Thomas R. Schroeder, Libor Pokorny ; consultant, Phyllis B. Pitluga.

8:50      Credits: Visuals and graphics, Franklin G. Smith, Dave M. Brugge, Charles Colley ; Spanish translation and narration, Maritza Arrigunaga ; music, Ron Dilulio ; script consultants, David J. Weber, Charles Colley.

8:51      Biographical information compiled by Jane Ryerson.

8:52      Graphics for the slides were prepared by C. Townley, J. Joseph, and M. Kalbaugh.

8:53      Manual by Barbara Thompson ; flash card illustrations by Jesse T. Hummingbird.

8:54      Lesson plan / by Sr. Jeanne d'Arc, R.S.M.

8:55      Created under the guidance of the U.S. Sewing Products Division of the Singer Company.

8:56      "Produced in cooperation with the Cornell University Wind Ensemble, Marice Stith, conductor"--Teacher's guide.

8:57      Filmed in cooperation with Hillcrest Kidney Disease Treatment Center, Tulsa, Okla.

8:58      "Funded by Iowa State University Research Foundation."

8:59      "Produced under a grant from the National Endowment for the Humanities."

## EDITION AND HISTORY (8.7B7)

8:60      Adapted from: A visit to William Blake's inn / Nancy Willard.

8:61      Adapted from: The wide-mouthed frog / written and illustrated by Rex Schneider.

8:62      An audiovisual text supplement adapted from: General carpentry / William P. Spence.

8:63      Adapted from the book of the same name by Edna Miller.

8:64      Adapted from the motion picture of the same name.

8:65      Adapted from the 1974 motion picture of the same name.

8:66      Adapted from the 1982 motion picture: An Upper room and a garden.

8:67      Adapted from the 1962 Universal Pictures motion picture: Freud--the secret passion, starring Montgomery Clift and Susannah York.

8:68      Adapted from the classic British film, produced in 1951 by Renown Film Productions.

8:69      Adapted from episode 6 of the PBS television series: Life on earth.

8:70      Based on: The New Larousse encyclopedia of animal life.

8:71      Based on: Le petit prince / Antoine de Saint-Exupéry.

8:72      Based on: All the president's men / Carl Bernstein and Bob Woodward.

8:73      Based on: The fall of the house of Usher and The pit and the pendulum / Edgar Allan Poe.

8:74        Based on the book: Anatomy of an illness as perceived by the patient / by Norman Cousins. Boston : G.K. Hall, 1980, c1979.

8:75        Based on books by Donald J. Sobol.

8:76        Based on the book of the same name by H.A. Rey.

8:77        Based on the book of the same name by Margret and H.A. Rey.

8:78        Based on the book of the same titles by Mercer Mayer.

8:79        Based on stories by Frank Muir.

8:80        Based on research by H.B.D. Kettlewell.

8:81        Based on the character, Annie, of cartoons, stage, and motion picture.

8:82        From the book: Brian Wildsmith's birds.

8:83        Edited from the 1976 Warner Brothers' motion picture of the same name.

8:84        Made from the motion pictures: House of Usher / Alta Vista Productions. 1960 and Pit and the pendulum / Alta Vista Productions. 1961.

8:85        Taken from: The New Larousse encyclopedia of animal life.

8:86        Taken from: The CIBA collection of medical illustrations / Frank Henry Netter.

8:87        Taken from: The Pretend Indians / edited by Gretchen M. Bataille, Charles L.P. Silet.

8:88        Taken from Dr. Carl Sagan's television series of the same name.

8:89        Duplicates the photographs in the book of the same title. (Slide)

8:90        Painted by Hilda Scott from an illustration by Ernest H. Shepard in The house at Pooh Corner by A.A. Milne.

8:91     Painted by the artist while a student at the Major Bent Elementary School, Steelton, Pa.
  (Art original)

8:92     Date on work: 14 January 1904.

8:93     Updated ed. of: Aorto-iliac and peripheral occlusive disease. 1973.

8:94     Updated and rev. version of: New York : Butterick Publishing, 1975. (Housing and home furnishings--your personal environment).

8:95     Updated and rev. version of: Making changes. New York : Butterick Publishing, 1976. (Lifestyles--options for living).

8:96     Rev. version of the filmstrips: Tracheostomy care. 1966; Introduction to tracheostomy care. 1972; Tracheostomy care--the cuffed tube. 1972.

8:97     Rev. version of the filmstrips issued in 1974 under their individual titles.

8:98     Rev. version of the 1971 filmstrip of the same title.

8:99     Rev. version of the slide set: Oral hygiene. 1972.

8:100     Rev. version of the 1972 slide set of the same name.

8:101     French version of: France in North America, Saint Pierre and Miquelon.

8:102     Version for intermediate school students issued under title: Myths and legends of ancient Greece.

8:103     Issued also as secondary level version.

8:104     Issued also in version for junior high school through adult.

8:105     First ed. issued as single set in 1972 under title: Chronic pulmonary diseases.

8:106     Subsequently issued as slide set in 1983 by: IBIS Media.

8:107     Correlated with the textbook: The Social sciences, concepts and values.

8:108    Correlated with: Sportsmanlike driving / prepared by the American Automobile Association.

8:109    Companion program: House of Representatives, voice of the people. 1971.

8:110    Designed to accompany the motion picture: Remembering names and faces.

8:111    For use with: Spelling our language books, 1-4; may also be used with: Writing our language.

8:112    Supplement to: Basic arrhythmias / Gail Walraven.

8:113    Supplements the text and laboratory manual: Structure and function in man / Stanley W. Jacob, Clarice Ashworth Francone, Walter J. Lossow. 5th ed.

## PUBLICATION, DISTRIBUTION, ETC. (8.7B9)

8:114    Slides and booklet, c1974; audiotapes, c1976.

8:115    The snow goose published in 1980 by Knopf.

8:116    Made in 1975.

8:117    Made in Canada.

8:118    First released in England.

8:119    A foreign slide set (England).

8:120    A foreign filmstrip (France).

## PHYSICAL DESCRIPTION (8.7B10)

8:121    Scale: 8:1.
    (Technical drawing)

8:122    Scale: 1/8 " = 1 '0 ".
    (Technical drawing)

8:123    Scale 1/4 in. to 1 ft.
        (Technical drawing)

8:124    Scale varies.
        (Technical drawing)

8:125    Scales vary from 1:50 to 1:200.
        (Technical drawing)

8:126    "No scale."
        (Technical drawing)

8:127    With captions.

8:128    Captions hand lettered on frames.
        (Transparency)

8:129    In binder: 28 cm.
        (Slide)

8:130    In box (6 x 11 cm.) with script (8 p. ; 25 cm.).

8:131    In container (11 x 12 x 4 cm.).

8:132    Filmslip and booklet in glassine envelope (24 x 11 cm.).

8:133    In folder.
        (Postcard)

8:134    In 4 plastic pages (29 cm.).

8:135    In plastic sheets (29 cm.) in binder.

8:136    In plastic sleeves (28 x 22 cm.) punched for 3-ring binder.

8:137    Inserted in plastic sleeves with 5 p. of critical reviews, in
loose-leaf binder.
        (Photograph)

8:138    Slides in plastic container (7 x 12 cm.).

8:139    Reels in pocket in front of study guide.
        (Stereograph)

8:140    In portfolio.
        (Photograph)

8:141    Slides in carousel tray.

8:142    In 6 carousels, for use with 2 projectors and dissolver unit.

8:143    Slides mounted in 2 Kodak carousel cartridges.

8:144    Loop film mounted in cartridge.

8:145    With cardboard frame (27 x 26 cm.).
         (Transparency)

8:146    Mounted in projection frame.
         (Transparency)

8:147    Mounted on spring roller.
         (Wall chart)

8:148    Mounted on wooden easel.
         (Chart)

8:149    Glass mounted.
         (Slide)

8:150    Unmounted.
         (Art print)

8:151    Issued in 2 parts.

8:152    Issued in 4 modules.

8:153    Issued in 2 units.

8:154    Size when framed: 53 x 43 cm.

8:155    Size when framed: 70 x 56 cm. (27 1/2 x 22 in.).

8:156    Frame: Brown wood.

8:157    Frame: Black velvet on wood, gold edges.

8:158    Beige driftwood frame with linen liner.

8:159    Each print has attached overlay.

8:160        Posters printed on both sides.

8:161        Charts fold to 28 cm. x 22 cm. and are 3-hole punched for student notebooks.

8:162        Wall calendar, with holes at corners for pinning.

8:163        Sound accompaniment for automatic operation only.

8:164        Sound accompaniment for manual operation only.

8:165        Sound accompaniment compatible for manual and automatic operation.

8:166        Sound accompaniment (English and Spanish) for automatic operation only.

8:167        Sound accompaniment (English) compatible for manual and automatic operation, sound accompaniment (French) for automatic operation only.

8:168        Sound accompaniment in English (19 min.) and in Spanish (15 min.) compatible for manual and automatic operation.

8:169        One side of sound cassette contains general level narration (ca. 60 min.), other side contains advanced level narration (ca. 60 min.).

8:170        Sound cassette side 1 without signal, side 2 with automatic advance.

8:171        Sound disc side 1 with audible advance signal, side 2 with automatic advance.

8:172        Cassette has audible pulses on one side, inaudible pulses on the other.

8:173        Programmed stops allow unrestricted response time.

8:174        Each flash card contains a strip of audiotape with student track and prerecorded teaching track.

8:175        Issued also as set of 106 slides with 2 sound cassettes.
             (Physical description area reads: 74 slides : col. + 1
             sound cassette)

## ACCOMPANYING MATERIAL (8.7B11)

8:176      Instructions for use on box.

8:177      Narration on inside cover of container.
    (Filmstrip)

8:178      Notes and guide inside cover of folder.
    (Art print)

8:179      Study guide on cover of container.

8:180      Issued with 104 slides containing same content.

8:181      Issued with 116 col. slides containing same content.

8:182      Issued with filmstrip containing same content.

8:183      Issued with filmstrip under set title of the same name by:
Guidance Associates.

8:184      With background reading materials for teacher and
students.

8:185      With: Guide to the Thomas Penn papers (17 p. : ill. ;
22 cm.).

8:186      With: Teacher's study guide card.

8:187      Accompanied by a "slide viewer."

8:188      For use with Micro-Slide-Viewer.

8:189      Requires viewer.

8:190      Transparencies are animated when used with Photo
Motion Activator.

8:191      For use with Audiotronics Tutorette 800 and 800-P
recorders.

8:192      For use on a flannel board.

## SERIES (8.7B12)

8:193     "An Associated Press special report."

8:194     "A BSCS single topic inquiry film."

8:195     Series on box: Music appreciation series.

8:196     "Series ga III."

8:197     Part 2 in a series. Part 1: To dream with open eyes. 1980.

## AUDIENCE (8.7B14)

8:198     Intended audience: General.

8:199     Intended audience: Hospital personnel at all staff levels.

8:200     Intended audience: Nurses and nursing students.

8:201     Intended audience: Nurses and other allied health professionals.

8:202     Intended audience: Remedial reading classes.
          (Flash card)

8:203     Intended audience: Senior high school through college and adult and industrial trainees.

8:204     Intended audience: Sixth grade pupils.

8:205     For individual or a pair of players.
          (Perception task card)

8:206     A complete learning program designed for the Industrial Arts curriculum.

8:207     Work sheets intended to be duplicated for students.
          (Physical description area shows accompanying material: + 2 work sheets)

## OTHER FORMATS AVAILABLE (8.7B16)

8:208          Issued also as 16 mm. filmstrip in cartridge.

8:209          Issued also as 16 mm. filmstrip in cartridge and as slide set.

8:210          Issued also as 16 mm. filmstrip in cartridge and as slide set and as videorecording.

8:211          Issued also in 16 mm. cartridge and as slide set and as videorecording.

8:212          Issued also as filmstrip and as videorecording.

8:213          Issued also as filmstrip by: Human Relations Media.

8:214          Issued also as filmstrip under title: Understanding earthquakes.

8:215          Issued also as slide set and as videorecording.

8:216          Issued also as slide set by: IBIS Media.

8:217          Issued also as slide sets under individual titles by: Center for Humanities.

8:218          Issued also as videorecording.

8:219          Issued also as videorecording and as slide set.

8:220          Issued also with sound accompaniment on disc.

8:221          Issued also with sound accompaniment on disc, as 16 mm. filmstrip in cartridge, and as slide set.

## SUMMARY (8.7B17)

8:222          Summary: Adaptations of four well-known fairy tales, which personify the seasons and the holidays that highlight them.

8:223   Summary: Each card has Spanish word on one side, with its English equivalent on the reverse. Lists irregular verb forms, derivatives, compounds, etc., designed to develop a basic vocabulary of over 2,000 words.

8:224   Summary: Each chart has twenty-four pictures (6 x 8 cm.) of instruments and families of instruments.

8:225   Summary: Drawings of court, throws, and other techniques of basketball. Suitable for bulletin board use.

8:226   Summary: A foreign-language teaching filmstrip which offers information about the Soviet Union.

8:227   Summary: Photographs of artworks created by children, adolescents, and adults in art therapy sessions and in programs for mental health and retardation, drug and alcohol abuse, gerontology, and children's service.
          (Slide)

8:228   Summary: Photographs of furnishings and accessories reproduced from the original objects in the Winterthur collections.

8:229   Summary: Photographs of paintings and archival maps and objects in various museums and private collections.

8:230   Summary: Photographs of selected drawings from the Public Archives of Canada's 1972 exhibition of the same name.

8:231   Summary: Photographs of the moai (statues) on Easter Island.

8:232   Summary: Photomicrographs of plants that reproduce without flowers, such as yeasts, mushrooms, mosses, ferns, and conifers.
          (Filmslip)

8:233   Summary: The sounds that a medical student needs to hear in learning to diagnose diseases of the chest are provided.
          (Slide with sound)

8:234    Summary: This starter set of informal assessment activities is designed to assist teachers in gathering information about children's development in skill understanding and application.

8:235    Summary: The author and illustrator introduces and reads the brief texts of his picture books.
(Filmstrip with sound)

8:236    Summary: Author-illustrator Mercer Mayer introduces and reads each of his four books, from which these filmstrips are adapted. The stories are printed on the screen.

8:237    Summary: Consists of twenty-six letter patterns, flat letter pieces to assemble upper case letters.
(Perception task card)

8:238    Summary: Describes the structure and function of the coronary artery and its diseases.

8:239    Summary: Discusses why the Greek myths began, how they developed, and why they are still important in our literature, art, and even science.

8:240    Summary: Examines representative members of the reptile family.

8:241    Summary: Illustrates the entire vertebral column along with individually labeled vertebra from each of the major vertebral regions.

8:242    Summary: Teaches young children the fundamentals of the Russian language.

8:243    Summary: Presents interviews with well-known personalities and others regarding their work styles and life-styles.

8:244    Summary: Serves as a convenient medium from which both reading and speaking vocabulary may be developed.

8:245    Summary: Takes viewers to Mexico City and shows the bullfights, modern squares, buildings, streets, and monuments. Also visits the opera house and catches some of the city's old-world traditions.

# CONTENTS (8.7B18)

8:246     Biographical material on reverse side.
          (Art print)

8:247     A guide for teachers follows each sound segment.

8:248     Notes on bottom of each picture.

8:249     Notes and guide on verso of each picture.

8:250     Teacher's notes on verso of each picture.

8:251     Descriptive text on the back of each picture.

8:252     Text on verso of each print.

8:253     Text on versos of maps.
          (Title proper: Alpha map transparencies)

8:254     Includes discussion guide, lesson plan, and quiz.

8:255     Includes pictures of Lincoln and his family, political
          cartoons, and assassination conspirators and scenes.

8:256     Includes work sheet master and discussion manual,
          including script and lesson plan.

8:257     Teacher's guide includes bibliography.

8:258     Contents: Reproduction process, thermal copy --
          Reproduction process, diazo copy.

8:259     Contents: Picture map of the Roman Forum -- Roman
          Forum : view A -- Roman Forum : view B -- Circus
          Maximus -- Colosseum -- Basilica of Maxentius --
          Mausoleum of Hadrian.

8:260     Contents: Curriculum outline and guide to supplementary
          materials. Student's workbook / compiled by Dorothy M.
          Bywaters -- The junior précis practice pad. Exercises in
          précis reading / Paul W. Lehmann -- A spelling workbook /
          by Mildred B. Plunkett -- The Johnson handwriting program
          -- The snow goose / by Paul Gallico -- Phonetic word cards.
          Phonics drill cards / Anna Gillingham -- Affix and root
          cards / by Dorothy M. Bywaters.

8:261        Contents: Assessment and planning (22 min., 43 sec.) --
The infant and toddler years (21 min., 20 sec.) -- The
preschool years (17 min., 57 sec.) -- The school age years (16
min., 47 sec.).

8:262        Contents: Evolution : the 4 billion year legacy (159 fr., 20
min.) -- The origin of life (103 fr., 12 min.) -- Intelligent life
in space (148 fr., 18 min., 30 sec.).

8:263        Contents: Rapunzel (68 fr., 8 min., 55 sec.) -- The elves
and the shoemaker (40 fr., 4 min., 40 sec.) -- The selfish
giant (61 fr., 11 min.).

8:264        Contents: The wildest of all wild creatures (182 fr.) --
Partners (189 fr.) -- The mystery horse (193 fr.).

8:265        Contents: 1. The ear -- 2. Cells of the blood -- 3. The
animal cell -- 4. Skin -- 5. The eye (2 charts).

8:266        Contents: A. Computing your expenses -- B. Making a
profit -- C. Banking and taxes -- D. Credit -- [E.] Personnel
-- [F.] Bookkeeping.

8:267        Contents: A. Basic theory of heat (74 fr.) -- B. Conversion
of heat into useful work (88 fr.) -- C. Effects of heat (78 fr.)
-- D. Heat as radiant energy (68 fr.).

8:268        Contents: ga 45-4. The genesis of lithography in America
-- ga 46-4. Genre in American lithography -- ga 47-4. The
human figure and Labor and industry.

8:269        Contents: lesson 1. Geography (81 fr., 9 min., 4 sec.) --
lesson 2. History (90 fr., 15 min., 9 sec.) -- lesson 3.
Industry (91 fr., 14 min., 32 sec.).

8:270        Contents: module 1. Introduction to interpretation of the
12 lead ECG (65 fr., 17 min., 47 sec.) -- module 2. Complex
arrhythmias (76 fr., 26 min., 38 sec.) -- module 3. Deter-
mination of electrical axis (66 fr., 20 min., 38 sec.).

8:271        Contents: program 1. Faces of depression (90 fr., 19 min.)
-- program 2. Signs & disguises of depression (97 fr., 20
min.) -- program 3. Roots of depression (114 fr., 27 min.).

8:272        Contents: pt. 1. Facts about drinking -- pt 2. Facts about
coping.

8:273    Contents: pt. 1. The penicillins, clindamycin, and chloramphenicol (78 slides) -- pt. 2. The tetracyclines, rifampin, and the aminoglycosides (62 slides).

8:274    Contents: pt. 1, module 1. Introduction to coma (28 min.) -- pt. 1, module 2. General assessment of the comatose patient (22 min., 57 sec.) -- pt. 1, module 3. Physical assessment of the comatose patient (26 min., 39 sec.) -- pt. 1, modules 4-5. Intracranial causes of coma, pts. A-B (47 min., 7 sec.) -- pt. 2, module 1. Metabolic coma, an overview (23 min., 2 sec.) -- pt. 2, modules 2-3. Endogenous causes of metabolic coma, pts. A-B (61 min., 49 sec.) -- pt. 2, module 4. Exogenous causes of metabolic coma (31 min., 12 sec.).

8:275    Contents: section 1. Anatomy and embryology -- section 2. Physiology -- section 3. Radiology -- section 4. Diseases and pathology.

8:276    Contents: set 1. Brazil (12 min.) Argentina (13 min.) Chile (11 min.) Paraguay and Uruguay (12 min.) Guyana, Surinam, and French Guinea [i.e. Guiana] (16 min.) -- set 2. Peru (13 min.) Ecuador (11 min.) Venezuela (13 min.) Colombia (13 min.) Bolivia (10 min.).

8:277    Contents: StoryStrip 1. First glimpse of the subconscious -- StoryStrip 2. Psychoanalysis -- StoryStrip 3. Oedipus complex.

8:278    Contents: unit 1. Setup & safety, pts. 1-2 (31 fr., 38 fr.) Spot tacks & beads (32 fr.) -- unit 2. Butt weld with filler rod (30 fr.) Flange edge weld (31 fr.) Corner weld (30 fr.) -- unit 3. Lap weld (29 fr.) Tee weld (32 fr.).

## NUMBERS (8.7B19)

8:279    Identifying mark: GLS/3/13.

8:280    Microslide set 211.
             (Filmstrip)

8:281    Order no.: 39201GR.

8:282    Print no. 4324.

8:283        "Program no. 171"-- Script.

8:284        Publisher no. 86788.


## COPY BEING DESCRIBED AND LIBRARY'S HOLDINGS (8.7B20)

8:285        Library's copy autographed.

8:286        Fifteenth of 100 prints, signed by artist in pencil.

8:287        Library's copy imperfect: Brittle, with upper right-hand corner lacking.

8:288        Some of the photographs are faded and slightly stained.

8:289        Library's copy lacks script.

8:290        Library's set lacks pt. 1 (slides 1-12).


## NOTES RELATING TO ORIGINAL (8.7B22)

8:291        Reproduction of: Chevaux de course. 1883. 1 art original : pastel, col. ; 54 x 63 cm. In National Museum of Art, Ottawa.

8:292        Reproduction of detail of painting on silk of Chinese Sung dynasty, 960-1280.

8:293        Reproduction of illuminated manuscript of Persian Turkman period, ca. 1480.

8:294        Reproduction of mosaic (Byzantine school) 6th century.

8:295        Reproduction of painted limestone stela, 2134-1001 B.C.

8:296        Reproduction of the artist's fresco painting, ca. 1290-1299.

8:297        Reproduction of the artist's lithograph.

8:298      Reproduction of the artist's painting in egg tempera.

8:299      Reproduction of the artist's painting in oil; youthful work
of artist, date uncertain.

8:300      Reproduction of the artist's photography, 1931.

8:301      Reproduction of the artist's stone sculpture, 1943.

8:302      Reproduction of a painting, in the National Gallery,
Washington, D.C., by a 19th and early 20th century
American artist.

8:303      Reproduction of a painting, in the Tate Gallery, London,
by a 15th century Florentine artist.

8:304      Original in cave at Lascaux, France.

8:305      Original in the Church of St. Matthew, Northampton,
England.

8:306      Original in the Metropolitan Museum of Art, New York
City.

8:307      Original in collection of Mrs. Andrew Wyeth.

8:308      Original in private collection, New York.

8:309      Original painted in 1890.

8:310      Museum designed, 1943-1946; built, 1956-1959.
(Art reproduction depicting Solomon R. Guggenheim
Museum)

# 9

# Machine-Readable Data Files

## NATURE AND SCOPE (9.7B1)

9:1        Tutorial.

9:2        Adventure game.

9:3        War simulation game for 1-6 players.

9:4        Simulation model of a nuclear power plant accident structured after the Three Mile Island incident.

9:5        Computer transcription of Roman poet Virgil.

9:6        Mail list package.

9:7        Bookkeeping package for a small business.

9:8        A complete general statistics package with database management.

9:9        Demonstration version of dBASE II which is limited to 15 records in a database file.

9:10       Covers international literature on water.

9:11       Records relate to technical reports written in the United States

## LANGUAGE, ETC. (9.7B2)

9:12        Written in ALC and COBOL.

9:13        Written in Applesoft, a BASIC derivative.

9:14        Programming language: PL/M Assembly.

9:15        FIELDATA character set.

9:16        Contains Hebrew and Arabic characters.

9:17        Transcribed from Old Church Slavonic in the medieval
            manuscript tradition.

9:18        Language of text: Spanish.

9:19        Multiple languages, more than 50.
               (Database)

## SOURCE OF TITLE PROPER (9.7B3)

9:20        Title from cassette label.

9:21        Title from codebook.

9:22        Title from container.

9:23        Title from directory.

9:24        Title from disk label.

9:25        Title from documentation.

9:26        Title from manual.

9:27        Title from printed source.

9:28        Title from report.

9:29        Title from tape layout.

9:30        Title from technical paper.

9:31        Title from user's guide.

9:32    Title from brochure provided by producer.

9:33    Title from data sheet supplied by programmer.

9:34    Title from: Harfax technical memorandum HD-10.

9:35    Title from: Geological reference file / prepared by American Geological Institute.

9:36    Title from: A Guide to the databases of the Schuylkill Valley Consortium. 2nd ed. p. 92.

9:37    Title supplied by cataloger.

9:38    Title supplied from correspondence with creator of file.

## VARIATION IN TITLE (9.7B4)

9:39    Title in manual: The Wizard & the princess.
        (Title proper: The Wizard and the princess)

9:40    Title in narrative notes: COXIST.

9:41    Title on cartridge and container: Pinochle and bridge.
        (Title proper: Bridge and pinochle)

9:42    Title on disk and manual: Star gazer's guide.
        (Title proper: Astronomy)

9:43    Titles on disk label: DOS 3.3 system master for II, II +, and IIe and DOS 3.3 sample programs for II, II +, and IIe.

9:44    Titles on manual: Electric bread board, Electronic bread-board.

9:45    Also known as: D-REF.

9:46    Also known as: BamBam.

9:47    Also known as: 1975 Wilderness area user's simulation model.

9:48    Also known as: WDROP, and WaterDROP.

## PARALLEL TITLES AND OTHER TITLE INFORMATION (9.7B5)

9:49    Title on producer's catalog: Bibliografia nazionale italiana.

9:50    Subtitle: A scheduling and predicting tool for manufacturing/industrial control/project management.

9:51    AGRICOLA is short for AGRICultural OnLine Access.

## STATEMENTS OF RESPONSIBILITY (9.7B6)

9:52    Credits: Game design, Steve Blake and Robert Hall ; program, Steve Blake.

9:53    Additional contributors to program: Charles Balz and Richard Stanwood.

9:54    Associated programmers: Gerald Rounds, Charles Kuljian, and Vincent Kovalic.

9:55    Designed by Edward Zeidman.

9:56    Conceived and designed by Alan Miller.

9:57    Developed by Speicher Systems, with design input by Clifford Jones ; Dr. Jennifer Alison developed the string functions and modified the character manipulation capabilities.

9:58    Written by Richard Ewing and John Unger Zussman ; program by Creative Computer Applications.

9:59    Compiled in collaboration with Canada Centre for Mineral and Energy Technology.

9:60    Sponsored by the National Science Foundation in conjunction with the Artificial Intelligence Laboratory and the Division for Study and Research in Education, M.I.T.

9:61    Course developed by Gayle J. Yaverbaum ; text by Melvin H. Wolf.

9:62      "The 40 Hi-Res portraits were created by artist Saul Bernstein"--P. 3 of Teacher's guide.

9:63      Simulation reprogrammed in COBOL by Frank Corcoran.

9:64      Data collected in collaboration with Robert W. Surridge, Pennsylvania State Data Center, Middletown.

## EDITION AND HISTORY (9.7B7)

9:65      First ed. called: BAM.
          (Game; title proper: Beneath Apple Manor)

9:66      1969 ed. corr. 1980 using update program received 1974.

9:67      Updated by semiannual meeting of finance ministers.
          (Title proper: Price setting tables)

9:68      Updated triennially.

9:69      Data collected July 1980-Dec. 1982, Jan. 1983.

9:70      Oral history interviews from 1965-1972.

9:71      Time period: 1861-1945.
          (Title proper: The effects of war on the combat soldier)

9:72      Machine transcription originally produced by Computer Systems Research, 1982.

9:73      Transcribed from: Travelling sketches / Anthony Trollope. London : Chapman and Hall, 1866.

9:74      Contains a subsample of cases surveyed in the 1969 health care facilities study.
          (Title proper: 1982 hospitals/nursing homes study)

9:75      Based on the BBC-TV series of the same name.
          (Game)

9:76      Based on: Quo vadis : a narrative of the time of Nero / by Henryk Sienkiewicz. Boston : Little, Brown, 1925.

9:77        Teaching module taken from data file entitled: Central
            American elections survey / conducted by Gregory
            Cunningham.

9:78        Source of data: Trade competition : worldwide markets /
            Center for Strategic and International Studies. 1981.

9:79        Related reference: World trends in science education /
            editor, Charles P. McFadden. Halifax, N.S. : Atlantic
            Institute of Education, 1980.

9:80        Companion program to: Stock tracker.


## PROGRAM (9.7B8)

9:81        Program will compile on PASCAL compiler.

9:82        FORTRAN V, level E.

9:83        Reading DMT, version 1, release 1, level 1.

9:84        SPSS, version H, release 9.1.

9:85        UNAMAP, version 4.

9:86        Reference manual for version 1.3, c1982.

9:87        Vol. 3 is version 2.6.


## PUBLICATION, PRODUCTION, DISTRIBUTION, ETC. (9.7B9)

9:88        Published in Canada for the Canadian Library Association
            by Canadian European Systems.

9:89        Distributed in the U.K. by: London : Caxton Software.

9:90        SEAST is solely distributed and supported by the bureau.

9:91        Thesaurus distributed solely by: Edmonton, Alta. : Boreal Institute for Northern Studies.

9:92        Producer: ESCCOMATE.

9:93        Producer and copyright: Hartley Data Systems.

9:94        Copyright by California Energy Commission.

9:95        Software copyright: Richard T. Scott.

9:96        Program contents, c1983; packaging, c1984.


# FILE DESCRIPTION AND PHYSICAL DESCRIPTION
## (9.7B10)

9:97        Contains ca. 60 million words.

9:98        File size varies, ca. 32,000 logical records per file.

9:99        Size of file not verified, ca. 500,000 definitions.

9:100       File size not verified, received as 35 reels of tape. Printed version contains 50,000 citations and 128,000 keywords.

9:101       File size unknown.

9:102       Undetermined number of program statements, documentation reads: SCAM requires ca. 15,000 words of storage for program statements.

9:103       Number of program statements not ascertained, 64K of core space required.

9:104       One disk contains course offerings, one the names and addresses.

9:105       30 plastic bank cards with magnetic strip on back.

9:106       Number of variables: 632.

9:107       Unit of analysis: Editors of refereed journals.

## ACCOMPANYING MATERIAL (9.7B11)

9:108    Codebook also issued as: Demographics survey of the
Soviet Union applications manual.
(Title proper: Demographics survey of the Soviet Union)

9:109    Documentation: AABB technical manual. 8th ed.
Washington, D.C. : American Association of Blood Banks,
1981.

9:110    Manual entitled: Communicating with Electronic
messenger / John P. Schucker. Philadelphia : Drexel University, 1984.

9:111    Manual written by Javed Aslam and Sonoma Softworks.

9:112    Reference card and user's guide by Thomas Malinowski.

9:113    Codebook produced by the Artificial Intelligence
Laboratory, M.I.T.

9:114    Documentation stamped: Preliminary.

9:115    Codebook numbered: ISBN 0-85296-266-5.

9:116    Manual includes index.


## SERIES (9.7B12)

9:117    "Video casino."

9:118    "An interactive learning system."

9:119    "Microcomputer software for business."

9:120    Originally issued in the series: Superwheels & thrill sports.


## AUDIENCE AND RESTRICTIONS ON ACCESS (9.7B14)

9:121    Intended audience: Stock traders, investors, advisors, and
brokers.

9:122     Intended audience: Water resources engineers; users are required to understand structure of data and file content to be run in conjunction with WATSIM.

9:123     Program designed for novices and professionals alike who have an interest in creating hobby and entertainment software.

9:124     Users require no knowledge of computer programming, but the program is patterned to those with expertise in human factors engineering and/or industrial design.

9:125     For 1-4 players.

9:126     For 2-5 players or teams.

9:127     Two board games for 2-5 players, for high school and college business administration courses.

9:128     Contains 12 games for 1 or 2 players.

9:129     For ages 6-8.

9:130     File copyrighted, restricted to researchers in the field.

9:131     Available only to students, faculty, and staff of Slippery Rock University.

9:132     Available only to high energy laboratories in collaboration with DESY.

9:133     Available for lease only.

9:134     Access by subscription only.

9:135     May be duplicated, original not to be removed from the library.

9:136     Special licensing allows student multiple copies.


## MODE OF USE (9.7B15)

9:137     Mode of use: IBM Personal Computer.

9:138    Mode of use: Batch, programmer operated.

9:139    Mode of use: Batch (disk storage); on-line (teletype terminal).

9:140    Mode of use: Batch, end-user or programmer operated; IBM 360/40 computer, DOS 26.3, POWER II level; 96K bytes storage; printer plotter.

9:141    Mode of use: On-line interactive end-user operated; operative computer: Honeywell H-2040A, OS-2000; requires raster scan display.

9:142    System requirements: 64K; APDOS; N-BASIC.

9:143    System requirements: 56K RAM; 2 160K disk drives; Microsoft BASIC-80; 24 x 80 video with cursor addressing; 132 column printer.

9:144    System requirements: Commodore VIC-20.

9:145    System requirements: Apple II/III + , 48K; DOS 3.3; graphics printer.

9:146    System requirements: Atari 800; television or monitor, paddle controllers.

9:147    One side of disk for IBM PCjr, other side for Apple IIc.

9:148    Requires PKSO interface board.

9:149    A 16-sector scratch file disk must be used when saving data on disk files.

9:150    Compatible with TRS-80 Model II.

9:151    "Also runs on Commodore 64."

9:152    Also runs on: Apple II or II + ; 48K DOS 3.3 or 3.2.1.

9:153    Dedicated terminal system: Available only through The SOURCE.

9:154    Technical details: Data prepared using the Unix NROFF/TROFF formatter.

9:155 Disk characteristics: Floppy, dual sided, double density, hard sectored.

9:156 Optional accessories: Game paddles, light pen, and/or printer.

9:157 Joystick controller optional.

## OTHER FORMATS (9.7B16)

9:158 Available in disk or cassette.

9:159 Also available in microfiche and hard copy print.

9:160 Available on cassette for TRS-80, on disk for Apple IIe.

## SUMMARY (9.7B17)

9:161 Summary: Program designed to develop understanding of mathematical principles using on-screen graphics to represent relationships between abstract symbols and amounts they represent.

9:162 Summary: Package develops ancillary data series used in analysis and forecasting techniques. Future trends can be predicted using current time series relationships.

9:163 Summary: Inventories parts in stock, calculates the number of finished goods to be made with the parts, and generates invoices.

9:164 Summary: Studies interactions between flowering plants, enabling a student to plan an investigation and carry it out without actual elapsed-time growth experiments. Treatments include crowding above and below ground and growth measurements.

9:165 Summary: A group of five programs on science topics for grade levels 6-9 including: FISH, a simulation of blood circulation in a two-chambered heart; MINERALS, an identification guide to thirty minerals; and QUAKES, a tutorial on locating the epicenter of an earthquake.

9:166    Summary: An orientation program to the University libraries including introduction to the card catalog, LC classification, subject search, main and branch library locations, reference and circulation services, and serials holdings.

9:167    Summary: A multi-level maze game; player must rescue four imprisoned humans locked in boxes on each maze level.

9:168    Summary: Sixty-six versions of a video game for one or two players using joystick controls; includes some versions for young children.

## CONTENTS (9.7B18)

9:169    Contains information on 18 campuses only.

9:170    Includes 7 practice programs: 3 on notation, 2 on rhythm, and 2 on pitch.

9:171    Federal records include housing and population data; state records include population data only.

9:172    Contents: Appleopoly -- Mah jong -- Microgammon.

9:173    Contents: Spy in the sky (5 games) -- Bug in the rug (6 games).

9:174    Contents: Patient billing -- Insurance claim processing -- Patient history -- Patient recall.
        (Menu)

9:175    Contents: Program 1: Add or terminate employee. Enter payroll information. Print checks -- Program 2: Print quarterly reports. Print W-2 forms. Year-end master file cleanup -- Compute -- Address.
        (Includes menu)

9:176    Contents: 1. Spanish (grades 3-6) -- 2. French (grades 3-6) -- 3. French (grades 7-9) -- 4. Latin (grades 9-12).

9:177 Contents: file 1. Physicians (1,150 logical records) -- file 2. Librarians (974 logical records) -- file 3. Attorneys (1,224 logical records).

## NUMBERS BORNE BY THE ITEM (9.7B19)

9:178 "CX 2617."

9:179 "AG-003."

9:180 DVS no.: 416-1966.

9:181 Initial study number: PSL248; final study number: PSL262.

## COPY BEING DESCRIBED AND LIBRARY'S HOLDINGS (9.7B20)

9:182 Library's copy of user's manual signed by the programmer.

9:183 For library's holdings consult Reference Desk.

9:184 Consult Printed catalog of computer programs at PSU for library's holdings.

9:185 Library's holdings consist of records for Capitol Campus only.

# 10

# Three-Dimensional Artefacts and Realia

## NATURE OF THE ITEM (10.7B1)

10:1        Authorized facsimile.

10:2        Replica of the original.

10:3        Replica of a bust of Samuel Langhorne Clemens, signed
Rom Tomson 70.

10:4        Funerary statuette.

10:5        Sculpted figure in mummy wrappings, bearing a prayer in
Egyptian hieroglyphic characters.

10:6        Caps of indeterminate age and origin, probably Near
Eastern or Mediterranean. Three different designs are
represented including an intricate colored knit.
    (Title proper: Skull caps)

10:7        Samples of seashells and articles made from seashells.

10:8        Group of barnyard animals.
    (Title proper: Play animals)

10:9        Push-button toy with 11 keys, made in England.

10:10        Bingo-type game.

10:11        French word-formation game.

10:12        Mathematical skills game.

10:13        Simulation game of the Yalta Conference.

10:14        Antique 19th century slide.
             (Microscope slide)

10:15        Features composition of mounted butterfly scales and
             diatoms.
             (Microscope slide)

10:16        Sectionalized representation.

10:17        Simplified cross sections.

10:18        Cross section of the skin.

10:19        Four-color cross section of adult heart.

10:20        Partially cross-sectional, showing both the internal and ex-
             ternal structures of the vertebral column.

10:21        Sagittal section of a permanent lower first molar.

10:22        Section of brain.
             (Title proper: Anatomy of the human cerebrum)

10:23        Bones of the hand and arm.

10:24        Eye set in skull orbit.

10:25        Shows internal structures of cranial vault; on base.

10:26        Shows 4 stages of tooth development.

10:27        Adult, life-size.


## SOURCE OF TITLE PROPER (10.7B3)

10:28        Box cover title.

10:29        Title from box.

10:30        Title from container.

10:31        Title from contents page laid in.

10:32        Title from label on container.

10:33        Title from stock list.

10:34        Title from supplier's catalog.

10:35        Title supplied by cataloger.

10:36        Title and imprint from box.


## VARIATIONS IN TITLE (10.7B4)

10:37        Caption title: Cambarus, crayfish.

10:38        Title on container: Ear model (hear).

10:39        Title on container: Foreign edition Scrabble.

10:40        Publisher's catalog title: Tooth development.

10:41        Title in Nystrom's catalog: Human development models.

10:42        Formerly published as: Bulge.
             (Game)

10:43        Also made in Sri Lanka and distributed by Childcraft with
             the title: People shapes.

10:44        Frequently referred to as the Death mask of Agamemnon,
             son of Atreus, King of Mycenae.


## PARALLEL TITLES AND OTHER TITLE
## INFORMATION (10.7B5)

10:45        Parallel title on case: Spinal column.

10:46          Subtitle on container: A game to sharpen the memory.


## STATEMENTS OF RESPONSIBILITY (10.7B6)

10:47          Museum Extension Project of the W.P.A.

10:48          Joint effort of S.E.S. and the Unitarian Universalist Association.

10:49          Much of the research in developing the WFF games was done on ALL Project (Accelerated Learning of Logic) at Yale Law School.

10:50          "Developed by Pose Lamb of A[ccelerated] L[earning] of L[ogic]."

10:51          "Developed by Abt Associates under the editorial supervision of Paul McKee and M. Lucile Harrison."

10:52          Inventor: Colin L. Proudman.
                  (Statement of responsibility does not appear on chief source of information)

10:53          Knitted by: Erica Wilson.
                  (Statement of responsibility does not appear on chief source of information)

10:54          Prepared for display by the library.
                  (Diorama)

10:55          Guide by Jack Megenity.

10:56          Lesson plan by Alvin Quinn.

10:57          Lesson plan author: Arnold R. Chalfant.

10:58          Teacher's manual authors: Illa Podendorf, Alice Moses.

10:59          Construction manual: Marionette assembly / by Mary H. Bucher.

## EDITION AND HISTORY (10.7B7)

10:60    Based on scenes from the novel/movie by Samuel Fuller.
(Game)

10:61    Based on the Coronet study print series: Discovering
vertebrates.
(Game)

10:62    Correlated with the kit: Ginn oral language development
(GOLD).
(Game)

10:63    The original, carved of Ohio pipestone in the form of a
dwarf in head dress, ear ornaments, and loin covering, was
used as a tobacco pipe.

10:64    Replica of a sculpture in black basalt carved in Egypt during the Middle Kingdom.

10:65    Replica of the original wood figure of the Ancon or
Chavin culture of ancient Peru, 1200-400 B.C. Original is in
the Art Institute of Chicago.

10:66    Replica of a carved stone figure typical of southern Vera
Cruz, probably an idol. The marble original is in the
Smithsonian Institution, Washington, D.C.

10:67    Replica of the bust modeled from life in Paris in 1786
during Jefferson's term as ambassador to France.

10:68    Authorized facsim. in patined caststone of a bust modeled
after the Lincoln Memorial statue, Washington, D.C.

10:69    Replica of the Adena pipe, an example of prehistoric
American Indian art, discovered in Chillicothe, Ohio, in
1901. Adena Indians lived in Ohio between 1000 B.C. and
700 A.D., and the pipe dates from late in that period.

10:70    Reproduced from the original set of 19--, modeled after
N.C. Wyeth illustrations.

10:71    Recast in metal from the original bronze Canaanite idol of
about 1000 B.C. Original is in the Walters Art Gallery,
Baltimore, Md.

10:72          Replica of funeral mask found by the Heinrich
               Schliemann excavation of the royal graves at Mycenae, 1876.
               (Model)

10:73          Gathered in Okefenokee swamp, December 1983.

## PUBLICATION, DISTRIBUTION, ETC. (10.7B9)

10:74          Made in West Germany.

10:75          Locally produced; title supplied by cataloger.

10:76          Place and date of manufacture derived from hallmark on
               bottom.

10:77          Manufacturer inferred from foundry mark on blade.

10:78          Guidebook, c1955; gameboard, c1954.

## PHYSICAL DESCRIPTION (10.7B10)

10:79          Embedded in paraffin.
               (Microscope slide)

10:80          Embedded in plastic, may be viewed from 4 sides.

10:81          Natural bone, hinged.

10:82          Smear.
               (Microscope slide)

10:83          Methylene blue stain shows compound eye of grass
               shrimp.
               (Microscope slide)

10:84          Surface treated for marking with erasable ink.

10:85          Designed to be used with permanent or temporary mark-
               ing pens.

10:86        Operated by 2 D-cell alkaline batteries.

10:87        Portable, with cutout handle, contoured to fit a child's lap.

10:88        Scale 1:3.

10:89        Scale model dissected into 3 sections.

10:90        Actual size.
                 (Mock-up)

10:91        Life-size.

10:92        Slightly enlarged. This model consists of 5 pieces which can be disassembled for demonstration purposes. Median section shows thyroid gland and muscles. Tongue and lower jaw are removable.

10:93        Consists of cross-sectional view of the skin, 70 times life-size.

10:94        Skull has calvaria cut and jaw is springheld. Skeleton is painted on one side to show muscle origins in red and insertions in blue.

10:95        Consists of the life-size head and torso of a 12-year-old boy, with a clear plastic shell representing the muscle structure.

10:96        Consists of a large tooth which opens to reveal a cross section of the internal tooth structure, attached stand resembles the jaw bone.

10:97        Pattern: Double wedding ring.

10:98        Red heart on chest; signed O'Neill.
                 (Kewpie doll)

10:99        Red cap of cotton and wool with black tassel and cotton liner. Of indeterminate age, the remains of label show origin as Egypt, probably Cairo.
                 (Title proper: Fez)

10:100       Handle is gold-plated.
                 (Shaving brush)

10:101      Parts of the eye are numbered.

10:102      Pictures on posters and study guide identical.

10:103      Backs of cards contain various color scenes of Florence, Venice, and Rome.
            (Playing cards)

10:104      Bones disconnected, with hinged wire rack for assembly.

10:105      Includes removable parts and is mounted on rollaway stand (41 x 41 x 178 cm.).

10:106      Issued in a case and housed in container (9 x 19 x 8 cm.).

10:107      Wood and glass box (32 x 25 x 25 cm.) contains model of 2 Indians building a wigwam.

10:108      Scene of an Indian family in front of a tepee, in wood and glass box (32 x 25 x 25 cm.).

10:109      Puzzle pieces fit within frame on cardboard base.

10:110      Container forms the playing boards.

10:111      Includes 2 large demonstration boards (72 x 98 cm.) with mounting legs.

10:112      Contains original candy.

10:113      Includes parts for construction and directions for use.

10:114      Consists of half crown, florin, shilling, and sixpence.

10:115      Includes one-dollar-bill stamp, five-dollar-bill stamp, and ten-dollar-bill stamp.
            (Rubber stamps)

10:116      Includes hand ax, horse head engraving, broad blade, flint blade, harpoon, salamander carving, and sculpture of mammoth.

10:117      Includes runic stone, runic coin, military diploma, Rosetta stone, Greek inscription, and seal of King Darius.

10:118      Each game includes sheets of detachable game cards and duplicator masters.

10:119        Contains 12 logic cubes, 2 playing mats, and 1 timer.

10:120        Contains 1 barn (red, white, blue, and yellow ;
              21 x 28 x 21 cm.) with 4 sets of doors that open and close.

10:121        Contains 1 game board, 6 clue lists, 1 rule book, 1 discus-
              sion sheet, 1 logic sheet, 24 pawns, and 4 sets of guide cards.

10:122        Contains 1 playing board, 100 wooden letter tiles, 4
              wooden tile racks, and 1 rule book.

10:123        Contains 1 teacher's manual, 1 game board, 1 packet of
              play money, 1 deck of 16 chance cards, 3 pollution in-
              dicators, 48 program cards, and 24 program sheets.

10:124        Contains 1 career score wheel, 4 pawns, 1 pair of dice, 24
              opportunity cards, 5 combination score forms, and 1 book
              of rules for playing.

10:125        Contains bottle of developer fluid; 1 each of magnetic
              tape, disk, and core plane; various output samples (punched
              cards, paper tape, magnetic ink characters, microfiche,
              teletype, line printer, plotter); 3 circuit boards (vacuum,
              transistor, integrated); manufacturers' booklets and
              brochures; other booklets; and activity guide in container (47
              x 38 x 10 cm.).

## ACCOMPANYING MATERIAL (10.7B11)

10:126        Directions for use on container.

10:127        Directions in cover of box.

10:128        Description sheet mounted on case.
                 (Microscope slide)

10:129        Game rules printed on envelope.

10:130        Instructions inside container lid.

10:131        Instructions on box lid.

10:132        Instructions printed on back of game board.

10:133      List of chemical compounds and experiments on inside of container lid.

10:134      Rules inside container lid.

10:135      Teacher's notes mounted in container lid.

10:136      With directions for assembly.

10:137      With instructions for operation.

10:138      With lesson plan: Script and its development / by Donald E. Stephan (6 p. on 1 accordion folded leaf : ill., map ; 28 cm.).

10:139      "Rules of the game": [2] p. accompany cards.

## AUDIENCE (10.7B14)

10:140      Intended audience: Grade 2.

10:141      Intended audience: Grades 5-6.

10:142      Intended audience: Primary grades.

10:143      Intended audience: Upper level elementary and junior high grades.

10:144      Intended audience: Secondary school students.

10:145      Intended audience: Supervisors and middle managers.

10:146      For ages 6 to 18 months.

10:147      For teens and adults.

10:148      For ages 8 to adult, 2 to 10 players.

10:149      For children 4 to 6 years old.

10:150      Not for children to play with.

10:151      Kit 1 for primary grades or remedial practice; kit 2 reinforces intermediate skills and reviews earlier skills.

10:152        For board display and group play.

10:153        For 2 players.

10:154        Designed for easy use by the handicapped.
              (Game)


# SUMMARY (10.7B17)

10:155        Summary: "Designed by an educator to create an interest
              in letter groupings, spelling, reading, and increasing
              vocabulary. Will develop auditory and visual discrimination
              abilities . . . "--Publisher's catalog.

10:156        Summary: Designed to develop in children concepts of
              color, dimension, shape, and balance. Stackable drums can
              also be used to teach manual dexterity.

10:157        Summary: Designed to give students hands-on experience
              with computer-related items.

10:158        Summary: For use in a variety of activities involving
              money, including counting and making change.

10:159        Summary: Using the general format of checkers, students
              reinforce math concepts and skills.

10:160        Summary: "The object of the game is to become the
              wealthiest player through buying, renting and selling
              property"--Instruction booklet.

10:161        Summary: Contains models of early forms of writing on
              stone.

10:162        Summary: Depicts days of the Aztec calendar.

10:163        Summary: Teaches the chant and actions of the ancient
              game of Ti Rakau.

10:164        Summary: Tells the present and foretells the future accord-
              ing to an ancient Chinese oracle.

10:165        Summary: After an adult has installed a picture panel on
              the pressure-sensitive keyboard, the child follows instructions

from the electronic "voice" by pressing appropriate areas of the panel. The voice recognizes correct responses and encourages another choice in the event of an incorrect response. Designed to assist in the language/vocabulary development of preschool children. Basic activities deal with colors, shapes, and objects.

10:166     Summary: A word game for two to four players. The play consists of forming interlocking words, cross-word fashion, on the playing board.

10:167     Summary: A simulation designed to interest students in the nomination, campaign, and election processes related to seeking the office of President of the United States.

10:168     Summary: A three-dimensional representation of the sun and nine planets to provide an understanding of sizes, distances, colors, and speeds at which the planets travel around the sun.

10:169     Summary: Four patterns, fit onto a pegged sorting board to establish shape discrimination concepts.

10:170     Summary: Cast figures representing statuary found in Aesclepion at Bergama, Turkey. They represent Asclepius, Greek god of medicine or health; Telesphorus, the boy genius of healing; and Asclepius's daughters, Hygieia, the goddess of health, and Panacea.

10:171     Summary: Puppets include one toddler, two children, and two adults; for enacting family interpersonal relationships.

10:172     Summary: Weights range from one kilogram to one gram, designed to demonstrate comparison of mass size and mass measurement.

10:173     Summary: Manila capital letters for stenciling, sign making, etc.

10:174     Summary: Cardboard wheels give independent practice in all four arithmetic processes.

10:175     Summary: Hardwood drilled cylinder block and blunt wooden needle dowel with four feet of cotton cord for demonstrating threading to three- to six-year-old children.

10:176     Summary: Basic column on flexible metal rod to demonstrate complete rotation, nerve impingement, lordosis, scoliosis, and kyphosis. Femoral and sciatic nerves are added in green vinyl plastic.

10:177     Summary: Demonstrates the structures and functions related to hearing and balance; ear drum, semicircular canals, and cochlea are removable.

10:178     Summary: Separate models show a dissection of the kidney (3x), an enlarged detail of the nephron (120x), and an entire glomerulus (700x).

10:179     Summary: Working model uses a colored liquid and air pressure to demonstrate blood circulation to the lungs, head, trunk, legs, and heart.

## CONTENTS (10.7B18)

10:180     Lesson plan includes bibliography.

10:181     Contents: Vowels-Up (Multiple spellings of sounds) -- Sylla-Build (Syllables) -- Lett-a-Score (Visual letter sequence).

10:182     Contents: model 1. Grades K-6 -- model 2. Grades 5-10.

10:183     Contents: [game 1] Masquerade party -- [game 2] People and places -- [game 3] When I grow up -- [game 4] People working together.

10:184     Contents: game S. Spelling ie-ei words -- game T. Possessives -- game U. Contractions -- game V. Commas.

## NUMBERS (10.7B19)

10:185     Registered design no.: 263851.

10:186     Serial no.: BS-1.

10:187     Patent no.: 222,401.

## COPY BEING DESCRIBED AND LIBRARY'S
## HOLDINGS (10.7B20)

10:188        Recipient's name engraved on base.

10:189        Library's set imperfect: 1 black rook missing.
    (Chess set)

10:190        Glass stopper damaged: Top half missing.
    (Perfume bottle)

10:191        Leather strap attached to iron ring, cracked but intact;
clapper missing.

10:192        Lacks original wooden chest.

10:193        Library has LF703, LF705, LF709.

10:194        Donated by the class of 1960.

# 11

# Microforms

## PREVIOUSLY PUBLISHED ITEMS

*Examples 11:1-13, in accord with LC policy, relate to microreproductions of previously published printed materials; the other examples in this chapter relate generally to original edition microforms but may apply, in some cases, to microreproductions that require further descriptive information. For LC's interpretation on cataloging macro- and micro-reproductions, see Cataloging Service Bulletin, no. 14, fall 1981, p. 56-58.*

11:1    Aperture card. Endicott, N.Y. : International Business Machines, 1964. 15 aperture cards ; 9 x 19 cm.

11:2    Microfiche. [Springfield, Va.? : National Technical Information Service?], 1978. 2 microfiches : negative ; 11 x 15 cm.

11:3    Microfiche. Ann Arbor, Mich. : University Microfilms International, 1982. 1 microfiche ; 11 x 15 cm. (Adelaide Nutting historical nursing collection ; AN 1109).

11:4    Microfiche. Glen Rock, N.J. : Microfilming Corp. of America, 1975. 6 microfiches ; 11 x 15 cm. (The Gerritsen collection of women's history ; P63).

11:5    Microfiche. Wiesbaden, D.F.R. : Harrassowitz Microfiche Service, [1977]. 51 microfiches ; 11 x 15 cm. (Micro bibliotheca asiatica).

11:6    Microfiche. Cambridge, Eng. : Chadwyck-Healey, Teaneck, N.J. : Somerset House, 1977.        microfiches ; 10 x 15 cm. (European official statistical serials on microfiche).
        (Serial)

11:7    Microfilm. Westport, Conn. : Greenwood Press, Microform Dept., [1976]. 1 microfilm reel ; 5 in., 35 mm.

11:8    Microfilm. New Haven, Conn. : Research Publications, 1975. 1 microfilm cartridge ; 35 mm. (History of women periodicals).

11:9    Microfilm. Woodbridge, Conn. : Research Publications, 1972. 2 microfilm reels (with Essais, reel 1) ; 35 mm.

11:10   Microfilm. Bloomington, Ind. : MCPL, 1982.         microfilm reels ; 16 mm. High reduction.
        (Serial)

11:11   Microfilm. Washington, D.C. : University Publications of America, 1978-            microfilm reels. 35 mm.
        (Serial)

11:12   Microfilm. Ann Arbor, Mich. : University Microfilms, 1974-            microfilm reels ; 35 mm. (Current periodical series ; no. 7845).
        (Serial)

11:13   Microopaque. New York : Readex Microprint, 1970. 2 microopaques ; 23 x 15 cm. (Landmarks of science).


# NATURE, SCOPE, OR ARTISTIC OR OTHER FORM OF AN ITEM (11.7B1)

11:14   Newspapers.

11:15   "Selections of the publications of the Library of Congress, Legislative Reference Service [i.e. Congressional Research Service]."

11:16        Collection of articles from the Library of American civilization.

## SOURCE OF TITLE PROPER (11.7B3)

11:17        Title from boxes.

11:18        Title from envelope.

11:19        Title from publisher's prospectus which has title: The Microbook library of American civilization.

## VARIATIONS IN TITLE (11.7B4)

11:20        Also known as: The Microbook library of the works of Henry James.

11:21        Title on binder: Women's studies.

11:22        Title on reel containers: The Gladstone papers.

## STATEMENTS OF RESPONSIBILITY (11.7B6)

11:23        At head of title on microfiche: Malthus Library--Jesus College.
           (Microreproduction of previously published work)

11:24        Produced by the Canadian Institute for Historical Microreproductions.

11:25        Sets for 1968/75-        compiled and edited by the Catalog Publication Division, Library of Congress.
           (Serial)

## EDITION AND HISTORY (11.7B7)

11:26        Continues the print edition.

## PUBLICATION, DISTRIBUTION, ETC. (11.7B9)

11:27        Sets for 1968/76-1968/77 not published.
             (Serial)

## PHYSICAL DESCRIPTION (11.7B10)

11:28        Ultra high reduction.

11:29        Diazo film.

11:30        Reproduced from holograph ; 1 score (78 p.).

## ACCOMPANYING MATERIAL (11.7B11)

11:31        Accompanied by: Pre-1900 Canadiana, title list.

11:32        Accompanied by Biblioguide which provides subject
             access, Author catalog, and Shelf list.

11:33        Accompanied by a guide which includes reel and subject
             indexes.

11:34        Accompanied by a guide edited by John Moscato and
             compiled by Robert Lester.

11:35        Accompanied by: A Guide to . . . listing the contents of
             the reels (printed matter).

11:36        Accompanied by: Guide to the microfilm edition of
             TCA / Jeffrey Andrews. 1982. (25 p. ; 22 cm.).

11:37        Microfilm reels for 1976-78-        accompanied by a
             booklet: A Guide to major studies and issue briefs of the
             Congressional Research Service . . . Supplement.
                 (Serial)

11:38        In binder with hard copy introduction.

11:39        Issued in binders with introductory pamphlets.

## OTHER FORMATS AVAILABLE (11.7B16)

11:40    Library has also volumes in printed form and on
microfiche.
(Microfilm)

## SUMMARY (11.7B17)

11:41    Summary: Chiefly a collection giving information about
availability of out-of-print rare and used books, prints,
maps, and manuscripts.

11:42    Summary: "A comprehensive collection of the source
material in the history of science comprising the significant
contributions to the advancement of science and
technology."

11:43    Summary: "The Library of Religion in America is one of
a series of MICROBOOK Libraries published by Library
Resources, Inc., a subsidiary of Encyclopaedia Britannica. It
is one of a much larger collection, The Library of American
Civilization"--Introd. to Biblioguide.

11:44    Summary: Set contains monographs and pamphlets span-
ning three and a half centuries of Canadian development.
Provides material for the study of Canadian culture, politics,
ethnology, sociology, history, economics, literature,
botanical and natural history, geography, and law.

## CONTENTS (11.7B18)

11:45    Contents: American mercury, 1784-1820 (213 microopaques) -- Boston gazette, 1719-1798 (237 microopaques) --
Freeman's journal, 1781-1792 (45 microopaques) -- Pennsylvania ledger, 1775-1778 (12 microopaques).

11:46    Contents: [reel 1] A tale of two cities. Oliver Twist -- [reel
2] David Copperfield. Great expectations.

## NUMBERS (11.7B19)

11:47       ED 119 729.

11:48       Microfiches are identified by Library of American civiliza-
            tion (LAC) numbers.
            (Title proper: Library of religion in America)

## COPY BEING DESCRIBED AND LIBRARY'S HOLDINGS (11.7B20)

11:49       Library's copy imperfect: Scattered frames illegible.

11:50       Microfilm copy lacks occasional issues.
            (Serial; microreproduction of previously published
            work)

11:51       Microfilm copy lacks all issues between Jan. 4, 1898, and
            Aug. 30, 1898, as well as other scattered issues.
            (Serial; microreproduction of previously published
            work)

## "WITH" NOTES (11.7B21)

11:52       Filmed with: Dun's review, v. 39-41, no. 2057; and, Dun
            and Bradstreet's monthly review, v. 41, no. 2061-2069.
            Filmed together subsequent to publication.
            (Serial; 11:52-56 are examples for microreproductions of
            previously published works)

11:53       Filmed with: United States news, v. 24, no. 1-2; and, U.S.
            news and world report, v. 24, no. 12-13; and, U.S. news &
            world report, v. 24, no. 14-16. Filmed together subsequent
            to publication.
            (Serial)

11:54       Filmed with: Dun's review, v. 39-41, no. 2057; and, Dun
            and Bradstreet's weekly review, v. 41, no. 2058-2060; and,
            Dun's review, v. 45-46. Filmed together subsequent to
            publication.
            (Serial)

11:55   Vols. 45-46 filmed with: Dun and Bradstreet's monthly review. Filmed together subsequent to publication.
     (Serial)

11:56a   Filmed with: The Bouquet celebration on Bushy Run Battlefield in Westmoreland County, Pa., August 6, 1883 / edited by Cyrus Cort. Lancaster, Pa. : Steinman & Hensel, 1886 -- Memorial of Enoch Brown and eleven scholars / edited by Cyrus Cort. Lancaster, Pa. : Steinman & Hensel, 1886. Filmed together subsequent to publication.
     (Title proper: Col. Henry Bouquet and his campaigns . . . ; note on first item)

     *For LC's interpretation on the use of "With" notes see Cataloging Service Bulletin, no. 22, fall 1983, p. 20*

11:56b   Filmed with: Col. Henry Bouquet and his campaigns of 1763 and 1764 / by Cyrus Cort. Lancaster, Pa. : Steinman & Hensel, 1883. Filmed together subsequent to publication.
     (Note on second and subsequent items)

11:57a   With: Online searching / Ann Jamison. -- Online cataloging / Paul Wild.
     (Note on first item of original edition microfilm; title proper: Bibliographic instruction; examples 11:57a-b illustrate AACR 2 rule 11:1G4)

11:57b   With: Bibliographic instruction / Jane Bristol.
     (Note on second and subsequent items of original edition microfilm)

# 12

# Serials

## FREQUENCY (12.7B1)

12:1       Triennial.

12:2       Biennial.

12:3       Published every other year in quarterly volumes, updating the center's 14 indexes published in the alternate years.

12:4       Annual.

12:5       Semiannual.

12:6       Semiannual, with annual (the 2nd issue of each year) and quinquennial cumulations.

12:7       Half-yearly bulletin on ongoing and planned research activities.

12:8       Quarterly.

12:9       Bimonthly.

12:10     Monthly.

12:11     Semimonthly.

12:12     Fortnightly (16 times, Sept.-May).

12:13     Weekly.

12:14     Weekly issues devoted to 10 specialties.

12:15     Eleven issues yearly.

12:16     Nine issues yearly,     -1975.

12:17     Ten issues yearly.

12:18     Twice a year.

12:19     Published twice yearly.

12:20     Five times a year.

12:21     Issued at least once a year.

12:22     Three times a year during the academic year.

12:23     Published 3 times a year with the 3rd volume an annual cumulation.

12:24     Sixteen issues yearly (monthly, July-Feb.; semimonthly, Mar.-June).

12:25     Quarterly (Sept. through June).

12:26     Monthly from Sept. through June (except Jan. and Feb.).

12:27     Monthly (July-Aug. combined).

12:28     Monthly (except semimonthly in Mar.).

12:29     Monthly (except June and Aug.).

12:30     Monthly (except Feb., Oct., and Dec.).

12:31     Weekly (except last week of the year), Apr. 20, 1981-

12:32     Weekly except for Fridays that follow or fall on July 4th and Christmas Day.

12:33     Quarterly, the 4th issue being an annual cumulation.

12:34      Quarterly, with the last issue being cumulative for the year.

12:35      Monthly, with cumulative volume issued annually.

12:36      Ten monthly issues with 2 semiannual cumulations.

12:37      Monthly, with an extra issue in Apr.

12:38      Monthly, with annual summary.

12:39      Monthly, with annual summary called no. 13.

12:40      Quarterly reports with annual supplements.

12:41      Biweekly, with semiannual references.

12:42      Vol. 1-      published monthly Mar. through Dec.; Jan./Feb. issue is an annual publication which includes a yearly economic profile.

12:43      Annual (irregular).

12:44      Quarterly (irregular).

12:45      Bimonthly (irregular).

12:46      Three issues yearly (irregular).

12:47      Semiannual (irregular), spring 1953-spring-fall 1959; annual, 1960-1961; semiannual, spring 1962-

12:48      Monthly, 1977-      ; 10 issues yearly, 1980-

12:49      Three issues yearly      ; 2 issues yearly,

12:50      Monthly      ; monthly (with a 2nd issue in July and Dec.), July 10, 1979-

12:51      Six issues yearly, 1978-1979; 4 issues yearly, spring 1980-

12:52      Monthly,      -Apr. 1974; quarterly, 1974, 3rd quarter-

12:53      Monthly (except Dec.), 1975; monthly (except combined Jan./Feb. issue), 1976-

12:54     Three issues yearly, Sept.-Dec. 1973-May-Aug. 1974; annual, Jan.-Dec. 1975-

12:55     Quarterly, 1980-      ; monthly, with quarterly and annual cumulations, Jan. 1981-

12:56     Monthly, 1948-Feb. 1950; semiannual, Mar./Aug. 1950; monthly (except June and July) and cumulating semiannually Feb. and Aug., Sept. 1950-

12:57     Quarterly (with additional issue dated Jan.)      ; bimonthly, Oct. 1980-

12:58     Irregular, summer 1977-      ; semiannual,

12:59     Irregular.

12:60     Occasional.

12:61     Frequency varies.


## LANGUAGES (12.7B2)

12:62     Arabic and English, 1978-      ; English, 1980-

12:63     English only, 1967-May 1969; English and French, June 1969-1971.

12:64     In French, 1978; Arabic and French, 1979-

12:65     Some issues in Afrikaans with English summary.

12:66     Reports for the years 1968-      have parallel texts in German and English.

12:67     Text in English and French; French text on inverted pages, 1976.

12:68     Text in English and French, each issue with special t.p. and separate paging. French text on inverted pages.

12:69     Text in English only, except when the English and French eds. are combined in one.

12:70     Some issues have text in English and French.

12:71     Romanized record.

12:72     Title in colophon of dai 2-geo, published in 1982 in romanization: Haiku Bungakkan kiyo.

12:73     First issue each year devoted to translations into English; the 2nd issue, into all other languages.

## SOURCE OF TITLE PROPER (12.7B3)

12:74     Caption title.

12:75     Cover title.

12:76     Masthead title.

12:77     Title from caption.

12:78     Title from contents page.

12:79     Title from cover.

12:80     Title from masthead.

12:81     Title from p. 1 of memorandum.

12:82     Title from table of contents page.

12:83     Title transcribed from the publisher's statement, issue no. 1, p. 2.
          (Newspaper)

## VARIATIONS IN TITLE (12.7B4)

12:84     Added title page title: Egyptian exporters directory.

12:85     Added title page title: Nuclear-hydrogen energy and technology.

12:86        Added title page title: Etudes, no. 7/10-

12:87        Added title page title: Journal of Oriental languages and cultures studies, May 1977-

12:88        Added t.p. in Malay.

12:89        French title appears on added t.p., 1975/76.

12:90        Caption title: Annual report.

12:91        Caption title: APBA roster.

12:92        Caption title: Seatrade guide to Arab shipping, 1978-

12:93        Cover title: Psychology and pedagogics.

12:94        Cover title: Public water supplies for the State of Oklahoma, South Central District.

12:95        Cover title: Données économiques et sociales, Provence-Alpes-Côte d'Azur.

12:96        Cover title: Directory / American Psychological Association.

12:97        Cover title: Irrigation Association . . . directory and industry buyer's guide.

12:98        Cover title: Annual report for the . . . season.

12:99        Cover title: Gouvernement du Canada : programmes et services.

12:100       Cover title: Budget, 1965-1968.

12:101       Cover title: Georgia's amended budget report,        -1979.

12:102       Cover title: Indicadores econômicos,        -Dec. 1976--Indicadores econômicos Mato Grosso, Jan. 1977-

12:103       Cover title: New Jersey public school racial/ethnic information, 1976-1977--New Jersey school racial/ethnic data, 1977-1978-

12:104   Cover and spine title: University/Industry/Government Microelectronics.

12:105   Distinctive title: Silver dollars, 1981.

12:106   Distinctive title: New directions in teacher preparation, 1976-1977.

12:107   Distinctive title: Decisions of the Civil Aeronautics Board, v. 2, 5--Economic decisions of the Civil Aeronautics Board, v. 3, 4, 6-12, 14-16--Safety decisions of the Civil Aeronautics Board, v. 13--Economic and safety enforcement cases of the Civil Aeronautics Board, v. 17-46--Economic cases of the Civil Aeronautics Board, v. 47-

12:108   Other title: Accent.

12:109   Other title: Aerial photography summary record system state-base graphics.

12:110   Other title: Best's executive data service, experience by state and line.

12:111   Other title: S.O.W.P. amateur call book.

12:112   Other title: Science and Education Administration, agricultural views and manuals. Northeastern series.

12:113   Other title: Supplementary report of the Canadian Wheat Board on the pool accounts. Wheat, oats and barley.

12:114   Other title: Agricultural sector, Queensland . . . Section 1, Rural land use, general activity, and value of production.

12:115   Other title: Arab shipping guide, 1978-

12:116   Other title: Natural resources and energy newsletter, no. 1-

12:117   Running title: Report of the Film Classification.

12:118   Running title: IMTJ.

12:119   Running title: I.U.F.C. blue yodel.

12:120   Running title: Convenience store merchandiser's . . . equipment buyer's guide.

12:121      Running title: Car collector, Jan. 1980.

12:122      Running title: Backstage TV/industrial film & tape directory, 1976-1978--Backstage TV/film & tape directory, 1979-

12:123      Spine title: Money saving car care.

12:124      Spine title: Madjalah B.N.I., July 1967-

12:125      Translated title: The World.
            (Newspaper; title proper: Le Monde)

12:126      Title romanized: Chung-kuo nien chien.

12:127      Title varies slightly.

12:128      Title alternates irregularly: Relatório.

12:129      Sometimes published as: Memoranda from the Occupational History Study.

12:130      Sometimes published as: Weekly Steelton news.
            (Newspaper; title proper: Steelton weekly news)

12:131      Sometimes published as: The Penny saver, Oct. 3-30, Dec. 2-31, 1956; Feb. 3-28, Apr. 4-30, 1957.
            (Newspaper; title proper: The Palmyra penny saver)

12:132      Each issue has a distinctive title.

12:133      Each issue has also a distinctive title.

12:134      Each no. has also a distinctive title.

12:135      Issue for 1979-80 has a distinctive title.

12:136      Some issues have individual titles, 1979-        : Investing in Colorado.

12:137      Issues for v. 86-87 of 1977-1978 also bear individual titles (Chemical sciences, Earth and planetary sciences, etc.) indicating contents of the issue.

12:138      Some no. have title: Expansion régionale.

12:139      Some no. have title: Bulletin / Division of Engineering Research.

12:140    Some issues have title: Prince George's County Genealogical Society newsletter.

12:141    Vols. for even-numbered years have title: National accounts.

12:142    Alternate issues titled: Geology and geography; Geophysics and geodesy.

12:143    Spring issue published as: Pacific packers report, formerly a special issue of National fisherman.

12:144    Issue for 1977/78 entitled: One- and five-year plan for vocational education for fiscal years 1978-1982.

12:145    Monthly issues and annual cumulations for 1975-1979 issued under title: Municipal bond prospectus library index. These were replaced by the 1975/80 cumulation.

12:146    Vols. for 1982-    carry in the title the year of issue, i.e. Compensation 82.

12:147    Issue for 1973/74 has titles in reverse: Rapport annuel. Annual report.

12:148    Cited as ALR 4th.

12:149    Issued in 2 pts.: Abstracts and Indexes.

12:150    Published in 2 v.: Report volume and detailed statistical tables volume.

12:151    Issued in 2 sections: Foreign and international bonds and Publicized Eurocurrency credits.

12:152    Issued in 2 v.: v. 1. General construction trades; v. 2. Mechanical and electrical trades.

12:153    Survey for 1981 issued in 2 v. called: Property - casualty and Life - health.

12:154    1970 ed. issued in 2 v.: v. 1. General subjects; v. 2. Geographic sources.

12:155    Vols. for 1980-    issued in 2 sections: section 1. Northern Europe; section 2. Southern Europe.

12:156    Vols. for 1976-    issued in 2 v.: v. 1. Transport and the activity of the Conference; v. 2. Resolutions of the Council of Ministers of Transport and reports approved.

12:157    Vols. for 1964/65-1974 issued in 2 pts.: pt. 1. Surface water records; pt. 2. Water quality records.

12:158    Vols. for    issued in 2 v.: v. 1. USSR and RSFSR; v. 2. Union Republics; vols. for    issued in 3 v.: v. 1. National organizations; v. 2. RSFSR; v. 3. Union republics.

12:159    "Weekly issue may contain two parts: I. Community documents and instruments; II. Community publications and studies."

12:160    Lacks specific section title.
          (Title proper: JGR. Journal of geophysical research. B.)

12:161    Numbers for June 1950-1951 lack title.

12:162    Some issues lack title.

12:163    Some issues printed without title, 1979-

12:164    Some no. issued without title.


## PARALLEL TITLES AND OTHER TITLE INFORMATION (12.7B5)

12:165    At head of title,    : Medicare/Medicaid.

12:166    At head of title, 1978-    : Committee print.

12:167    At head of title, 1972/76-    : Media report to women.

12:168    Title in English only, 1981-

12:169    Title also in the association's other official languages.

12:170    Added title in Arabic, 1969-1980.

12:171    Parallel title: The Swedish post.
          (Newspaper; appears only in publisher's statement)

12:172    Parallel title varies slightly.

12:173    Added parallel titles in Greek and Russian, 1983-

12:174    Some issues combine English and French eds. in a bilingual ed., issued under title: Social development = Développement social.

12:175    "Bed and breakfast places, farmhouses, and university accommodation"--Vol. 2.

12:176    "An annual devoted to the ancient and medieval cultures of Europe."

12:177    "Carleton University annual papers on classical antiquity and the Middle Ages."

12:178    Subtitle varies.

12:179    Subtitle varies slightly.

12:180    Vols. 1-5 have subtitle: Review of events & digest of opinion.

12:181    Vols. for        have subtitle: Student Body statutes.

12:182    Composed of alternately issued volumes with subtitles: Fundamentals, Applications, Equipment, and Systems.


## STATEMENTS OF RESPONSIBILITY (12.7B6)

12:183    At head of title,        -1953: Illinois nature preserves systems.

12:184    At head of title, 1980-1983: NODC.

12:185    At head of cover title: the University of Florida Department of Chemical Engineering.

12:186    On cover: Building Cost File Inc.

12:187    On cover,        : New Jersey Business & Industry Association.

12:188     "Water Resources Division"--Verso of t.p.

12:189     Full name of the institute: Scientific Institute for the Study of the Panda.
           (Title proper: Transactions of the Scientific Institute)

12:190     Issued by: the Associated College Libraries of Central Pennsylvania.
           (Title page transcription: In the know / ACLCP)

12:191     Official journal of: Group Health Association.

12:192     Official journal of: the Vernacular Architecture Group.

12:193     Official journal of: the Instituto de Artes of the Universidade Federal de Goiás, Jan./June, 1980-

12:194     Official publication of: Motorcycle Trades Association, Inc.

12:195     Official publication of: the Chi Epsilon, National Civil Engineering Honor Fraternity.

12:196     Official publication of: the National Knitwear and Sportwear Association; and, the Knitted Textile Association.

12:197     Official magazine of: AAPA, American Association of Port Authorities, Inc.; ICHCA-USA, Int'l Cargo Handling Coordination Ass'n./U.S. Nat'l Committee; FCC, Foreign Commerce Club of New York, Inc.

12:198     Official membership roster of: the Nashville Area Chamber of Commerce.

12:199     Membership directory of: Public Relations Society of America.

12:200     Official organ of: Ring Deutscher Berginenieure.

12:201     Organ of: the División de Bibliotecas, Universidad Nacional de Trujillo.

12:202     International journal of: Seventh-Day Adventist Ministerial Association.

12:203     Journal of: the Anthropology Club, California State University, Chico.

12:204    "The Journal of the International Association for Wind Engineering."

12:205    Newsletter of: the Department of Archaeology, University of Ghana.

12:206    Proceedings of the North American Sawmill & Panel Clinic.

12:207    "A service of Johnson & Johnson Health Care Division," Mar. 1980; "A service of Johnson & Johnson Products Inc.," June 1980-

12:208    Analyses for June 8, 1976-June 6, 1978 by Legislative Analyst.

12:209    Issued also as the journal of the Surveyors Institute of Zambia, Mar. 1979-

12:210    Includes reports by Jamaica Bauxite Mining Limited . . . [et al.].

12:211    Vols. for 1981-82-    by S. Haggart and D. Porter.

12:212    Vols. for 1981-1982-    by F. Hammel, assisted by R. Pollack.

12:213    Authors: Flora Crater, Elizabeth Vantrease, Meg Williams, 1979-

12:214    Editor: J.A. Seabury.

12:215    Editor: Karl Maramorosch.

12:216    Editor: v. 1-12, William Osler.

12:217    Editor: 1976-    R.H. Millenson.

12:218    Editor: 1979-1980, C.A. Frazier.

12:219    Editors: J. Dumont and J. Nunez.

12:220    Editors: O.S. Margolis & D.J. Cherico.

12:221    Editors: 1980-    L.J. Otte and R.L. Ingram.

12:222    Editors: 1980-    Scott G. McNall and Gary N. Howe.

12:223    Editors: 1982-    J. Robert Connor and the staff of Business week.

12:224    Editors: 1980/81-    Glen Beeson, Reuben E. Slesinger.

12:225    Editors: 1973-1980, G. Spelvin; 1981-    R. Arny.

12:226    Editors: v. 18-    G.M. Paterson (v. 19-    with J.E. Hardy).

12:227    "Edité par la Société internationale pour l'étude de la philosophie médiévale."

12:228    "Assembled and edited by the Geographical Studies and Research Center, Department of Geography, Eastern Kentucky University, Richmond, Ky."

12:229    Compiled by: T.O. Brooke.

12:230    Compiled by: Business Guides, Inc.

12:231    Vols. for    include statistical data compiled by the bureau under its later name: Commonwealth Bureau of Census and Statistics.

12:232    Vols. for    compiled and edited by A.J. Heim.

12:233    Vols. for    compiled and edited by the Catalog Publication Division, Library of Congress.

12:234    Compiled and published by: Martha Nell Craig.

12:235    Compiled and published by: Economics and Markets Branch, Ministry of Agriculture, Zimbabwe, July-Dec. 1979-

12:236    Selected by: Thomas Moult.

12:237    Founded by: Eugene Fodor.

12:238    Founded and for some years edited by H. de Lacaze-Duthiers.

12:239    Founded, edited, and published by Sylvia Beach.

12:240    Prepared by: Office of Libraries and Learning Technologies.

12:241      Prepared by: the staff of the Legal/Claims Division.

12:242      Prepared by: English class, Adel De Soto High School.

12:243      Prepared by: Division of Administration & Finance, State
            Dept. of Education,        -1974-75; School Finance and
            Statistics, 1975-76-

12:244      Prepared by: the Wyoming State Highway
            Department,        ; the Wyoming State Highway Depart-
            ment, Planning Branch, 1974-

12:245      Vols. for FY 1982-        prepared by AgRISTARS Pro-
            gram Management Group, National Aeronautics and Space
            Administration, Lyndon B. Johnson Space Center.

12:246      Vol. for 1981 was produced by the National Foreign
            Assessment Center; 1982-        by the Central Intelligence
            Agency.

12:247      One of a series of surveys of financial reporting practices
            prepared by Peat, Marwick, Mitchell, & Co.

12:248      Prepared with: Labor Area Research Dept., 1981/82-

12:249      Vols. for 1980/81-        prepared with C.P. Stickney and
            R.L. Weil.

12:250      Vols. for        prepared with South Carolina Agricultural
            Experiment Station, Dept. of Agricultural Economics and
            Rural Sociology cooperating with United States Dept. of
            Agriculture, Economics, Statistics, and Cooperatives Service.

12:251      Prepared in cooperation with the State of Illinois and
            other agencies.

12:252      Vols. for        prepared in cooperation with Universitas
            Sjiah Kuala.

12:253      "Prepared with the cooperation and approval of the Con-
            necticut Energy Advisory Board"--Letter of transmittal.

12:254      Prepared in affiliation with: U.S. Employment and Train-
            ing Administration,

12:255      A joint effort of the International Agency for Research on

Cancer and the German Cancer Research Center, within the framework of the International Cancer Research Data Bank Program of the National Cancer Institute of the United States.

12:256    Published by Ronsetsu Shiryeo Hozonkai    ; issued 1970-    by the society under its later name: Cheugoku Kankei Ronsetsu Shiryeo.

12:257    Issued by: Foundation of Thanatology.

12:258    Issued by: the Illinois Office of Education.

12:259    Issued by: University of Waterloo, Faculty of Mathematics.

12:260    Issued by: Society of Amateur Cinematographers,

12:261    Issued by: the Statistical Office, Denver Service Center, U.S. Dept. of the Interior, National Park Service, 1979-

12:262    Issued by: Asia Electronics United, no. 26-33.

12:263    Issued by: Boycot Outspan Aktie, Komitee Zuidelijk Afrika, and Werkgroep Kairos.

12:264    Issued by: Charities Aid Fund, 1968-1973; Charities Aid Foundation, 1975-

12:265    Issued by: Chicano Graduate Association, Stanford University, summer 1975-    ; Stanford University, winter 1976-

12:266    Issued by: the Twentieth Century Fund, 1931-1934; Raymond Rich Associates, 1939-1948.

12:267    Issued by: Dept. of Commercial Intelligence and Statistics, Apr. 1965-    ; Directorate General of Commercial Intelligence and Statistics, Apr. 1975 to Mar. 1976-

12:268    Issued by: United States Travel Service, Office of Research and Analysis, 1974-    ; United States Travel Service, Office of Policy and Research, 1977-    ; United States Travel Service, 1979-

12:269    Issued by: United States Department of Agriculture, Economic Research Service, June 1975-1977; by USDA,

Economics, Statistics, and Cooperatives Service, Jan./Feb.
1978-Oct. 1980; by Economics and Statistics Service, United
States Department of Agriculture, Nov. 1980-June 1981; by
the Economic Research Service, July 1981-

12:270        Issued cooperatively by: U.S. Dept. of Agriculture,
Statistical Reporting Service and Tennessee Dept. of
Agriculture, 1963-        and by: U.S. Dept. of Agriculture,
Economics, Statistics, and Cooperatives Service and Ten-
nessee Dept. of Agriculture, 1978-

12:271        Vols. for 1948-Apr. 1949 issued by the Wisconsin University Library School.

12:272        Vols. for        issued by the Rural Manpower Services
Division;        by the Employment Data and Research
Division.

12:273        Vols. 8-17 issued by the Ministère des finances; v. 18-30,
no. 349 by the Ministère de l'économie et des finances; v.
30, no. 350-352 by the Ministere de l'économie; v. 30, no.
353/354-v. 31 by the Ministèrès de l'économie et du budget.

12:274        No. 1-142 issued by the Bureau of Agricultural
Economics; no. 143-187 by the Agricultural Marketing Ser-
vice, no. 188-        by the Economic Research Service; Feb.
1979-        by the Economics, Statistics, and Cooperatives
Service;        -Oct. 1980 by the Economics and Statistics
Service.

12:275        Vols. for 1896-Oct. 1913 issued by the Massachusetts
Association Opposed to the Further Extension of Suffrage to
Women (called Massachusetts Association Opposed to the
Extension of Suffrage to Women, 1896-1899).

12:276        Vols. for        issued by the foundation under its later
name: Arthritis Foundation.

12:277        Vol. 1976-1977, t. 2 issued by Departamento de
Estadísticas Económicas, Instituto Nacional de Estadística.

12:278        A joint publication of: the World Meteorological
Organization . . . [et al.].

12:279        Issued with the collaboration of: the Société historique
polonaise, Commission d'histoire médiévale.

12:280    Vols. for    issued jointly with the Federal Judicial Center and the Administrative Office of the United States Courts.

12:281    Some no. issued jointly with the Bureau of Domestic Commerce, Dec. 1977; with the Bureau of Domestic Business Development, 1978-Oct. 1979; with the Bureau of Industrial Economics, Nov. 1979-

12:282    Published on behalf of the Faculty of Law, University of Oxford.

12:283    Prepared for: U.S. Dept. of Energy, Office of Facility Planning and Support, Oct. 1980-

12:284    A report submitted to North Carolina Energy Institute and U.S. Department of Energy.

12:285    Vols. for    submitted to the State of Florida Dept. of Administration, Division of State Planning;    to the Dept. of Community Affairs;    to the Dept. of Veteran and Community Affairs.

12:286    Published under the auspices of the London Institute of World Affairs.

12:287    Published under the auspices of the Rutgers Institute of Jazz Studies, 1982-

12:288    Issued under the auspices of the Federal Financial Institutions Examination Council, 1979-

12:289    Sponsored by: the American Association for Applied Linguistics and the British Association for Applied Linguistics.

12:290    Sponsored by: the Association for Computing Machinery, Special Interest Group on Automata and Computability Theory, with the cooperation of the IEEE Computer Society Technical Committee on Mathematical Foundations of Computing, and various host universities.

12:291    Sponsored by: Air Force Office of Scientific Research and Army Research Office, 1977; by Office of Naval Research and others, 1978-

12:292    Vols. for Feb. 1980-    sponsored by Arbetslivscentrum.

12:293       Conferences for 1979-      sponsored by the Associação Brasileira de Artistas Plásticos Profissionais.

12:294       Conferences for      -1973 sponsored by the Tribunal de Contas of the State of Pará; 1975-      by the Tribunal de Contas of the State of Paraíba.

12:295       Institutes for 1972-      sponsored by the International Oil and Gas Educational Center, Southwestern Legal Foundation.

12:296       Cosponsored by: the Medical Library Association.

12:297       Cosponsored by: University of Colorado, Graduate School of Business Administration and Colorado Division of Commerce and Development, 1966-      ; University of Colorado, College of Business and Administration and the Colorado Division of Commerce and Development, 1980-

12:298       Sponsored jointly by: Rensselaer Polytechnic Institute, the University of Delaware, and the University of Florida.

12:299       Sponsored in part by: the Association of Pacific Fisheries.

12:300       Supported in part by: the Association of Academic Health Sciences Library Directors.

12:301       Partially funded by: the Weatherhead Foundation.

12:302       "Authorized by Governor Frank White and the seventy-third General Assembly."

12:303       "Approved by the World Food and Agricultural Outlook and Situation Board"--P. 3.

12:304       Hosted by: the Department of Art, UCLA.

12:305       Vols. for Nov. 1981-      presented by: the Century City Bar Association.

12:306       Collected by: Office of Management Information.

12:307       Developed by: the Library and Information Services Division, Environmental Science Information Center.

12:308       Work performed by the Science Communication Division, George Washington University, under grant SRS-16-

P-56803/3-09, in cooperation with the George Washington University Medical Rehabilitation Research and Training Center.

12:309    "Co-principal investigators: Dinesh O. Shah and Robert D. Walker, Jr."

12:310    " . . . from the working files of Berger & Associates Cost Consultants."

12:311    English translation by: Royer and Roger Inc.

12:312    Translated by Royer and Roger Inc., Mar. 1958-    ; by the International Division of Royer and Roger Inc., -Apr. 1961; by Scripta Technica Inc., May-Dec. 1961.

12:313    Chairman: 1942/43-    Herb Breau.

12:314    Name of the Minister of Finance varies in later issues.

12:315    "The journal is not affiliated in any way with the Federal Government."


## RELATIONSHIPS WITH OTHER SERIALS (12.7B7)

12:316    Translation of: Mekhanika kompozitnykh materialov.

12:317    Selected translation of: T'ien wen hsüeh pao; and, T'ien t'i wu li hsüeh pao.

12:318    Includes translations from the Nepal press reports, Nepal gazette, and of articles from newspapers and periodicals.

12:319    Continues: Annual review of new American architecture.

12:320    Continues: Appearances and activities of leading Chinese officials during . . .

12:321    Continues: Mortgage banking . . . financial statements and operating ratios (1974).

12:322    Continues: Abstracts of Bulgarian scientific literature. Geology and geography.

12:323    Continues: Trends in the hotel business. International ed.

12:324    Continues: Statistik Kabupaten Daerah Tingkat II Banjarneagra [sic].

12:325    Continues: Cinemagic (Baltimore, Md.).

12:326    Continues: Information bulletin (Australian Institute of Criminology).

12:327    Continues: Statistical abstract (United States. National Park Service).

12:328    Continues: Vital statistics (Alaska. Bureau of Vital Statistics. Data Services).

12:329    Continues: Minería y metalurgia (Asociación de Ingenieros de Minas, Metalurgistas y Geólogos de México).

12:330    Continues: Indice de preços ao consumidor (Ceará (Brazil : State). Secretaria de Planejamento e Coordenaçao. Departamento de Estatística).

12:331    Continues: Carnegie Dunfermline Trustees. Report for . . .

12:332    Continues: Cyprus. Forest Dept. Annual report of the Forest Department for the year . . .

12:333    Continues: American Academy of Arts and Letters. [Report of activities].

12:334    Continues publication with the same title: Screen achievement records bulletin.

12:335    Continues the 8 monthly statistical issues of Sugar and sweetener report, ISSN 0362-9511.

12:336    With: Humanities index, ISSN 0095-5981, continues: Social sciences & humanities index, ISSN 0037-7899.

12:337    With: Journal (Association of Teachers of Colonial History), continues: Broadside and town crier.

12:338    With: Institute of International Education. Annual report, continues: Reports on international study.

12:339    With: Bottin . . . produits et services, continues: Bottin professions. Liste alphabétique nationale des entreprises.

12:340    With 12 or more similar titles, continues: Statistical register of Western Australia.

12:341    Continued by: SAC movie news.

12:342    Continued by: Annuaire des sociétés des opérateurs du port et des principaux importateurs-exportateurs du Sénégal.

12:343    Continued by: Tennis . . . buyers guide, 1982.

12:344    Continued by: Carnegie Dunfermline Trustees. Report for . . . and retrospect . . .

12:345    Continued by: Target (Warminster, Pa.).

12:346    Continued by: Atlantic (Boston, Mass. : 1932), ISSN 0160-6506, July 1932.

12:347    Continued by: Indice de preços ao consumidor (Fundação Instituto de Planejamento do Ceará. Coordenadoria de Estatística e Informática).

12:348    Continued in 1970 by: Polish feature films.

12:349    Continued by a section in: Flight controllers' bulletin.

12:350    Merger of: Latin America political report; and, Latin America economic report.

12:351    Merger of: Tanzarchiv; and, Ballett-Journal.

12:352    Merger of: Sea (Eastern edition); and, Sea (Southern edition).

12:353    Merger of: Sea (Western edition); and, Pacific skipper.

12:354    Merger of: Statistiques du commerce extérieur de Madagascar. Importations; and, Statistiques du commerce extérieur de Madagascar. Exportations.

12:355    Merger of: Canadian cartographer, ISSN 0008-3127; and, Cartographica, ISSN 0317-7173, and continues the numbering of the former.

12:356   Merger of: Estadística de los negocios de seguros
(Dominican Republic. Oficina Nacional de Estadística); and,
Estadística bancaria (Dominican Republic. Oficina Nacional
de Estadística).

12:357   Merger of: Gujarat (India). Chemical Analyser. Annual
report; Gujarat (India). Directorate of Health and Medical
Services. Annual administration report on mental hospitals;
and, Gujarat (India). Directorate of Health and Medical
Services. Civil hospitals and dispensaries, annual administration report.

12:358   Merger of: Asbestos, ISSN 038-5778; Copper and nickel
production, ISSN 0380-6952; Gold production, ISSN
0318-7977; Iron ore, ISSN 0318-7969; Production of
Canada's leading minerals, ISSN 0008-2619; Salt, ISSN
0318-7918; and, Silver, lead and zinc production, ISSN
0318-7926.

12:359   Previously issued in 3 pts.: Friendly societies, industrial
assurance companies and general; Building societies; Industrial and provident societies.

12:360   Merged with: Pacific skipper, to become: Sea & Pacific
skipper.

12:361   Merged with: Nation and athenaeum, to become: New
statesman and nation.

12:362   Merged with: Instructor (Dansville, N.Y.), to become:
Instructor and teacher.

12:363   Merged with: National union catalog; Monographic series;
Subject catalog, to become: NUC. Books.

12:364   Merged with: List of Canadian hospitals and related
facilities, ISSN 0703-9298, to become: List of Canadian
hospitals and special care facilities, ISSN 0225-5642.

12:365   Merged with: Statistiques du commerce extérieur de
Madagascar. Importations, to become: Statistiques du commerce extérieur de Madagascar (Institut national de la
statistique et de la recherche économique (Madagascar) :
1970).

12:366      Merged with: Asbestos, ISSN 0380-5778; Copper and nickel production, ISSN 0380-6952; Iron ore, ISSN 0318-7969; Production of Canada's leading minerals, ISSN 0008-2619; Salt, ISSN 0318-7918; and, Silver, lead and zinc production, ISSN 0318-7926, to become: Production of Canada's minerals, ISSN 0709-292X.

12:367      In 1981 one section merged with: APICS news, to become: Production & inventory management review & APICS news.

12:368      Earlier reports issued in: Louisiana. Dept. of Conservation. Biennial report.

12:369      Earlier data published in Weather, crops and markets; and, National weather and crop bulletin.

12:370      Continues in part: Environmental pollution.

12:371      Continues in part: Bulletin signalétique. 170, Chimie.

12:372      Continues in part: Across the board (California Library Services Board).

12:373      Continues in part: Statistiques du commerce extérieur de Madagascar (Malagasy Republic. Service de statistique : 1957).

12:374      Continues in part: Brisbane City Council. Annual report.

12:375      Continues in part the Transactions of the Faraday Society and adopts its volume numbering.

12:376      Split into: Domestic arrivals and departures; and, Foreign arrivals and departures.

12:377      Split into: Adults under community supervision; and, Children under community supervision.

12:378      Split into: Statistiques du commerce extérieur de Madagascar. Exportations; and, Statistiques du commerce extérieur de Madagascar. Importations.

12:379      Split into: Annual reports on the progress of chemistry. Section A, Inorganic chemistry; and, Annual reports on the progress of chemistry. Section C, Physical chemistry.

12:380     Split into: Indiana. Laws of a general nature passed and published at the . . . session of the General Assembly of the State of Indiana; and, Indiana. Laws of a local nature, passed and published at the . . . session of the General Assembly of the State of Indiana.

12:381     Continued by: ASHRAE handbook. Fundamentals; ASHRAE handbook. Applications; and, ASHRAE handbook. Equipment.

12:382     Product directory section continued by: ASHRAE product specification file, which accompanies each volume of ASHRAE handbook.

12:383     Split into 3 separate publications of the Indian Academy of Sciences: Proceedings. A, Part I, Chemical sciences; Proceedings. A, Part II, Earth and planetary sciences; and, Proceedings. A, Part III, Mathematical sciences.

12:384     Dec. issue called Green book buyers' guide, issued separately, 1979-

12:385     Separated from: Knitting times.

12:386     Separated from: Price policy recommendations for the agricultural price review, 1978.

12:387     Separated from: American Institute of Mining, Metallurgical and Petroleum Engineers. Transactions of the American Institute of Mining, Metallurgical and Petroleum Engineers.

12:388     Continues the "Letters to the Editor" section of: Journal of materials science.

12:389     Formerly issued as a section of: Directory : home centers & hardware chains, auto supply chains.

12:390     Previously published as a section in Ontario history, ISSN 0030-2953, called: Book notes.

12:391     Previously published as a separately paginated section in: Water & sewage works.

12:392     Absorbed: Galaxy, Feb. 1878.

12:393    Absorbed: Bulletin of the Mineralogical Society of Southern California, Nov. 1934.

12:394    Absorbed: Standard & Poor's register of corporations, directors and executives. Geographical index. United States and Canada.

12:395    Absorbed: Monthly bulletin (International Juridical Association), ISSN 0098-7700.

12:396    Absorbed: Museum of the City of New York. Annual report.

12:397    Absorbed: Youth, Community Recreation, and National Fitness Council (W.A.). Report of the Youth, Community Recreation, and National Fitness Council.

12:398    Absorbed: Klüter Blätter, 1982; and, Politischer Zeitspiegel, 1982.

12:399    Absorbed: Acid rain studies; and, in part, Atmosphere and pollution.

12:400    Absorbed by: Gems and minerals.

12:401    Absorbed by: Instruments and automation, 1956.

12:402    Later reports included in the Lunacy Section annual reports.

12:403    Absorbed in part by: Deutsche Monatshefte (Berg, Starnberg, Germany : 1982).

12:404    Reprint. Originally published: Brussels : The Association, 1887-1903.

12:405    Reprint, with an introd. Originally published: México : Editorial "Vida Mexicana".

12:406    Reprint, with an introd. Originally published in London, 1934-1935.

12:407    Reprint. Originally published monthly.

12:408    Reprint. Originally published quarterly: Shillong : Directorate of Research.

12:409    Reprint. Originally published quarterly: Hyderabad, Deccan : Islamic Culture Board.

12:410    Reprint, with an introd. Originally published monthly (irregular): Mexico : [s.n.].

12:411    Reprint. Originally published monthly: The Accounting historian.

12:412    Reprint. Originally published monthly: Interurban newsletter. Fort MacArthur, CA : I.L. Swett.

12:413    Reprinted with: Nuestro México, t. 1, no. 1 (marzo 1932)-t. 2, no. 8 (nov. 1932).

12:414    Reprinted with: Vida mexicana (Mexico City, Mexico : 1922), t. 1, no. 1 (dic. 1922)-t. 1, no. 2 (marzo 1923).

12:415    Reprint of a periodical.

12:416    Reprint of the publication with same title.

12:417    Reprint of selected volumes of various publications on early cars.

12:418    Reprint of the Aug. issue of Art in America.
          (Item is an annual guide to galleries, museums, artists)

12:419    Reprint from copies in the New York Historical Society Library of the original periodical published in Philadelphia by John Doughty.

12:420    Vols. 8-20 are a reprint of a periodical published quarterly by: Southern Association of Teachers of Speech, 1942-      ; Southern Speech Association,      -1971.

12:421    Contents reprinted from: AIA journal.

12:422    Contains collected reprints of articles from: Parasitology.

12:423    Consists of articles on selected topics reprinted from: Molecular and cellular biochemistry.

12:424    "Taken in part from the Guiness book of world records."

12:425    English ed. of: Rā'idah.

12:426    English ed. of: Debatte van die Bophuthatswana Wetgewende Vergadering.

12:427    Spanish ed. of: Latin-American integration process in . . .

12:428    French ed. of: An Index to Government of Canada programs and services available to the public in Canada, ISSN 0707-9583.

12:429    Also published in French under title: Sommaire des communications, ISSN 0226-7489.

12:430    Issued also in English under title: Statistical year book.

12:431    Issued also in French under title: L'économie au Nouveau-Brunswick, ISSN 0383-3208.

12:432    Issued also in English under title: IDRC reports, and in French under title: CRDI explore.

12:433    Cumulated as: How to evaluate education programs / Arlene Fink.

12:434    Published also in Russian.

12:435    Also issued in French only, 1976 under title: Rapport de l'Auditeur général du Canada à la Chambre des communes, ISSN 0705-534X; 1977 under title: Rapport du Vérificateur général du Canada à la Chambre des communes, ISSN 0705-5323.

12:436    Spanish ed. of: Miami herald.

12:437    Published also in French, Spanish, German, and Dutch editions.

12:438    Also published in Dutch and German editions.

12:439    Issued also in French.

12:440    Issued also in a U.S. edition.

12:441    Also issued in English edition.

12:442    Also issued in limited editions with lists of headings in Spanish and Portuguese.

12:443    Also available in Danish, Dutch, French, German, and Italian editions.

12:444    Chinese edition also exists. Cf. v. 8, no. 1.

12:445    Includes some no. in both English and French editions.

12:446    Issued in alternating Japanese and European editions with the even no. being Japanese and describing Japanese cars and the odd no. being European, describing European cars.

12:447    Issued in 4 editions: Central ed., Eastern ed., Southern ed., Western ed., 1956-        ; in various regional commodity editions, 1977-

12:448    Sunday edition called: Sunday union, Jan. 11-May 1, 1891.
          (Newspaper edition that is named but not cataloged separately)

12:449    On Sunday published as: Sunday Patriot-News.
          (Newspaper edition that is named but not cataloged separately)

12:450    Other editions available: Trends in the hotel industry. USA edition.

12:451    Other editions available: Hammond almanac, 1979-80.

12:452    Other editions available: Développement social, ISSN 0316-3148.

12:453    Numerous editions.

12:454    Supplement to: Bangkok post.

12:455    Supplement to: Joel Whitburn's Top LP's, 1945-1972.

12:456    Supplement to: Industria azucarera (Buenos Aires, Argentina).

12:457    Supplement to: World agricultural situation (Washington, D.C. : 1970), ISSN 0084-1358.

12:458    Supplement to: National Governors' Association. Policy positions.

12:459    Vols. for    issued as a supplement to: Consumption of energy in New York State, 1960-1970 / Olaf Hausgaard.

12:460    Supplement to: Monthly record meteorological observations in western Canada; Monthly record, meteorological observations in northern Canada; and, Monthly record, meteorological observations in eastern Canada.

12:461    Supplement to: Série A/Série B, Série C, and Série D of Comptes rendus des séances de l'Académie des sciences, 1979-1980; Série I, Série II, and Série III of Comptes rendus des séances de l'Académie des sciences, 1981-

12:462    Supplement: Latin America Newsletter Ltd. book news.

12:463    Supplement: Annual economic review (Bangkok, Thailand).

12:464    Supplements a statistical compilation on the misuse of drugs published in the Home Office statistical bulletin series.

12:465    Issues a literary supplement called: Volksrath.
         (Newspaper supplement that is named but not cataloged separately)

12:466    Special issue of: Apparel industry magazine.

12:467    Annual June special issue of: Euromoney.

12:468    Published as a special issue of: Adweek (New York, N.Y.).

12:469    Mar.-Dec. 1980 (Vol. 1) published as special monthly issues of the weekly publication: Knitting times.

12:470    Vols. for    issued as a special number of: Chiffres pour l'Alsace.

12:471    "Numéro spécial du Bulletin de l'Afrique noire."

12:472    Issued as a special number of: Conjoncture économique régionale; and, Sud information économique.

12:473    Vols. for    published as a section of: Propeller.

12:474    Issued as a section of Journal of molecular structure, and included in its numbering also.

12:475      Issued every July as the "Directory issue" of: Public relations journal.

12:476      Updates Pochtovik, P.D. Miniatkilurnye knigi SSSR, published in 1975, which covers books until 1975.

12:477      Issued in conjunction with: Newsletter (Australian Institute of Aboriginal Studies).

12:478      Companion publication to: Res mechanica letters.

12:479      To accompany: Ohio statewide comprehensive outdoor recreation plan (SCORP). Assessment and policy plan.

12:480      Beginning Sept. 28, 1960 each issue accompanied by: Science teacher's world.

12:481      Ten times a year it is accompanied by an insert: Scott chronicle of new issues, Nov. 1982-    ; 12 times a year, 1984-

12:482      Issues for July 1952-1964 accompanied by: Statistical supplement, formerly included in statistics section of the Review, and was continued in 1965 by: Bulletin of labour statistics.

12:483      Vol. 2 of the Annual report issued separately as: Merger decisions.

12:484      Comprises 1 of 2 volumes of a survey; v. 1 entitled: Magazine total audiences.
         (Note on v. 2 of survey; with distinctive title; cataloged separately)

12:485      Includes: Harris Indiana buyers industrial directory, also issued separately.

12:486      Each issue contains the abstracts and reviews on subjects gathered separately from 2 v. of Zentralblatt für Mathematik.

12:487      Vol. 6 in Livestock business.

12:488      Vols. for     -1958 constitute supplement D of part 1 of Bibliographie de la France.

12:489    Vols. for 1981-        consist of proceedings of the 3rd and 4th-        Annual Symposium on Recent Advances in Clinical Therapeutics, held respectively on Dec. 1-2, 1979 and Oct. 8, 1980-

12:490    Beginning with 1909/10 the reports are also issued in the Annual report of the President of the Board of Trustees of the Institute.

12:491    Vol. 2, no. 3/4 is a combined issue with Porcepic, v. 1, no. 2.

12:492    Vol. 9, no. 5 is Proceedings of the 9th Conference (1958) of the institute.

12:493    Also issued as individual numbers of: Linguistics.

12:494    Index to: Municipal securities document library (called 1975-        Municipal bond prospectus library).

12:495    Vol. 64 is an index to: Societas pro Fauna et Flora Fennica. Notiser ur Shallskapets pro Fauna et Flora Fennica förhandlingar; and, Societas pro Fauna et Flora Fennica. Meddelanden af Societatis pro Fauna et Flora Fennica.

12:496    Numerous supplements.

12:497    Supplements tipped into 1978-79.

12:498    Supplements accompany some numbers.

12:499    Supplements accompany some issues; some supplements issued by Conseil international des économies régionales.

12:500    Supplements accompany June and Dec. issues, June 1977-

12:501    Supplements called Annexes accompany some numbers.

12:502    Some volumes accompanied by supplements.

12:503    Some numbers accompanied by addendum.

12:504    Includes special supplements.

12:505    Includes an annual supplement.

12:506    Includes semiannual supplement for Jan.-June 1971.

12:507    Includes supplementary material for the CETA prime sponsor area.

12:508    Vol. for 1948 includes material supplementary to volume for 1939/47.

12:509    Vol. for 1937 issued as a supplement to 1936.

12:510    Vols. for 1977-        prepared as a supplement to the foundation's annual report.

12:511    Vols. for        issued as supplementary part of the biennial report.

12:512    First supplement covers 2 years.

12:513    Supplement published in the alternate year.

12:514    Update issued between editions.

12:515    Vols. 1-2 are updated annually; v. 3 will be revised only as necessary.

12:516    Bimonthly updating supplements are issued between editions.

12:517    Kept up-to-date between editions by the biannual: Supplement to the directory of the American right, ISSN 0164-2510.

12:518    Kept updated by annual publication called Books in print supplement, ISSN 0000-0310, 1972/73-        ; and bimonthly issues of Forthcoming books, ISSN 0015-8119, 1966-

12:519    Updating supplements published April, July, and October.

12:520    Kept up-to-date by occasional supplements.

12:521    Kept up-to-date by pocket supplements.

12:522    Material for later cases issued in pocket continuation.

12:523    Accompanied by updates in a loose-leaf format: Canadian customs and excise reports : customs, excise, sales tax, antidumping : [service volume].

12:524    Updated by continuing supplementary material and cumulated irregularly.

12:525    Kept up-to-date between 5-year cumulations by quarterly and annual supplements.

12:526    Cumulates the monthly publication.

12:527    Cumulates the bimonthly publication: The Foundation grants index bimonthly.

12:528    Cumulation of the 12 monthly issues of: Abridged index medicus.

12:529    Annual cumulation of a bimonthly publication with the same title.

12:530    Quinquennial cumulations issued as volumes of the quinquennial cumulations of: National union catalog, ISSN 0028-0348.

# NUMBERING AND CHRONOLOGICAL DESIGNATION (12.7B8)

12:531    Began with 1978 volume.

12:532    Began with 1976/77 volume.

12:533    Began with 1912/13? issue.

12:534    Began with volume for 1968.

12:535    Began with edition published in 1926.

12:536    Began with issue for 1968 through 1970.

12:537    Began with Nov. 1963 issue.

12:538    Began with July/Dec. 1971 issue.

12:539    Began with Nov. 1978/Jan. 1979 issue.

12:540    Began with spring 1980 issue.

12:541      Began with issue for summer 1975.

12:542      Began with 1st (1966).

12:543      Began with nr. 1 in 1972.

12:544      Began with v. 27, fiscal years 1977, 1978, and 1979.

12:545      Began with production area and sales, 1976 and 1977, intentions for 1978.

12:546      New series began with no. 1, July/Aug. 1965.

12:547      Began in 1969. Cf. New serial titles.

12:548      Began and ceased in 1891.

12:549      Began in 1977; ceased in 1981.

12:550      Began with v. 1, no. 1, Oct. 1899; ceased with v. 6, no. 3, July 1905. Cf. Union list of serials.

12:551      Began publication with 22. année (1900); ceased publication with 33. année (1911).

12:552      Numbering irregular.

12:553      Vol. numbering irregular: v. 28 repeated.

12:554      Vol. numbers irregular: v. 1 repeated, 1977.

12:555      No. 925 repeated in numbering.

12:556      Vol. numbering irregular: v. 20-58 omitted in numbering.

12:557      No. 25 omitted in numbering.

12:558      37th omitted in numbering.

12:559      Nov. 1977 issue not numbered.

12:560      Some issues lack chronological designation.

12:561      Some issues lack monthly designation.

12:562      Vols. numbered      -6 are undated; Bd. 7-      dated 1978-

12:563    Beginning with 1982 Directory, the date on the title page agrees with the date of publication; therefore there is no Directory bearing the date 1981.

12:564    Chronological designation dropped beginning with v. 1, no. 5.

12:565    Vol. for 1981 lacks numeric and chronological designation.

12:566    Annual summary lacks numbering.

12:567    Vol. 1, no. 2 called Directory of Indiana college English teachers; it lacks both the title of the serial and any volume numbering.

12:568    Issues for 1977-1979 lack volume designations but constitute v. 1-3.

12:569    Vol. numbering dropped beginning with Sept. 1971 issue.

12:570    Beginning with no. 3 volume numbering was dropped.

12:571    New series designation dropped with v. 7, 1980.

12:572    Beginning with July 1888 the designation New series was discontinued.

12:573    Numbering begins with no. 2.

12:574    Numbering begins in 1976.

12:575    Numbering irregular: also called issue no., no., issue; issues for 1976-1977 called also v. 2; issue 7/8 (spring 1978) called also year 4.

12:576    Publications designated AFPR-1; ESCS-AFPR-2--ESCS-AFPR-3; AFPR-4--

12:577    Numbering begins each year with 1.

12:578    Vol. 153/no. 1 (Oct.-Dec. 1981) is only issue published in 1981; numbering in 1982 starts with v. 154/no. 1 (Jan.-Mar. 1982).

12:579    Later issues have volume and numbering designations also.

12:580        Alternate volume numbering with the Transactions of the Metallurgical Society of AIME and the Transactions of the Society of Petroleum Engineers of AIME.

12:581        Beginning with        alternating issues are also designated A or B, i.e., Nov. 1978 issue called v. 52A, no. 6.

12:582        Issues for 1970 and 1972 called v. 2. Began consecutive numbering with issue no. 8, Feb. 1973.

12:583        Vols. 1-12 have internal numbering only; whole numbering begins with v. 13.

12:584        Vol. designations correspond to years, issues are numbered consecutively without regard to volume.

12:585        Has also whole numbers (odd numbers 589-
assigned to Faraday transactions 1; even numbers assigned to Faraday transactions 2).

12:586        Vols. for 1947/48-1956 called also nouv. sér. d'Archeion, t. 27-35 in continuation of the numbering of that journal.

12:587        Vol. 1, no. 1-4 called v. 104, no. 1-4 in continuation of the numbering of the Journal of experimental psychology.

12:588        Errors in numbering: v. 31, no. 2-3, Feb.-Mar. 1981 called v. 30, no. 2-3; v. 31, no. 5, May 1981 called v. 31, no. 4.

12:589        Vols. 8-10 misnumbered 18-20.

12:590        Vol. 2, no. 4 incorrectly called v. 2, no. 3.

12:591        Numbering irregular: no. 3-5 called also no. 2-4 on covers.

12:592        Issue for Dec. 14, 1981, erroneously numbered v. 4, no. 37, following the numbering sequence of: NAHB builder.

12:593        The 44th regular session of the General Assembly was designated as the 45th regular session. The error in numbering has been continued by all the following assemblies.

12:594        Vol. for 1979 constitutes 17th, but incorrectly marked 16th.

12:595        Issues for 1966-1967 called no. 1-2, but constitute v. 2-3.

12:596    Issue for Jan. 1-15, 1978, called Inaugural issue, but constitutes v. 1, no. 2.

12:597    Preceded by unnumbered pilot issue, Feb. 1980.

12:598    Vol. 1, no. 1 preceded by pilot issue dated Oct. 1980.

12:599    Vol. 1, no. 1 preceded by an issue called Spring 1981.

12:600    Unnumbered preliminary issue precedes v. 1, no. 1.

12:601    Issue for June 1980 called Inaugural issue.

12:602    Vol. 1, no. 1 called also Inaugural issue.

12:603    Oct./Nov. 1981 called also Premier issue.

12:604    Introductory no., called CERO, was issued in 1977.

12:605    An introductory issue numbered v. 1, no. 0 was issued June 14, 1967.

12:606    Vol. for 1978 called no. especial, but constitutes no. 1.

12:607    Vol. 1, no. 3 (winter 1973) called Special issue.

12:608    2nd ed., 1970, called 1st ed.

12:609    Issue for winter 1980 called also winter 1981.

12:610    Vol. 2, no. 2 called also winter 1980 issue.

12:611    Issue for 1976-1977 called also Bicentennial edition.

12:612    Published as: Bicentennial edition, 1975.

12:613    Vols. for 1973-1977? called also Appendix B.

12:614    Issues for 1947 (June 1-Dec. 31)-1955 called 10th-18th annual reports.

12:615    Issues for Feb. and May 1978: no. 2 and no. 3, respectively.

12:616    Issues for 1st quarter, 1981-2nd quarter, 1981 called also v. 22, no. 1-v. 22, no. 2.

12:617    Ser. 6, v. 1-3 also numbered v. 51-53; ser. 7, v. 1 also numbered v. 52.

12:618    No. 7/10-    called also v. 5-

12:619    Issues for 1977-    called also no. 1-

12:620    Vols. 1-    called also v. 27-

12:621    Vols. for 1979-    called also t. 288-

12:622    Issues for May 1946-July 1948 called also año 1-3.

12:623    Issues for    -Apr. 1974 called also anul    -9.

12:624    Issues for July/Aug. 1974-    called also año 2-

12:625    Issues for 1972-    called also jaarg. 34-

12:626    Vols. for    called also    éd.

12:627    S. prt. 98-11 called S. prt. 98-1.

12:628    Vols. for 1872-    called ser. 1-    , but constitute v. 1-

12:629    Vols. for July 1921-May 1934 called also new ser., v. 1-13.

12:630    Series 2 called New series.

12:631    Vols. 4-    called n.s.

12:632    Each issue carries also numbering derived from the initials of its author, e.g., NNM-1-'82.

12:633    Carries also the volume numbering of: Zentralblatt für Mathematik.

12:634    Carries the volume numbering of the former: Transactions of the American Society of Mechanical Engineers, which ceased publication in 1958.

12:635    Most issues carry also the numbering of its monthly publication, e.g., volume for 1972 called v. 13, no. 11.

12:636    Vol. for 1982 issued as v. 32, no. 13 of: Printing impressions.

12:637     Resumes the volume numbering of: Review of books and religion (Belmont, Vt.).

12:638     Resumes the numbering of: Rudder (v. 93, no. 4-97, no. 10 not published).

12:639     Assumes the series and volume numbering of: Bollettino della Unione matematica italiana. Sezione A, and Sezione B.

12:640     Vol. 1-     called also v. 10-     in continuation of the numbering of: Proceedings of the Indian Association for the Cultivation of Science.

12:641     Called [Part] C, 1973-1979; the first 3 issues each year called [Part] C, and the last 3 called [Part] D, 1980-

12:642     One issue each year consists of a buyers' guide called Green book.

12:643     Dec. issue is the Buyers guide.

12:644     In Dec. has an extra number called Special directory issue.

12:645     Includes special unnumbered issues.

12:646     Includes occasional unnumbered special issues.

12:647     Includes an unnumbered issue published in 1939.

12:648     Some combined issues.

12:649     Some issues published in combined form.

12:650     Some volumes issued in combined form.

12:651     Reports for some years issued in combined form.

12:652     Some sessions issued in multiple numbers.

12:653     Some years issued together.

12:654     Journals for 1946 combined in 1 issue.

12:655     Reports issued in combined form for 1973-78.

12:656     Issued in combined form, 1975-76 and 1976-77-

12:657  First report combines the reports for 1976/77 and 1977/78.

12:658  Vols. for the 4th-5th conferences issued in combined form.

12:659  Vols. for 1966-67 issued combined; for 1968-70, combined; for 1974-75, combined.

12:660  Vol. 1 complete in 1 issue.

12:661  Vol. 26 consists of 1 no.

12:662  Each volume consists of 1 no. only.

12:663  Vol. 1 contains 5 issues; v. 2-  begins with May/June issue.

12:664  Four issues constitute a volume.

12:665  Some volumes issued in parts.

12:666  Each volume issued in parts.

12:667  Report issued in several volumes a year.

12:668  Published in more than 1 v.

12:669  Each issue published in 2 v.

12:670  Some reports issued in 2 or more parts.

12:671  Some no. published in more than 1 v.

12:672  Issued in 3 or more volumes.

12:673  Issued in 2 or more Bd. a year.

12:674  Vols. for 1977 issued in 2 sections.

12:675  Issue for 1977 published in 2 v.

12:676  Publications for 1979-  issued in 2 v.

12:677  Issues for 1981-  published in 2 v.

12:678  Issues for 1974-  issued in 10 v.; 1977-  in 3 v.; 1979-  in 1 v.

12:679    Issues for 1976/77-    published in 2 v.

12:680    Vols. for Apr. 1975 to Mar. 1976-    issued in 2 or more volumes.

12:681    Vols. for    issued in 2 tomes.

12:682    Issues for    published in 4 or more volumes.

12:683    Reports for    issued in 3 or more volumes, each volume prepared by a different office, e.g., pt. 1. Office of Wastewater Pollution Control.

12:684    Each report issued in several volumes covering various subjects.

12:685    Vols. for    issued in parts, each covering a different topic.

12:686    Vols. for 1968-    published in several issues, each issue covering one county.

12:687    Issued in parts continuously paged and supplied with a general t.p. and subject index to form a volume.

12:688    Beginning with 1975/80 each cumulation covers 1975 to the present.

12:689    Each year the list is cumulative from 1961.

12:690    Each volume is cumulative from 1957.

12:691    Each issue cumulative from the beginning of the calendar year.

12:692    Each issue cumulates the previous issue, culminating in a final ed. for each Congress.

12:693    Cumulation of the monthly publication: The Official Washington post index.

12:694    Cumulation of the monthly publication: Media report to women, ISSN 0145-9651.

12:695    Cumulation of pocket parts.

12:696       Cumulates the abstracts and indexes originally published in monthly issues Jan.-Dec., generally covering publications issued Oct.-Sept.

12:697       Data were cumulated quinquennially in: Surface water supply of the United States.

12:698       Each annual issued supersedes all previous issues.

12:699       Subsequent issues of each volume constitute revisions of previous ones, which they supersede, 1981-

12:700       Report year irregular.

12:701       Report year irregular; 1st report covers Jan. 1938-Sept. 1939.

12:702       Report year ends June 30.

12:703       Report year ends Jan. 31, for 1959/60-1968/69; and June 30, for 1969/70-

12:704       Report year ends Dec. 31; report for 1979/80 covers the period July 1979-1980.

12:705       Report covers fiscal year.

12:706       Report covers the school year.

12:707       Period covered by reports ends June 30.

12:708       Vol. for 1978 covers the period 1971-1978.

12:709       Vol. for May 1981 covers FY 1982.

12:710       First report covers period July 1949-1950.

12:711       "This [first] report covers only the second half of calendar year 1979. Subsequent reports will cover complete calendar years"--P. 1.

12:712       The 1st issue, v. 1, no. 7-12, covers 5 months.

12:713       In some issues the period covered by report is the year following the date of issuance, e.g., Mar. 31, 1973 covers period from Apr. 1, 1973-Mar. 31, 1974.

12:714    Contents of each issue cover the previous year (i.e., 1978 issue covers year 1977).

12:715    Each issue covers currency from 1845 to date.

12:716    Each issue covers 3 fiscal years with the table volume appearing approximately 1 year before the report volume.

12:717    Each volume covers a 5-year period and consists of 20 no., e.g., v. 18, no. 1-20, 1972-77.

12:718    Vols. include retrospect for 2 preceding years, 1979-

12:719    Vols. for 1926-1936 include data retrospective to 1918; 1937-1959 include data for preceding 20 years; 1961-1967 include data for preceding 15 years.

12:720    Not published 1971-1974.

12:721    Suspended with v. 42.

12:722    Suspended 1944-1947.

12:723    Suspended publication 1973-1975.

12:724    Publication suspended        -1977; resumed with new ser., v. 1, no. 1, winter 1978.

12:725    Publication suspended 1874-1903, 1905-1909, 1915-1924; no numbers issued for 1866, 1913, 1930, 1932, 1934-1935.

12:726    1978 volume not published.

12:727    Vol. for 1981 not published; vol. for 1982 issued as v. 3.

12:728    No volume published for 1979.

12:729    Vol. 7, 1971, never published.

12:730    None published for 1909/69.

12:731    None published between June 1 and Dec. 5, 1975.

12:732    No separate issue published for 1977-78.

12:733    No. 128 withdrawn by the publisher.

12:734   No more published.

12:735   No more published?

12:736   Ceased with FY 1957-58.

12:737   Ceased with v. 4, 1980. Cf. Letter from publisher.

12:738   Ceased with Mar. 1979.

12:739   Ceased with 1971.

12:740   Ceased in 1980.

12:741   Ceased with årg. 59, 1969?

12:742   Ceased with v. 5, no. 4, autumn 1982.

12:743   Ceased with summer 1980. Cf. Letter from publisher.

12:744   Ceased publication in 1981.

12:745   Ceased with July 1983 issue?


## PUBLICATION, DISTRIBUTION, ETC. (12.7B9)

12:746   Imprint varies: 1978, Ministry of Tourism and Small Business Development; 1979-     Ministry of Tourism, Policy, Development and Planning Branch.

12:747   Imprint varies: Boston, Mass., Nov. 1979-

12:748   Imprint varies.

12:749   Published: San Francisco, Calif., Apr./June 1975-

12:750   Published: Edinburgh, 1967-

12:751   Published: Lalitapur, Nepal, Oct. 1961-

12:752   Published in Kempten-Wiggenbach, Okt. 1978/79-

12:753   Issues for Nov./Dec. 1903 published in London.

12:754      Issues for        published in Midland Park, N.J.

12:755      Place of publication varies.

12:756      Place of publication varies slightly.

12:757      Publisher: Journal Publications, 1973-

12:758      Publisher: Genova : Studio editoriale di cultura,
Apr.-June 1979-

12:759      Published: Calabasas, Calif. : Trailer Life Pub. Co., 1978-

12:760      Published: Los Angeles : Barclays law monthly, Feb.
1979-

12:761      Published: Boston, Mass. : Ski Earth Publications, 1977-
            winter/spring 1980.

12:762      Published: Chicago, Ill. : Union of Democratic Thais, v.
1, no. 4 (Oct. 1977)-

12:763      Published: New York : Traditional Acupuncture Foundation, summer 1978-       ; Columbia, Md. : Traditional
Acupuncture Foundation, spring 1980-

12:764      Vol. 2-        published by the Beaver Island Historical
            Society.

12:765      Published by: University of Warwick Arts Federation,
            1975-        ; School of English and American Studies,
University of East Anglia, autumn 1980-spring 1981-

12:766      Published by: Federal Energy Regulatory Commission,
Office of Pipeline and Producer Regulation, 1976; Energy
Information Administration, Assistant Administrator for
Energy Data, 1977; Energy Information Administration,
Assistant Administrator for Energy Data Operations,
1978-1979.

12:767      Published by: the Institute of Physics, London, England,
in association with the American Institute of Physics, on
behalf of the European Physical Society.

12:768      Published by: the University of Chicago Press for the
Society for Research in Child Development.

12:769      Published by the societies of medical radiology in Denmark, Finland, Norway, and Sweden.

12:770      The issue of July 6, 1870, gives T.A. Brown as owner and proprietor. By Feb. 1, 1879, I.Z. Black had joined Brown as owner and publisher. Black sold his interest in the paper to Brown on June 13, 1888, and the paper began to be published by Brown and his son, T.A. Brown, Jr. H. Kapper became co-owner Mar. 28, 1889.

          (Newspaper: optionally, give a narrative publishing history)

12:771      Some numbers also published by Colorado Dept. of Health.

12:772      Published in cooperation with: Employment and Training Administration, U.S. Dept. of Labor, 1978-

12:773      Published in collaboration with: the College of Engineering and Applied Sciences of King Abdulaziz University.

12:774      Issued with: Job Market Research Service, 1979/80.

12:775      Issued with: the Agricultural Marketing Service, May 1928-Apr. 17, 1961; Dept. of Agriculture, Statistical Reporting Service, Apr. 21, 1961-1977; Dept. of Agriculture, Economics, Statistics, and Cooperatives Service, Jan. 19, 1978-Apr. 15, 1980; Economics and Statistics Service,
        ; and also with the World Food and Agricultural Outlook and Situation Board, Apr. 22, 1980-

12:776      Published with: United States, Dept. of Agriculture, Agricultural Marketing Service, Market News Branch, and State of California, Dept. of Food Agriculture, Division of Marketing Services, Bureau of Market News, 1977-

12:777      Vol. 1 published with Butterworths, London.

12:778      Vols. for 1978-     published with the Board of Governors of the Federal Reserve System and the Office of the Comptroller of the Currency.

12:779      Published on behalf of: Institute of Mathematics and Its Applications.

12:780      Available through DOCEX Project, Library of Congress.

12:781      Available from DOCEX Project, Library of Congress, or National Technical Information Service.

12:782      No. 2-3 published in 1978, no. 4 in 1983.

12:783      Pre-publication issue published July 1980.

12:784      First issue published, Mar. 1977, erroneously called no. 2.

12:785      Published on Friday, 1950-1972.
            (Newspaper)

12:786      Day of weekly publication is Wednesday.
            (Newspaper)

12:787      Many issues lack dates.


## PHYSICAL DESCRIPTION (12.7B10)

12:788      Large print.

12:789      Grade 2 braille.

12:790      Kept up-to-date by replacement pages.

12:791      Beginning with v. 2, current issues in loose-leaf format; each volume issued also in bound form after completion.

12:792      Issues for 1974/77 originally issued in loose-leaf format. These were later cumulated and reissued as 1974/77 bound volume.

12:793      In 3-ring binder which is arranged in 3 parts: Antiquarian list (printed), Specialties index (printed), and microfiches.

12:794      Issues for v. 87, though numbered sequentially, are paginated according to subject: Chemical sciences, Earth and planetary sciences, and Mathematical sciences.

12:795      Some volumes illustrated.

12:796      "With illustrations."

12:797    "All plates except the frontispiece in Volumes I and II and plate VII in Volume III were originally color plates and have been reproduced in black and white in this edition. These volumes have been reduced from their original size and were reprinted from the only available copies"--P. ii.

12:798    Size varies: no. 4 (2nd quarter 1973) is 19 x 26 cm.; no. 22 (1980) is 36 cm.

12:799    Vols. for 1967-    : 24 x 29 cm.

12:800    Arranged alphabetically by community as received.

12:801    Arranged by report number within numbered subject sections.

12:802    Each article is individually numbered following the numbering designation begun with Estudios CIEPLAN.

12:803    Errata slip inserted in 1981 edition.

## ACCOMPANYING MATERIAL (12.7B11)

12:804    Vol. 7 accompanied by magnifying glass.

12:805    Issue for winter 1980 accompanied by disc (45 rpm, mono. ; 7 in.).

12:806    Vols. for 1977-    accompanied by a loose-leaf solutions manual.

12:807    Vol. 10, no. 2 contains map (col. ; 25 x 42 cm.) in pocket.

12:808    Art print with each Oct. issue.

12:809    An annual Buyer's guide issued with 1980-

12:810    Issued with appendices.

12:811    Has separately issued support documents reproduced on microfiche.

## SERIES (12.7B12)

12:812     Vols. for 1973-     lack series statement.

12:813     Series romanized: Shih pao shu hsi.

12:814     Series on spine: Chin tai Chung-kuo shih liao ts'ung k'an hsü chi.

12:815     "A Seatrade guide."

12:816     "A Halsted Press book," 1973-1976.

12:817     Issued as part of the Mineral Policy Sector's Statistical series.

12:818     Issued in the series of Reports and papers of the House of Commons of Parliament.

12:819     Each volume has also subseries title and numbering.

12:820     Each issue numbered 2, 4, 6, 8, etc., in series.

12:821     Each issue individually numbered in series.

## AUDIENCE (12.7B14)

12:822     Intended audience: Junior and senior high school librarians.

12:823     For western yachtsmen.

12:824     For U.S. Government officials.

12:825     For members of the American Production and Inventory Control Society.

12:826     For those interested in the literature pertaining to running.

12:827     "An aid for disabled and elderly travelers."

12:828     "A detailed listing of primary subjects of interest to managerial personnel, with a record of sourcebooks, periodicals, organizations, directories, handbooks, bibliographies, on-line data bases, and other sources of information on each topic'' (varies).

12:829     Magazine for Atlantic and Gulf yachtsmen.

12:830     Magazine for parents and teachers of gifted/creative/talented children.
      (Title proper: G/C/T)

12:831     Circulated to selected practicing dentists.

12:832     Presented at the annual meeting of the Arizona Newspaper Association.

12:833     Consists of papers presented at a postgraduate course in advanced geriatric medicine in Glasgow, Nov. 1980-

12:834     Distribution restricted.

12:835     Limited distribution.

12:836     Limited to members.

12:837     ''Not for publication.''

## OTHER FORMATS AVAILABLE (12.7B16)

12:838     Available in microfiche.

12:839     Available on microfiche.

12:840     Available on microfiche from National Technical Information Service.

12:841     Available on microfilm from University Microfilms.

12:842     Available on microfilm from Johnson Associates, University Microfilms, and Princeton Microfilms.

12:843     Also issued on microfiche.

12:844     Issued also in microfilm.

12:845        Issued also on microfiche and microfilm.

12:846        Available also in microfiche, which includes supple-
              mentary material.

12:847        Vols. 1-5, 1974-1978, published on microfiche only.

12:848        Reprinted v. 1-40 available from Kraus Reprints; v. 37-
                    available in microfiche from J.S. Canner & Co. and
              Johnson Associates.

## INDEXES (12.7B17)

12:849        Indexes: No. 31 (1972)-42 (1975) 1 v.

12:850        Indexes: Vols. 1 (1967)-5 (1971) 1 v.; Vols. 1 (1967)-7
              (1973) 1 v.

12:851        Indexes: Vols. 1 (1857)-32 (1876) 1 v.; Vols. 1 (1857)-62
              (1888) 1 v.; Vols. 63 (1889)-68 (1901) 1 v.

12:852        Indexes: Vols. 1 (1907)-24 (1931) 2 v.; Ser. 2, v. 1
              (1932)-30 (1961) 3 v.

12:853        Indexes: No. 1 (Aug. 25, 1953)-300 (Nov. 6, 1959) 1 v.;
              No. 301 (Nov. 13, 1959)-450 (Jan. 4, 1963) 1 v.; No. 451
              (Feb. 1963)-600 (Feb. 1966) 1 v.

12:854        Indexes: Vols. 1 (1940)-3 (1943) with v. 3; Vols. 8 (1947)-9
              (1948) in v. 10; Vols. 10 (1949)-11 (1951) in v. 12; Vols. 12
              (1952)-13 (1953) in v. 14; Vols. 14 (1954)-16 (1956) in v. 16;
              Vols. 17 (1957)-18 (1958) in v. 18; Vols. 19 (1959)-20 (1960)
              in v. 20.
                    (To show location of the index in the set, use "in" if
                    index is included in the paging of an issue; "with" if
                    index is separately paged, or unpaged, and bound with
                    a volume of the serial)

12:855        Indexes: Vols. 1-2 (1970-71)-5 (1974) in v. 5.

12:856        Indexes: Vols. 1 (1947)-10 (1956) in v. 10; Vols. 1
              (1947)-25 (1971) in v. 25.

12:857    Indexes: Vols. 1 (1891)-10 (1900) with v. 9-10; Ser. 2, v. 1 (1901)-10 (1910) with ser. 2, v. 9-10; Ser. 3, v. 1 (1911)-6 (1920) in ser. 3, v. 3-6.

12:858    Indexes: Vols. 1 (1975)-4 (1978) in v. 5, no. 13.

12:859    Indexes: Vols. 1 (1948)-5 (1952) / v. (includes index to the journal under its earlier title); Vols. 6 (1953)-7 (1954) with v. 1-7; Vols. 8 (1955)-10 (1957) with v. 8-11.

12:860    Indexes: Vols. 1 (1933)-4 (1936) in v. 5, no. 3 (includes index to the journal under its later title).
          (Title proper: Oregon mineralogist; continued by Mineralogist)

12:861    Indexes Vols. 1 (1933)-4 (1936) in v. 5, no. 3 (includes index to the journal under its earlier title).
          (Title proper: Mineralogist; continues Oregon mineralogist)

12:862    Vol. 7, no. 1 contains a cumulative index to v. 1-6 of Rutgers journal of computers and the law.

12:863    Indexes: No. 1 (1967)-85 (1977) 1 v. (includes index to earlier title).

12:864    Index for FY 73-FY 80, published in 1 v., also covers serial under its earlier title: Federal program evaluations.

12:865    Indexes: Vols. 1 (1949)-18 (1967) 1 v. (includes index to Annual conference proceedings [of the] American Institute of Industrial Engineers).

12:866    Indexes: Vols. 1 (1849)-45 (1894) in v. 46 (includes index to the society's proceedings of the annual meeting); Vols. 1 (1849)-51 (1900) in v. 52 (includes index to the society's proceedings of the annual meeting).

12:867    Indexes: Vols. 1 (1849)-45 (1894) in v. 46, and Vols. 1 (1849)-51 (1900) in v. 52 of the Transactions of the Indiana State Medical Society.

12:868    Indexes: Vols. 1 (1875)-60 (1937) issued as v. 61.

12:869    Indexes: Topical index, v. 1 (1966)-12 (Oct. 1977) 1 v.

12:870        Indexes: Geographic index, v. 1-15, 2 pts.; Vols. 16-21;
              Vols. 22-45, 2 pts.; Vols. 46-60, 2 pts.; Vols. 61-75.

12:871        Indexes: Author index, no. 16 (Jan./Feb. 1968)-24 (May/
              June 1969) with no. 24.

12:872        Indexes: Subject index, v. 1 (1961)-3 (1963) with v. 3;
              Vols. 4 (1964)-7 (1967) with v. 7.

12:873        Indexes: Author index, v. 1-7 in v. 8.
                       Subject index, v. 1-7. 1 v.
                       Number index, v. 1-8 with v. 8

12:874        Index to ASTM standards issued as last part of each
              volume.

12:875        Every 5th volume is an index to all preceding volumes.

12:876        December issue contains index for year-to-date.

12:877        Final yearly issue includes index of special articles.
              Dec.-Mar. issues contain reports of snow and ice conditions.

12:878        Annual index published in no. 10 of each volume,
                       -June 1980.

12:879        Beginning with 17, each issue contains a cumulative author
              index.

12:880        Index published separately, 1978-

12:881        Index for 1975-1977 published separately.

12:882        Indexes covering every 4 v. (beginning with v. 20 and ex-
              cluding statistical volumes) issued with title: Index of reports
              on federal funds for R & D.

12:883        Cumulative index covering v. 1-5 issued separately in 1980.

12:884        Cumulative index regularly updated and reissued.

12:885        Cumulative indexes published semiannually;
              1980-          one semiannual index issued for Jan.-June.

12:886        Cumulative indexes issued from time to time, with title:
              Index digest of determinations of the impartial umpire under
              the AFL-CIO internal disputes plan.

12:887      Quarterly and annual cumulative indexes issued with title: Index chemicus.

12:888      Index issues, published monthly and cumulated semi-annually and annually, have title: Index chemicus; quadrennial cumulations have title: Encyclopaedia chimica internationalis.

12:889      Indexed by: American statistics index.

12:890      Indexed by: Subject guide to books in print, ISSN 0000-0159, 1957-

12:891      Indexed selectively by: Chemical abstracts, ISSN 0009-2258.

## CONTENTS (12.7B18)

12:892      Includes a handbook for the following year.

12:893      Includes preliminary data and projections for the following 2 years.

12:894      Includes a review of the year and the outlook for the following year.

12:895      Issues include revised data for previous years.

12:896      Each volume includes entries omitted from volumes for the previous years.

12:897      Each volume contains final data for 1 year and provisional data for the following year.

12:898      Some volumes include principles of medical ethics and/or rules of the Judicial Council.

12:899      Vols. for      include 4 special directory issues.

12:900      Vols. for      have preliminary forecast for succeeding years.

12:901      Vols. for 1909/72-      contain data on job vacancies.

12:902      Vols. for 1964-1967 contain papers of the Beef Cattle Science School; 1968-1974, papers of the Stockmen's School; 1975-      papers of the International Stockmen's School.

12:903      Includes: Etats financiers / Centre de recherche industrielle du Québec.

12:904      Includes section: Cosmetic & fragrance retailing, a "magazine-within-a-magazine."

12:905      Each issue includes a separate section with title: MetaData's legalnotes.

12:906      Includes: Section 1. Alphabetical listing of abbreviations -- Section 2. Definitions of military terms.

12:907      Includes: Harris Illinois buyers industrial directory, also issued separately.

12:908      Contains 2 sections: Coin news; and, Medal news, which have separate caption titles and pagings, 1981-

12:909      Each issue includes separate but continuously paged sections called: Nuclear medicine; and, Ultrasound.

12:910      Includes a separately paged section with the title: Pediatric infectious disease newsletter, v. 8, no. 1-

12:911      Vols. for 1981-      include: Cosmetic & fragrance price directory, issued as separately paged section of 2 issues each year.

12:912      Issues for 1959-1962 include a separately paged Abstracts section (also published separately), discontinued with the issue for Jan. 1963.

12:913      "Geographical highlights" as tear sheet in Jan. issue.

12:914      Includes occasional special issues called: Jamaica intercom annual.

12:915      Includes supplementary bibliographies called: Service de documentation; some numbered in regular series.

12:916    Beginning with 1947 each volume includes 1 or more separately issued parts called: Notes et revue.

12:917    Some volumes include: Instrument manufacturing. The . . . buyers' guide, issued separately in some years.

12:918    "Weekly issue may contain two parts: I. Community documents and instruments; II. Community publications and studies"--T.p. verso.

12:919    Issues for          include: Annual report of the National insurance scheme.

12:920    Vols. for Dec. 1953-          include: Proceedings of the Antiquarian Horological Society.

12:921    Vol. for Oct. 1977 contains: Index to reviews of bibliographical publications, 1976.

12:922    Vols. for June 1982-          include: Updata, Vol. 12, no. 6 (June 1982)-

12:923    Vol. 5-          also includes: Proceedings supplements, 12th-          annual meetings, 1968-

12:924    Issues for 1977-          include the proceedings of the Informatics conferences, previously published as single volumes by Aslib, entitled: Informatics 1-3.

12:925    Issues for Oct. 1979-Sept. 1980 include supplementary material such as Birds of prey of Wisconsin, and other publications issued by the department.

12:926    "Including the . . . Annual report on the Government Hospital for the Insane at Abbassia and the . . . Annual report on the Government Hospital for the Insane at Khanka."

12:927    Reports for          -1929 include the Annual report on the Government Mental Hospital at Abbâssîya and the Annual report on the Government Mental Hospital at Khanka; 1930 includes the Mental Hospitals of Abbâssîya and Khanka; 1931-          include the Mental Hospitals of Abbâssîya and Khanka, and Khanka Criminal Asylum.

## NUMBERS (12.7B19)

12:928    "FERC form no. 15"--1977.

12:929    "DOE/EIA"--1977-

12:930    "HUD-319"--P. [C-54].

12:931    GPO: Item 42-M.

12:932    GPO: Item 768-8-09 (microfiche).

12:933    GPO: Item 1039-A, 1039-B (microfiche).

12:934    Supt. of Docs. no.: HE 22.202:M46/

12:935    WI docs. no.: He 1 St. 6/2: A 5/1968-

12:936    Kansas State documents classification number: E5.39 : yr.

12:937    Issues for Feb. 1981-May 1981 were classed: A 105.20/2:(nos.).

12:938    Issues for Apr. 1980-July 1981 have Supt. of Docs. no.: A 105.10/4:(v. no. & no.).

12:939    Issues prior to Jan. 1976 have Supt. of Docs. no.: C 56.216:M 33 K.

12:940    Prior to Jan. 1976 issues were classed C 56.216:MQ-22 during the time the Census Bureau was subordinate to the Social and Economic Statistics Administration.

12:941    Prior to Jan. 1976 issues were classified (Supt. of Docs.) C 56.216:MA-38B during the time the Census Bureau was subordinate to the Social and Economic Statistics Adminis-tration.

12:942    Issues carry also United Nations publication sales number.

12:943    Issued 1950-1955 with no. M31L, 1956-1964 with no. M35L.

## COPY BEING DESCRIBED AND LIBRARY'S HOLDINGS (12.7B20)

12:944     Library has v. 2, no. 5 (May 1980)-

12:945     Library lacks v. 7, no. 3.

12:946     Located in library's microforms collection.

12:947     Earlier titles cataloged separately.

12:948     Vols. before v. 5 cataloged separately in this library.

12:949     Issues before t. 3 classified separately in this library.

12:950     Issues before no. 7/10 classified separately in this library.

12:951     Vols. before v. 7 which cannot be analyzed, cataloged separately in this library.

12:952     Separately cataloged in this library after v. 84.

## "WITH" NOTES (12.7B21)

12:953     Vols. for 1980-     with: Abstracts of Bulgarian scientific literature. Scientific communism, philosophy, sociology, science of science and scientific information.

12:954     Vols. 7-8 with: Agricultural sector. Livestock and livestock products; Agricultural sector. Land use, artificial fertilizers and other improvements; and, Agricultural sector. Values of agricultural commodities produced.

12:955a     With: Journal of experimental psychology. Animal behavior processes, ISSN 0097-7403; and, Journal of experimental psychology. Human perception and performance, ISSN 0096-1523. Bound together subsequent to publication.
     (Title proper: Journal of experimental psychology. General; note on first item)
     *For LC's interpretation on the use of "With" notes see Cataloging Service Bulletin, no. 22, fall 1983, p. 20*

12:955b     With: Journal of experimental psychology.  General, ISSN
0096-3445. Bound together subsequent to publication.
(Note on second and subsequent items)

## ITEM DESCRIBED (12.7B22)

12:956     Description based on: 1977; title from cover.

12:957     Description based on: 1982, pt. 7.

12:958     Description based on: 1980-1981 ed.; cover title.

12:959     Description based on: 1973/1974, v. 1A.

12:960     Description based on: 1977 & 1978.

12:961     Description based on: 79/80.

12:962     Description based on: 1973/74/75/76/77/78; title from
cover.

12:963     Description based on: July 1, 1978 through June 30, 1979;
title from text.

12:964     Description based on: 1 July 1978 to 30 June 1979.

12:965     Description based on: July 1, 1978-June 30, 1979 and
July 1, 1979-June 30, 1980.

12:966     Description based on: Year ended 30th Sept. 1976.

12:967     Description based on: For the year ended Aug. 31, 1980;
title from cover.

12:968     Description based on: Academic years 1976-77 and
1977-78.

12:969     Description based on: Calendar year 1979.

12:970     Description based on: Financial year 1979-80.

12:971     Description based on: FY/80.

12:972     Description based on: Water year 1979.

12:973       Description based on: Fall 1980.

12:974       Description based on: Winter 1976-1977.

12:975       Description based on: Season 1972/73.

12:976       Description based on: 1st quarter 1979; caption title.

12:977       Description based on: Summer quarter 1973, autumn quarter 1973, winter quarter, 1974, spring quarter 1974.

12:978       Description based on: Aug. 1979.

12:979       Description based on: 4, April 1979; title from cover.

12:980       Description based on: Week ending Jan. 13, 1979; caption title.

12:981       Description based on: Aug. 24-27, 1980.

12:982       Description based on: Monday, 2nd June, 1969 and Tuesday, 3rd June, 1969.

12:983       Description based on: Vol. 22, no. 2 (1978/1979).

12:984       Description based on: Vol. 2, no. 8 (Aug.-Sept. 1980); caption title.

12:985       Description based on: Vol. 7, no. 2 (Nov./Dec. 1981); title from cover.

12:986       Description based on: Vol. 8, no. 85       (Jan. 10, 1979); masthead title.

12:987       Description based on: Vol. 14, no. 1 (automne 1980); title from cover.

12:988       Description based on: Vol. 21 (ed. 1978).

12:989       Description based on: Vol. 28 (fiscal years 1978, 1979, and 1980), final report.

12:990       Description based on: No. 25 (Sept. 1979); title from caption.

12:991       Description based on: Pt. 1 (1977); title from cover.

12:992    Description based on: Bk. 111 (correct to 30 Apr. 1979).

12:993    Description based on: 5.

12:994    Description based on: 2/1980.

12:995    Description based on: 3 (nov.-dic. 1973); title from cover.

12:996    Description based on: 2nd (1978/1979).

12:997    Description based on: 36th (July 1, 1975 through June 30, 1976); title from p. [i] of text.

12:998    Description based on: 7th compilation (1981).

12:999    Description based on: 96th Congress (1979-1980).

12:1000    Description based on: 16th issue (1975).

12:1001    Description based on: 5th Legislative Assembly, 1st (16 July 1977).

12:1002    Description based on: 89th year (1981 ed.).

12:1003    Description based on: 251st year, 2nd session of 2nd Parliament, v. 6, no. 2.

12:1004    Description based on: 2ème année, no. 15 (déc. 1980); title from cover.

12:1005    Description based on: Beiträge 3. Jahrg. (1966); title from cover.

12:1006    Description based on: 4e éd. (1978); title from cover.

12:1007    Description based on: 2a. época, no. 83 (sept./oct. 1976); title from cover.

12:1008    Description based on: 135e jaarg., Vooraflevering 8.

12:1009    Description based on: al-Sahah 1., al-'adad 2. (Tishrīn Thān 1978); title from cover.

12:1010    Description based on: Sér. 2, no. 1 (oct.-nov.-déc. 1976).

12:1011    Description based on: Th. 1978-1979; title from cover.

12:1012    Description based on: Vyp. 3.

12:1013    Description based on: Zafra 1979; title from cover.

12:1014    Description based on surrogate.

12:1015    Description based on surrogate of: No. 5.

# Subject Index*

---

*Boldface numbers refer to chapters; lightface numbers refer to examples.

Project numbers *see* Numbers, contract, etc.

Pseudonyms, **4**:111-112

Publication, distribution, etc., **2**:363, 409, 450-495, 801; **3**:288-309;
      **4**:368-386; **5**:288-294; **6**:322-333; **7**:109, 120, 139-140, 153-165;
      **8**:106, 114-120, 183, 216-217; **9**:88-96; **10**:74-78; **11**:27;
      **12**:746-787
  date of *see under* Date(s)
  distributor, **2**:425, 475-478, 483-484; **3**:297-298; **6**:328-329;
      **7**:164-165; **9**:89-91; **10**:43; **12**:780-781, 840-842, 848
  on part of item, **2**:455-456, 463-464, 483-484, 487, 491-493
  place of, **2**:465, 475-478, 480-483; **7**:154-165; **8**:117-120; **9**:88-89
    change in, **12**:747-756, 758-763
    more than one, **2**:465, 475-476, 480; **5**:290-291; **7**:159, 165
  printer, **2**:412, 430, 447, 598, 800; **3**:293-294
  publisher, **2**:409, 428, 459, 461-464, 801; **3**:292; **6**:325-327; **8**:115;
      **9**:88; **12**:234-235, 239, 410
    change in, **12**:746, 757-762, 764-766
    change in name of, **12**:256, 763, 766
    joint, **2**:466-467; **3**:288-292; **12**:767, 769-778
  statement, source of, **2**:450-451, 453, 457-460, 472-474, 480-482;
      **3**:295-296; **5**:288-291, 293; **6**:322-324

Publication suspended *see* Not published; *see under* Serials

Publisher *see under* Publication, distribution, etc.

Publishers' numbers *see* Music, plate/publishers' numbers;
    *see under* Sound recordings

Quotations, source of, **2**:22, 65, 71, 75, 86, 253-255, 265, 280, 285, 448,
    477-478, 588, 761; **3**:21; **5**:89, 210, 222, 292; **6**:118, 357,
    460-461, 535; **7**:68-69, 273; **8**:56, 283; **9**:62; **11**:43; **12**:175, 253,
    928-930

Readers *see* Performers

Realia *see* Three-dimensional artefacts and realia

Reissues *see* Reprints

Related works, **2**:374-401, 520, 566, 571; **3**:230-233; **7**:149-152, 248-249;
    **8**:107-113; **9**:78-80; **10**:62; **12**:316-530

Videorecordings *see* Motion pictures and videorecordings

Views *see* Cartographic materials, map views

Vita, **2**:722-724

Vocalized, **2**:162-163

Voices *see under* Music, medium of performance

Wills *see under* Manuscripts

"With" notes, **1**:22-23; **2**:231, 426, 798-804; **3**:588-593; **6**:536-539; **7**:279-280; **11**:9, 52-57; **12**:953-955
  bound together, etc., subsequent to publication, **1**:22; **2**:798-801; **3**:592; **11**:52-56; **12**:955
  uniform title specified, **6**:539

Without special title, **2**:744

Workshops, etc. *see* Conferences

Year(s) *see* Date(s)

# Selected Bibliography

American Library Association. Committee on Cataloging: Description and Access. *Guidelines for Using AACR2, Chapter 9 for Cataloging Microcomputer Software.* Chicago: American Library Association, 1984.

Anglo-American Cataloguing Committee for Cartographic Materials. *Cartographic Materials: A Manual of Interpretation for AACR2.* Hugo L.P. Stibbe, general ed. Chicago: American Library Association, 1982.

Betz, Elisabeth W. *Graphic Materials: Rules for Describing Original Items and Historical Collections.* Washington, DC: Library of Congress, 1982.

*Cataloging Service Bulletin.* Washington, DC: Library of Congress, Processing Services, 1978-

Dodd, Sue A. *Cataloging Machine-Readable Data Files: An Interpretive Manual.* Chicago: American Library Association, 1982.

Hensen, Steven L. *Archives, Personal Papers, and Manuscripts: A Cataloging Manual for Archival Repositories, Historical Societies, and Manuscript Libraries.* Washington, DC: Library of Congress, Manuscript Division, 1983.

Intner, Sheila S. "Suggestions for the Cataloging of Machine-Readable Materials." *Library Resources & Technical Services* 27 (1983):366-370.

Olson, Nancy B. *A Manual of AACR 2 Examples for Microcomputer Software and Video Games.* Lake Crystal, MN: Soldier Creek Press, 1983.

Rogers, JoAnn V. *Nonprint Cataloging for Multimedia Collections: A Guide Based on AACR 2.* Littleton, CO: Libraries Unlimited, 1982.

Smiraglia, Richard P. *Cataloging Music: A Manual for Use With AACR2.* Lake Crystal, MN: Soldier Creek Press, 1983.

# ABOUT THE AUTHORS

Florence A. Salinger, associate librarian, is head of Technical Services at the Heindel Library of The Capitol Campus of The Pennsylvania State University in Middletown. She worked as a special librarian for IBM, Burroughs Corporation, and the School of Dental Medicine of the University of Pennsylvania.

Ms. Salinger holds an M.S. in library science from Drexel University and a B.S. in chemistry from College Misericordia. She is a member of Beta Phi Mu, International Library Science Honor Society, and a past chairperson of the Technical Services Round Table of the Pennsylvania Library Association. She was coauthor with Dr. Emerson Jacob of "Staff vs. Books in Academic Library Budgets," *Library Journal,* October 15, 1978.

Eileen Zagon, senior assistant librarian, is a cataloger at the Heindel Library of The Capitol Campus of The Pennsylvania State University. She received a B.S. in English from the University of Wisconsin-Madison and an M.A. in librarianship from the University of Denver where she was elected to Beta Phi Mu.

Ms. Zagon has worked in cataloging departments at the University of Wisconsin Center System Library and the Champaign (Illinois) Public Library and has been a serials cataloger at the University of Denver. She coauthored a series of bibliographies on opiates, endorphins, and the developing organism in *Neuroscience and Biobehavioral Reviews.*

Ms. Salinger and Ms. Zagon are the authors of *Monograph Cataloging Notes.*